Potsdam Conference 1945
Shaping the World

SANDSTEIN

Potsdam Conference 1945

SHAPING THE WORLD

Edited on behalf of the
General Direction of the
Prussian Palaces and Gardens
Foundation Berlin-Brandenburg
by Jürgen Luh
in collaboration with Truc Vu Minh
and Jessica Korschanowski

Contents

Dear Readers, the exhibition and the companion volume commemorating the seventy-fifth anniversary of the Potsdam Conference make clear that it takes a sound knowledge of history to understand the present and shape the future.

As a rule, historical events and processes have far-reaching consequences. They affect the lives of contemporaries and, most of the time, also those of the following generations. For us, this makes it all the more important to use our knowledge of the past to assume responsibility, for both our own lives and our democratic society.

Commemorating the end of the Second World War in Europe and Asia, the defeat of the murderous Nazi regime and the deliverance from war and fascism seventy-five years ago—for us, all this includes exhortation, reappraisal and educational work. We commemorate the millions of European Jews murdered. We pay tribute to those persecuted and to the victims who lost their lives in the Nazi extermination and forced labour camps, to those who died on the battlefields and those who fell victim to terror and war. We remember those who refused to participate in crimes and those who actively resisted such crimes. We urge the world not to forget or belittle war and terror. We are glad to live in peace, and we strive to preserve it. We exhort ourselves to be vigilant and to unambiguously oppose nationalism, extremism, anti-Semitism and warmongering.

For our commemorations and admonitions to remain strong and effective, it is imperative that we face our recent history and continue our educational work. Brandenburg practices a pluralistic, diverse and decentralised culture of remembrance. Museums, memorials, research institutes, voluntary initiatives, schools and municipalities provide educational opportunities and make history tangible "on site".

Not least because of its proximity to Berlin, the capital of the former Reich, Brandenburg has many important contemporary historical sites. The concentration camps at Ravensbrück and Sachsenhausen, numerous concentration subcamps, the jails in Brandenburg an der Havel and Cottbus, the Seelower Höhen and the Halbe Forest Cemetery are important places of remembrance when it comes to the Nazi dictatorship and the Second World War.

On the seventy-fifth anniversary of the Potsdam Conference, Cecilienhof Palace—the meeting place of the Big Three: Truman, Stalin and Churchill—comes to the forefront as a unique and symbolic place. It is not an exaggeration to say that world history was written here. In consideration of our European perspective, it is important to remember that the conference took place at a time between war and peace. The guns had fallen silent in Europe, yet fighting continued in East Asia, with the goal of putting a decisive end to Japan's struggle for supremacy. It is hard to bear the thought that the final orders for dropping the atomic bombs on Hiroshima and Nagasaki were given at Potsdam.

The exhibition and its companion volume throw light on the impact of the decisions and resolutions adopted at Potsdam, which was far-reaching in terms of both space and time. The significance of the Potsdam Conference for the Allies themselves, as well as for Germany and Poland, is specifically supplemented by the perspectives of other participants and affected parties who received little or no attention at the Cecilienhof conference table. These include, for example, China and Korea, Iran, and many European countries. I am particularly saddened by the fact that Holocaust survivors and displaced persons were hardly of any importance during the negotiations.

The Potsdam Conference had serious consequences for the people of Brandenburg. Because of the redrawing of Germany's borders, Brandenburg became part of the Soviet occupation zone and the GDR. It was only decades after the Allies' decision to democratise Germany that East Germans finally achieved the basic democratic rights that had long been taken for granted in West Germany.

The second German dictatorship and the Peaceful Revolution that supplanted it have left their mark on our state. Many citizens of Brandenburg had to put up with fractures in their lives that disrupted their daily existence and sometimes tore apart their families. Some Brandenburg memorial sites have a so-called multiple past: they have historical connections to both German dictatorships. What these locations of contemporary history show us—similar to the Potsdam Conference—is that anyone wanting to understand and communicate the development both of the world and of their country since the end of the Second World War will need to relate that development back to previous events and take a look far beyond Germany and Europe.

With the broad view presented here of the Potsdam Conference and its consequences, this exhibition and its companion volume help advance the scholarly discourse on the post-war period. Visitors to Cecilienhof can explore the actual setting of a significant historical event as though taking a journey through time. The companion volume offers a deepened and expanded understanding of the Potsdam Conference. I would like to thank all those who have brought to our attention this historical site and who have laid out for us the momentous event hosted here and its far-reaching consequences for us today.

In the summer of 1945, world history was given a new shape at Potsdam, and Germany's division was initiated. The Treaty on the Final Settlement with Respect to Germany was signed in Moscow forty-five years later, paving the way for German reunification. At the same time, after decades of uncertainty for our Polish neighbours, the Oder-Neisse border between Germany and Poland was finally established under international law. Long and difficult negotiations invariably preceded these historic changes. Victors and vanquished, friends and opponents, and sometimes enemies had to approach one another to build trust, negotiate and come to terms. This was successfully achieved in Potsdam and Moscow.

Talking to each other is the only way to resolve conflicts peacefully. This, for me, is the legacy of the Potsdam Conference. | CN

Foreword
Christoph Martin Vogtherr
General Director of the Prussian Palaces and Gardens Foundation Berlin-Brandenburg

When German Emperor Wilhelm II officially inaugurated the newly built Cecilienhof Palace—which had been under construction for several years—in Potsdam's New Garden on 9 November 1917, nobody was able to foresee that it would be the last palace built by the Hohenzollern dynasty. Nor were they able to predict the momentous future events that would be hosted here. The end of the German empire was near. One year later to the day, on 9 November 1918, the republic was proclaimed in Berlin, and the German monarchy ended.

After the troubled years of the Weimar Republic, the Nazi terror and the war-induced suffering of millions of people, Cecilienhof Palace—idyllically situated between the lakes Heiliger See and Tiefer See—was made the venue of what would come to be known as the Potsdam Conference, thereby becoming the centre of world attention in the summer of 1945. Immediately after the end of the war in Europe, the power balance and geopolitical fate of Germany as well as of numerous other states and regions in Europe, the Middle East and Asia were determined here. The leading roles were played by the heads of state of the victorious powers: Churchill (replaced during the conference by Attlee) for Great Britain, Truman for the United States and Stalin for the Soviet Union. These were the so-called Big Three. A similar meeting had already taken place a few months earlier, in February 1945, at the Crimean resort town of Yalta—with President Roosevelt representing the United States. What was at stake at Yalta, as would be the case at Potsdam, was the divvying up and reshaping of the post-war world. And much like at Potsdam, a former residence—Livadia Palace, the summer home of the last tsar, Nicholas II—had been chosen as the setting.

The Potsdam Conference and the decisions laid down in the Potsdam Agreement date back seventy-five years. Since then, time has continued apace, history keeps on being made, but is still shaped by the events of summer 1945. Set against this background, our exhibition commemorates a major milestone in history, one that impacted the fortunes of Germany as well as Europe and the entire world. We invite visitors to immerse themselves in the events that took place in late July and early August 1945, when Cecilienhof Palace was the focus of global interest. The Prussian Palaces and Gardens Foundation Berlin-Brandenburg is fortunate to be able to present the exhibition at its historical location, which offers opportunities far beyond those of neutral exhibition venues, such as museums. The rooms frequented by the three delegations for their work, the surrounding terraces and gardens where the heads of state would dwell, and the conference hall itself—all these make Cecilienhof Palace an important exhibit in its own right and an integral part of the show. The Potsdam Conference is brought back to life through diary extracts, loans from national and international collections such as the Hiroshima Museum, historical footage and other contemporary documents covering both the official points of view of conference delegations and the private perspectives of those immediately affected by the resolutions made in Potsdam—whether through flight and expulsion or by political or systemic changes. We are very pleased that the overall theme as well as the media of communication and some of the display objects themselves will, after the end of the exhibition, find their way into the permanent collection and will continue to make the topic more tangible to visitors.

For us as a foundation, the exhibition is a major occasion to highlight the importance of the palaces and gardens in our care, especially in the twentieth century and after the end of the monarchy. The formerly Prussian grounds, structures and parks not only served their princely patrons' and users' need for representation or retreat, but they later also became sites for historical events, such as Schön-hausen Palace in Berlin. Often, they were still used as loci of power. "Potsdam Conference 1945 – Shaping the World" illustrates once again how much this also holds true for Cecilienhof Palace.

I wish to thank all sponsors, supporters and partners for their decisive contributions to the success of this ambitious project; without their donations, the exhibition would never have come to pass. These include Minister of State and Federal Government Commissioner for Culture and Media Monika Grütters, along with the Ministry of Science, Research and Culture of the State of Branden-burg, the East German Sparkassenstiftung and the Mittelbranden-burgische Sparkasse. My thanks also go to the numerous employees in museums and science and research institutions in Germany and abroad as well as to the lending institutions and private lenders for their unfailingly good and reliable cooperation. With the support of all our colleagues from the Prussian Palaces and Gardens Foundation Berlin-Brandenburg, the 'Project Group Potsdam Conference' was responsible for the exhibition and its companion volume. I also wish to extend my thanks to all my colleagues for their great commitment, their creativity and their curiosity. Finally, I wish to thank Gestaltungs-büro beier + wellach, Berlin as well as the companies whose expert help and know-how have made the exhibition possible—Sandstein Verlag Dresden and our media and cooperation partners. |CN

The Potsdam Conference: About this volume

Jürgen Luh

Potsdam was the last of the three Allied war conferences, and although it took place after the surrender of the German Reich and was to decide the fate of many people, especially in Europe and Asia, the previous meetings of the Big Three in Tehran and Yalta are considered more important and are much better known than the Potsdam Conference. Information on the final encounter between Truman, Stalin and Churchill (later replaced by Attlee as British Prime Minister) as found in films, newspaper articles, photos and radio reports, is usually not presented under the keywords "Potsdam Conference" or "Potsdamer Konferenz" but under "Berlin Conference" and "Konferenz von Berlin". Berlin, the former capital of the Reich, which had been conquered by the Red Army after fierce fighting with many casualties, was not only more famous than tranquil Potsdam, located a few miles away from its gates and surrounded by water. Berlin is also given as the place of the "protocol" terminating the conference—and signed by the three heads of government on 2 August 1945 at 12:30 a. m. but dated 1 August.

The location of Potsdam and Cecilienhof Palace was the reason why the city near Berlin was chosen for the meeting of the three Allied heads of state. On one of the last days of the war, on 14 April 1945, it had suffered an air raid by 488 British bombers, which resulted in severe destruction of the old city. The New Garden and Cecilienhof Palace, however, had been spared major damage. The palace and villas in nearby Babelsberg offered enough space both for the comfortable accommodation of the Big Three and their delegations as well as the conference they convened for. The most important representatives were, on the Soviet side, the People's Commissioner for Foreign Affairs Vyacheslav M. Molotov, his deputy Ivan Maisky, Admiral of the Fleet Nikolai G. Kuznetsov, Chief of Staff of the Red Army General Aleksei I. Antonov, and Andrei A. Gromyko, Soviet Ambassador to the USA; on the American side, Secretary of State James F. Byrnes, Fleet Admiral William D. Leahy, Chief of Staff of the US Army George C. Marshall, Averell Harriman, American Ambassador to the USSR, and General of the Air Force Henry H. Arnold. On the British side, they included Foreign Secretaries Anthony Eden and Ernest Bevin, Field Marshal Sir Alan Brooke, Sir Charles Portal, Chief of the British Imperial General Staff and Marshal of the Royal Air Force, and Admiral Sir Andrew Cunningham.

The conference began at 5 p. m. on 17 July 1945 in the residence hall of Cecilienhof Palace and ended there on 2 August 1945 at 12:30 a. m. when Truman, Stalin and Attlee signed the "Protocol of the Proceedings of the Berlin Conference", which shortly thereafter found its way into the common usage as "Potsdam Agreement"—although it was neither an agreement nor a contract. Subsequent to the conference, the three Allies published their "Report on the Tripartite Conference of Berlin", an abbreviated summary of the "Protocol", which could be purchased for 30 pfennigs. Over the sixteen days of the conference, the three heads of state convened for

← The ruins of the Postdam City Palace with a view of St Nicholas Church a total of thirteen sessions, each starting at 5 p. m. and lasting approximately one to two hours. These sessions were preceded by preparatory discussions in committees consisting of the relevant representatives of each delegation, starting at 8 a. m., and the sessions of Foreign Secretaries Byrnes, Molotov and Eden or Bevin, together with their staffs, starting at 11 a. m.

A decision easily reached at the beginning of negotiations was the establishment of a Council of Foreign Ministers, which was to include, next to the representatives of the three statesmen convened at Potsdam, the foreign ministers of China and France. The Council was asked to take the the necessary preparatory steps for the peace treaties with the defeated former enemy states, the negotiation and conclusion of which was not meant to be the purpose of the conference.

The content of the Potsdam negotiations is reflected in the "Communiqué" issued by the three governments at the end of the conference. This Communiqué was primarily about the treatment of the German Reich, including the definition of how Germany was to be understood in terms of territory; the internal and external reorganisation of the country; its reparation payments and, finally, the German Navy and merchant fleet. The three governments also agreed on holding elections in Poland and on shifting Poland's border westwards. Pending its final determination in a peace settlement, the border was formed by "a line running from the Baltic Sea immediately west of Swinemunde, and thence along the Oder River to the confluence of the western Neisse River and along the western Neisse to the Czechoslovak frontier".[1] The Communiqué expressed the desire "that the present anomalous position of Italy, Bulgaria, Finland, Hungary and Rumania should be terminated by the conclusion of Peace Treaties" and declared the willingness to support "the admission of other states into the United Nations Organization".[2] It also included the agreement on the provisional treatment of Austria. Finally, the report announced, "the agreement on the removal of Germans from Poland, Czechoslovakia and Hungary".[3]

The "Protocol of the Proceedings of the Berlin Conference" and the conference documents of the three participating states was not published until 24 March 1947. They provide further and deeper insight into the negotiations, revealing the way they were conducted and what goals the respective governments pursued. They also reflect the diversity of the topics discussed, which cannot be inferred from the previously published Communiqué. Among other topics, these include the situation in Spain and the future dealings with the Franco government. In this context, they also cover Tangier, France, Italy, Yugoslavia and conditions in Greece, the Black Sea Straits, Syria and Lebanon and the future of Iran. Of these, only Iran, Tangier and the Black Sea Straits were included as independent sub-items in the "Protocol".[4]

The Potsdam talks carried political weight, both at the time and afterwards. They staked out influences and spheres of influence.

Opening session of the Potsdam Conference at Cecilienhof Palace, Potsdam

Because of their outstanding political, military and economic position in the world, it was, above all, the United States and the Soviet Union and, with far less authority, the United Kingdom that determined, or at least influenced, the progress of developments—both in the states whose conditions had been made an issue at the conference and in the countries and regions which had not been the subject of negotiations.

Further, there were discussions on the ongoing war in Asia, on how to end it as quickly as possible, and without heavy casualties among own forces, and how Japan should be forced to surrender unconditionally. For this purpose, the United States wanted the Soviet Union to enter the war. The Red Army was to tie Japanese troops in Manchuria and prevent them from defending Japan. On 26 July 1945, the heads of the United States, China and the United Kingdom declared their intention to deliver "the final blows" to Japan if it did not surrender. Otherwise they would be determined to exercise their military power, which would then entail "the inevitable and complete destruction of the Japanese armed forces and just as inevitably the utter devastation of the Japanese homeland".[5] Before the opening of the conference, President Truman had received news that the test of the atomic bomb had been successful. And only shortly after its end, on 6 and 9 August 1945, the first—and to date only—atomic bombs were dropped on Hiroshima and Nagasaki, respectively, with consequences previously unimaginable. Since then, human life and politics have been in the shadow of the nuclear threat.

This collection of essays assesses the diversity of topics discussed at the Potsdam Conference as well as their political significance for Europe after the war and still today. Its purpose is not to tell yet another story of the conference or how the change from active combat to the Cold War came about, since Herbert Feis, Robert Betzell, Charles L. Mee, Michael Dobbs and, most recently, Michael Neiberg (who takes his readers to the conference table, as it were) have already fully accomplished this task.[6] Neither does it primarily deal with Europe or the German question. These aspects, too, have been academically investigated and researched, by, among others, Herbert Kröger, Fritz Faust, Ernst Deuerlein and Michael Antoni.[7]

What were the hopes and expectations that politics and the public at large associated with the Big Three's conference at Potsdam? To answer this question, it is important to recall the venue of the event and to look at the objectives pursued by the three victorious powers. What ideas did people in Europe and Asia have about the new era and the new order emerging after the long years of devastating war? Did feelings of confidence and security return after the conference and the end of the war (for these two cannot be isolated from one another)? Did people take notice of the resolutions reached at Potsdam by a handful of politicians and, ultimately, by the Big Three alone? And, if so, did they perceive these decisions, in which they had had no say, as an opportunity for themselves and a better future?

The articles in this volume also look at the impact of the conference and its results—in the way they were made known to the world in the "Communiqué"—and at what these results meant for the people affected by the resolutions and those who had hoped for more, or more far-reaching, compassion with their fates. It is an attempt to broaden our perspective—focusing not only on the objectives of the three victorious powers or the impact of the conference results on Germany or Poland.

Against the background of the Potsdam discussions, which dealt with a large number of political issues and states worldwide, our aim here is to devote more space than usual to those issues which have not, or only incidentally, been included in the "Communiqué" and the "Protocol"—even if it has not been possible to deal with every aspect, nor deal exhaustively with the aspects taken into account. The importance of the Potsdam Conference should be considered and weighed with regard not only to the United States, the Soviet Union and the United Kingdom, on the one hand, and to Germany and Poland, on the other, but also to all those affected directly or indirectly by the decisions—the displaced persons and Holocaust survivors, who had no voice in Potsdam; the Chinese, the Japanese and the Koreans, who were still at war; the Persians whose fate was decided without consulting their interests or wishes; the French, who were among the victorious powers but had not been invited. Beyond a purely political analysis of the Potsdam consultations and resolutions which left many issues unresolved and indefinite, and yet created a new world order, a look at the impact of the conference and those directly affected by it makes for a better understanding of today's world and its problems. | CN

Notes
1 Report on the Tripartite Conference of Berlin, https://history.state.gov/historicaldocuments/frus1945Berlinv02/d1384 [accessed 20 January 2020]. / 2 Ibid. / 3 Ibid. / 4 Feis 1962, 333–34. / 5 1945, The Conference of Berlin (The Potsdam Conference), vol. 2, 1474–76. / 6 Feis 1960; Betzell 1970; Mee 1975; Dobbs 2012; Neiberg 2015. / 7 Kröger 1957; Faust 1960; Deuerlein 1961; Antoni 1985.

Choosing a Location for the Berlin Conference in Potsdam

Stefan Gehlen

Winston Churchill's suggestion that the Big Three should meet after hostilities had ended (and before the American troops had withdrawn from Europe) was accepted by both the new American President, Harry S. Truman, and Joseph Stalin in May 1945.[1] All three of them agreed on the code name "Terminal" and on holding the meeting on German territory. In contrast to the previous Big Three conference at Yalta, which had been preceded by tough negotiations on its location, finding a locale was fairly uncomplicated this time. Truman's initial idea of hosting a conference in Alaska had not been pursued—everybody knew that Stalin would not accept a location outside the Soviet sphere of influence. Churchill's first choice had been Jena. According to inter-Allied agreements, the city in Thuringia, which was conquered by the US armed forces, was to be handed over to the Soviets. Churchill wanted to delay the American withdrawal to prevent the advance of the Iron Curtain. But Truman declined, preferring to keep to the agreements made, thus being able to demand the same from Stalin.[2] So Churchill's idea was dropped.

The Soviets, in the meantime, had made their withdrawal from Berlin's western districts—which was to enable the other Allies to move into the sectors assigned to them—dependent on the withdrawal of the US Army. Since its conquest by the Red Army, Berlin, until 1 July 1945, was still completely under Soviet control—and would be governed by a joint Control Council only after its division into four Allied sectors.[3] The city centre and the government quarter in the Mitte district had been allocated to the Soviet sector and remained within the Soviet sphere of influence. Stalin therefore proposed Berlin as a conference location.[4]

The British and American sectors in the west bordered directly on the Soviet city centre. The western delegations and military escorts could have easily been billeted, and provided for, in their own respective sectors during the conference; Stalin, as its host, would still have remained in full control of the progress. When he submitted his proposal to Churchill on 27 May, Churchill immediately agreed, responding that he was looking forward to the meeting in Berlin— or, rather, in what was left of it.[5] In fact, the centre of Berlin was one of the districts most severely destroyed in the war. In July 1945, when Churchill, Truman and other conference participants took sightseeing tours here, it was still filled with the stench of corpses and sewers as well as the acrid smell of burning.[6]

The only other place where the British, American and Soviet spheres of power met, apart from Berlin's city centre, was Potsdam. The former Prussian residence city had not been incorporated into Greater Berlin in 1920. It was located in the Soviet-occupied zone surrounding the Allied sectors of Berlin, more precisely, on their southwestern edge. Only part of its cultural landscape, Glienicke and the Pfaueninsel, belonged to Berlin and the American sector. To the north, the village of Sacrow, which had been part of Potsdam since 1939, bordered on the Greater Berlin districts of Kladow and

← Cecilienhof Palace, view of the north side with conference hall

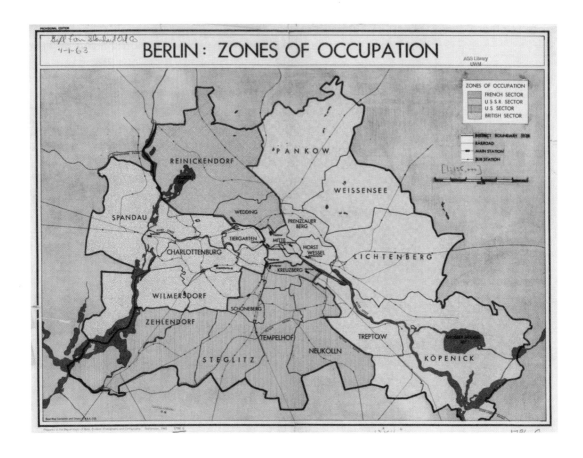

Occupation zones
Berlin 1945

Gatow, now belonging to the British sector. The Western Allies' major air and land corridors through the Soviet occupied-zone into Berlin —Gatow Airfield, used by the Royal Air Force, as well as highways to Magdeburg and Dessau—were located nearby. From a logistical point of view, Potsdam was thus a viable alternative to the destroyed centre of Berlin.

As the second residence of the Prussian kings and German emperors, Potsdam was not merely a conveniently located suburb but also a highly symbolic place—an emblematic follow-up to Versailles and other Paris suburbs (where the peace conferences after the First World War had been held) and to the Big Three's previous meeting at the Tsar's Crimean summer residence.[7] Another symbolic factor that spoke in favour of Potsdam was the goal of demilitarising Germany—after all, Potsdam was considered the cradle of German militarism.[8] Churchill as well as Stalin and General Lucius D. Clay are said to have been aware of Potsdam's significance as "the City of the Kings of Prussia, where German aggression had its origin".[9] Churchill's stance on Prussia, however, was ambivalent. On the one hand, he considered Prussian militarism to be one of the causes of National Socialism and a root of all evil, but on the other,

General Dwight D. Eisenhower and Lt. General Lucius D. Clay at Gatow Airfield, 20 July 1945

he still counted Prussia among the five major nations in Europe (Sanssouci was part of his visiting programme).[10] The restoration of (a reduced and weakened) Prussia as an independent state, which he had still advocated during the war, was no longer an issue since the Yalta Conference.[11]

Potsdam was less affected by the last great battle of the Second World War in Europe than the centre of Berlin, but its city centre, too, had been badly damaged. At Yalta, Stalin had asked the Western Allies for air support in the upcoming Battle of Berlin; and during the night of 14 to 15 April 1945, Royal Air Force bomber squadrons attacked militarily important communication routes between Potsdam and Berlin, destroying Potsdam's previously undamaged baroque city centre. It is a matter of dispute whether the so-called "Night of Potsdam" in 1945 was meant as an answer to the "Day of Potsdam" in 1933 or whether "Operation Crayfish" was aimed at the destruction of the city as a symbol of Prussian militarism.[12] It is also controversial whether the raid was flown to support the Soviet troops or to impress them by the strength of the Anglo-American air force. In order not to leave the prestigious capture of Berlin to the Soviets alone, Churchill had unsuccessfully urged US President Roosevelt,

shortly before his death in early April, to have American tank forma-
tions advance from the Elbe. Churchill was not interested in destroying Potsdam—shortly afterwards, indignant about the attack, he
asked: "What was the point of going and blowing down Potsdam?"[13]
He never received an answer.

The second wave of destruction ensued when the First Ukrain-
ian Front and First Belarusian Front under Marshal Ivan Konev and
Marshal Georgy K. Zhukov, respectively, advancing from the south
and north and closing the Soviet ring around Berlin to its southwest,
came against the boundaries of Potsdam.[14] After costly battles
around Potsdam, which had been declared a "fortress", parts of
the German troops had withdrawn eastwards via Berliner Vorstadt
across Glienicke Bridge, where they defended Wannsee Island in
fierce battles against Konev's assault until the Battle of Berlin had
ended on 2 May.[15] Through underground railway tunnels, Hitler's
political will could thus be smuggled out of the encircled *Führer-
bunker*, and thence be carried by seaplane from Wannsee out of the
Soviet ring. By now, the remainder of the hopelessly surrounded
German defenders in Potsdam had already made their way from Park
Sanssouci via Ferch to the Western Front, some 55 miles away, to be
taken prisoners of war by the Americans.

Both the bombing as well as the futile and absurd attempt to
defend Potsdam had destroyed about 50 per cent of the city centre's
historic buildings. Half of the houses in the entire city had become
uninhabitable. The residential areas in the suburbs and outskirts,
which the Red Army had taken without a fight, were still relatively
intact. Also, the palaces in the parks had largely been preserved.
With a view to seizing their inventory for transport to Moscow, they
had already been put under military administration by the Soviet
trophy brigade under Colonel General Ludshuveit.[16] Although large
parts of their valuable art treasures had been moved to external
locations during the war, the palaces offered a rich field of activity
for the trophy brigades which elsewhere dismantled industrial facilities as reparation.

The Prussian palaces and gardens lent themselves as a conference venue for the planned summit, where the question of reparations was high on the agenda. At the Crimea conference in Yalta, the
Soviets had deliberately laid out the Western delegations' access
routes through ruined landscapes to show them the war damage
suffered by the Soviet Union. At the planned conference in Germany,
on the other hand, the aim was obviously to show that the defeated
country was not yet completely bled and devastated and that high
reparation payments were therefore justified. In Potsdam's largely
undamaged suburbs and parks, hiding the true extent of the war
damage was made easy by the choice of location as well as the
restoration of accommodation, access routes, parks and gardens.[17]

Subsequent to the trophy brigade, further Soviet military facilities were installed in the former Prussian garrison town. Since May

Aerial view of Potsdam
shortly after the
Royal Air Force raid
of 14 April 1945

1945, Potsdam's numerous barracks—used by Reichswehr and Wehrmacht after 1918—had been gradually taken over by Soviet troops. The high command of the Soviet occupation forces in Germany was established in Potsdam-Babelsberg. Here, Marshal Zhukov, the first Commander-in-Chief of the occupying forces, and Ivan Serov, the People's Commissar for Internal Affairs in Germany (NKVD) and Head of the Civil Administration of the Soviet Military Administration in Germany (SMAD), had their offices and residences. Since 5 June, Zhukov, as head of the SMAD, exercised supreme authority in the Soviet zone; he was subordinate solely to the Council of People's Commissars in Moscow and thus to Stalin.[18] Zhukov was not to be sidestepped—neither by the Western Allies' advance commands when it came to the (complicated) occupation of their sectors, nor by the Moscow delegation in the localisation and preparation of the planned conference.

Stalin, for this purpose, had sent generals from the State Security Service and staff from the People's Commissariat for Foreign Affairs to Berlin. According to his memoirs, Zhukov managed to personally convince the delegation to choose a conference venue in the area surrounding Berlin instead of its centre, sending a group of rear service officers and the head of accommodation department to Potsdam, where they found what they had been looking for: "The heads of delegations, Foreign ministers and principal advisers and experts could be conveniently quartered in Babelsberg, a Berlin suburb which had been practically undamaged during the war."[19] During the Soviet attack on Wannsee Island in the last days of the war, numerous houses in this garden suburb on Lake Griebnitz had been confiscated, and their inhabitants expelled, by the Soviet billeting administration. For the conference, the residential area was divided into a Soviet, American and British sector. These, however, proved too small, so that numerous members of the western delegations were billeted in the nearby western sectors of Berlin. Three prestigious villas on the banks of Lake Griebnitz were selected for the Big Three. House Erlenkamp, which had been the home of publisher Gustav Müller-Grote and his family, was prepared for Truman and then became known as "Berlin White House" and "Little White House".[20] Churchill was given the house of banker Franz Urbig, which had been built by Mies van der Rohe; and Stalin took up quarters in the Herpich family's villa, built by Alfred Grenander.

The head of the secret police, Lavrentiy Beria, informed Stalin about the preparations and was concerned about his security. On 2 July, Beria reported to Stalin and Vyacheslav Molotov in Moscow: "Sixty-two villas have been made ready (10,000 square metres plus a two-storey detached house for Comrade Stalin of 400 square metres: fifteen rooms, an open veranda, a mansard roof). The house is completely equipped. There is a communications centre. Stocks of game, poultry, delicacies, groceries and drink have been laid in. Three supplementary sources of supply have been established seven kilo-

View of "Little White House" (Haus Erlenkamp), Truman's residence during the Potsdam Conference

metres from Potsdam with livestock and poultry farms and vegetable stores; there are two bakeries at work. All the staff is from Moscow. Two special aerodromes have been prepared. Seven regiments of NKVD troops and 1,500 operational troops will provide security. This will take the form of three concentric circles. Chief of security at the house will be Lieutenant General Vlasik. Kruglov will be in charge of security at the conference.

A special train has been prepared. The route is 1,923 kilo-metres in length (1,095 in the USSR, 594 in Poland, 234 in Germany). Security along the route will be provided by 17,000 NKVD troops and 1,515 operational troops. Between six and fifteen men will be posted at every kilometre of track. Eight armoured trains with NKVD troops will be patrolling the track.

A two-storey house of eleven rooms has been made ready for Molotov. There are fifty-five villas, including eight detached houses, for the delegation."[21]

The opposite bank of Lake Griebnitz had belonged to the American sector of Berlin since early July. During the conference, however, it was guarded by Red Army soldiers, who also directed the traffic on Glienicker Uferchaussee and the access routes. The Soviet guards were partly billeted on the site of the former presidential building of the German Red Cross (DRK) on Lake Griebnitz (the highest employer of the DRK, once it had been brought into line with the SS, was Heinrich Himmler). The large National Socialist building, designed by Norbert Demmel and Emil Fahrenkamp in 1943, had representative halls and numerous office and work areas; from September 1945 to 1951/52, it was used by the SMAD and as headquarters of the Soviet occupation troops in Germany. Since the building, in perfect condition, was located near the delegations' quarters, it could easily have served as conference venue.

Zhukov's officers, however, chose Cecilienhof Palace in the northeast of Potsdam, which was in the hands of the trophy brigade. After Zhukov had approved their choice, also Stalin agreed to the proposal.[22] On 18 June 1945, he told Churchill: "All three delegations will be accommodated in Babelsberg, southeast of Potsdam. The fourth room intended for the joint meetings is the German Crown Prince's palace in Potsdam."[23] Churchill, who at previous conferences had always been stubborn about Moscow's proposals, immediately agreed.

Cecilienhof Palace, built between 1913 and 1917 to plans of architect Paul Schultze-Naumburg in the English country house style and partly based on designs by Paul Ludwig Troost, had been the home of Crown Prince Wilhelm and Crown Princess Cecilie (born Duchess of Mecklenburg-Schwerin).[24] After his abdication in 1918 and a brief exile in the Netherlands, the former Crown Prince and his family had lived in the Palace from 1923 to February 1945—in 1926, the Prussian state had granted them right of residence for life. During this time, leading National Socialists—among them Hitler, Göring and Röhm—were guests at Cecilienhof. With his support for Hitler in the 1932 elections and his participation in the "Day of Potsdam" in 1933, Wilhelm had hoped in vain to get back on the throne. The Hohenzollerns' involvement with Hitler had already occupied General Lucius D. Clay's special adviser, James K. Pollock, who travelled to the former Crown Prince's residence at Hechingen six months after the conference, but was only informed of Hitler's 1933 visit to

Cecilienhof. Churchill, on the other hand, blamed Hitler's rise to power on the Allied-enforced abdication of the Hohenzollerns: "I am of opinion that if the Allies at the peace table at Versailles had not imagined that sweeping away of long-established dynasties was a form of progress, and if they had allowed a Hohenzollern, a Wittelsbach, and a Habsburg to return to their thrones, there would have been no Hitler."[25]

After Wilhelm's family had fled from the approaching Red Army in February 1945, Cecilienhof Palace was initially used as a military hospital. When the north of Potsdam was attacked in April, an amphibian unit of the First Belarusian Front unexpectedly landed on the shores of the Jungfernsee in the New Garden. The Palace thus fell into the hands of Zhukov's troops almost without a fight. In preparation for the conference, the palace was removed from the trophy brigade's administration in June. The building equipment was state-of-the-art. Other than the older palaces, it had modern sanitary facilities and kitchens; every room was equipped with electricity. In contrast to the narrowness of Livadia Palace in Yalta, Cecilienhof had a spacious conference hall as well as prestigious studies for the Big Three with adjoining consulting rooms, to which delegations and staff could retreat.

The area around the palace, the New Garden, the adjacent Nauener Vorstadt and all access routes were evacuated for safety reasons, and declared a restricted area.[26] The Big Three were thus spared the daily sight of floods of refugees which had so much depressed Truman during his trip to Berlin.[27]

The bridges, which had all been destroyed in the battle for Wannsee Island, had to be replaced or repaired.[28] Park bridge over the Teltow Canal was repaired for the three delegations to travel from Babelsberg to Glienicke. For the onward journey from Glienicke to Potsdam's Berliner Vorstadt, a wooden makeshift bridge had to be built next to the destroyed Glienicke Bridge. The delegations would separate once they had crossed Glienicke Bridge. To prevent them from coming too close to the destroyed city centre, the western delegates were channelled through Berliner Vorstadt around the Holy Lake to the main entrance of the New Garden.[29] For Stalin, on the other hand, a shorter route to and from Cecilienhof was built, and the Soviet delegation drove across Schwanenallee and the repaired Schwanenbrücke to the north terrace of Cecilienhof. Here, Stalin could enter the palace through a patio door leading directly to the Soviet reception room. A portal frame with a protective roof was installed on the outside to improve the simple window door into an entrance door. The Western Allies' limousines approached the Palace from the south. The American delegation was assigned a side entrance under the outer driveway; the English delegation took the passage to the court of honour and was allowed entry through the main entrance. In this way, the three delegations and the Big Three only met in the conference hall. A fourth driveway was designated for

the correspondents and the operating staff, who also had a separate access to the conference hall.

Inside the palace, separate functional areas had to be created for the delegations. Originally, the Crown Prince's and Crown Princess's living spaces had been added to the left and right, respectively, of the large central residential hall. In the adjoining wings, the Crown Prince had been allocated the dining room and the marshal's table as well as utility rooms and the courtyard, and the Crown Princess, the governess's and children's apartments around the prince's courtyard. For the conference, this bipartite floor plan was rearranged into three sectors. To the west of the conference hall, Churchill's and Truman's studies were set up in the library on the ground floor and in the Crown Prince's smoking room. To the east of the hall, the Crown Princess's parlour and writing room were converted into a reception room and study for Stalin. As a result, the Western Allies were brought closer together, standing opposite, as it were, the Soviet side, the only delegation to enjoy a spacious reception room of its own. Not each of the three studies, however, could be connected to the respective delegation room. While Truman and Stalin were each able to enter their delegation's back room, Churchill had to put up with a laborious route from his study via hallways and stairs to the rooms of the English delegation on the upper floor in the east wing. The similar arrangement of the three entrances to the conference hall was meant to express the equal rank of the Big Three, but the British were clearly disadvantaged in this regard.

Studies and delegation rooms were refurbished for the conference—according to Nikolay A. Antipenko's "Restoration Report", nothing much had been done in the palace in terms of renovation for many years: "There was a 'White Room' for the Soviet, a 'Blue Room' for the American, and a 'Red Room' for the British delegation. The conference hall was panelled with oak, and the panelling was carefully cleaned. The representatives of the USA and Great Britain closely monitored the repair work, and sometimes were very demanding. At their request, we had to decorate the walls in various rooms with coloured silk. The floors were covered with precious carpets everywhere.

It seemed to me that Stalin's rooms were to be furnished no less luxuriously, and something in this regard had already been done. But Moscow's representative, General Vlasik, said that the more modest the décor, the better. Instead of the expensive furniture brought in from other palaces, the furniture [in Stalin's room] is simple. Study, bedroom and reception room were painted in dark colours; instead of carpets, rugs were laid.

A round table with a diameter of 6.8 meters was produced for the conference hall by the Moscow furniture factory 'Lux'. Two rows of armchairs were placed around the table: the first row was intended for the heads and members of the delegations, the second for their assistants and consultants."[30]

Main entrance to Palace Cecilienhof with the flags of the Allied victors

31

Since the palace furnishings had already been removed by the Soviets, replacement furniture had to be brought in for the Western Allies' studies: for Truman's study, it was mainly taken from Babelsberg Palace; and, for Churchill's, from the Marmorpalais (Marble Palace). Zhukov, who also wrote a short report on the conference preparations, highlighted the participation of the Western Allies: "The Americans requested that the premises set aside for the President and his staff be finished in blue, the British, for Churchill, in pink. The Soviet quarters were finished in white."[31] General Floyd L. Parks had been entrusted with the supervision by American Commander-in-Chief of the Western Allied Forces in Europe, Dwight D. Eisenhower. There were, however, narrow limits to this participation. When the British advance command, led by Miss Joan Bright, criticised the circuitous route that Churchill had to take through the Palace and asked to unlock the double doors, the Soviets refused.[32] Apparently, they did not want to allow the British to make their entrance through the larger double doors and via the prestigious main staircase. Churchill already had the privilege of being able to use the central main access in the court of honour. There, however, a red star made of a thousand flowering geraniums was to remind him every day of who now had the say in Potsdam. | CN

Notes

1 Deuerlein 1963, 86–187; Badstübner 1985, 2–6; Görtemaker 1995, 58–95; Laufer 2009, 571–73; Simmich 2019. / **2** Jansohn 2013, 24–26. / **3** The division and occupation of Berlin by the Soviets and the two Western powers had already been agreed in 1944. From 1 July to August 1945, the Soviet occupying forces in Berlin evacuated the western sectors which, as from 4 July, were taken over by American and British troops. The French followed on 12 August. / **4** Sipols et al. 1985, 74; Ressing 1970, 57. / **5** Keiderling 1997, 87–102, here 87. / **6** Stalin, on the other hand, did not take part in the jaunt, saying that he was not a tourist. See Sebag Montefiore 2003, 507. / **7** Truman made explicit reference to Versailles in his opening speech at the Potsdam Conference. / **8** Bright Astley 2007, 193. Discussed most recently by Simmich 2019. / **9** Neiberg 2015, 145; Mee 1975, 70–71. / **10** Craig 1993. / **11** In July 1945, the Soviet Military Administration in Germany (German abbreviation: SMAD) had included two Prussian provinces in the country structure of its zone of occupation, the province of Mark Brandenburg and the province of Saxony (Saxony-Anhalt, as of 1946). After the formal dissolution of the Free State of Prussia in 1947, the provinces were transformed into "Länder". / **12** Jörg Friedrich advanced the controversial thesis that "Potsdam was destroyed in order to annul the history of Prussian militarism". The attack, according to him, was motivated less by military than by intellectual history. To his mind, it was directed at the "demon" associated with the name of Potsdam: "Each and every vessel that could offer the demon a future abode had to be broken in an attempt to track him down. With Potsdam's ruin on April 14, the bombers were hot on the demon's trail. The mythical stone of Potsdam and Nuremberg was triumphantly toppled." (Friedrich 2006, 466–67). / **13** Quoted after Klos 2018, 58. / **14** The ring around Berlin was closed on 25 April in Ketzin on the Havel, northwest of Potsdam. See Arlt und Stang 1995. / **15** Knöfel 2015. Since Wehrmacht officers refused to surrender the Pfaueninsel (Peacock Island) as the last German "bastion" in the Potsdam area, the civilians capitulated here on 2 May at 11.30 a. m. See Seiler 2015. / **16** Anders 1999, 47–55. / **17** For example, the Soviets planted 1,500 Thuja plants, silver fir and other shrubs as well as 50 flowerbeds. See Antipenko 1973, 305–07. / **18** The official SMAD headquarters was in Berlin-Karlshorst, but Zhukov mainly resided in the vicinity of the military in Potsdam. / **19** Zhukov 1971, 667. / **20** Mackay 2002. / **21** Quoted after Volkogonov 1991, 498–90. / **22** Antipenko 1973, 305. / **23** Quoted after Simmich 2019. / **24** The Crown Prince's architects, Schultze-Naumburg and Troost, later became Hitler's minions. / **25** In a letter of 26 April 1945, quoted after Churchill 1953, 643. / **26** The military secret service established on Pfingstberg remained in the so-called "Military Town No. 7" until 1994, when the last Russian armed forces left Potsdam. / **27** "But much more distressing than the ruined buildings was the long, never-ending procession of old men, women and children along the autobahn and the country roads. Wandering aimlessly and probably without hope, they clutter the roads carrying their small children and pushing or pulling their slender belongings. In this two hour drive we saw evidence of a great world tragedy—the beginning of the disintegration of a highly cultured and proud people." Log of the President's Trip to the Berlin Conference, Harry S. Truman Library and Museum, www.trumanlibrary.gov/calendar/travel_log/documents [accessed 18 October 2019]. / **28** According to Lieutenant General Nikolay A. Antipenko, two new bridges were built and two older ones repaired for the conference. See Antipenko 1973, 307. More recent reports from contemporary witnesses about another bridge in the Deep Lake have not yet been reconciled with Antipenko's statement. / **29** For travelling from Glienicke to Gatow Airfield, they used a pontoon bridge between Glienicke and Sacrow. / **30** Antipenko 1973, 305–06. / **31** Zhukov 1971, 668. / **32** Mee 1975, 40–41.

In the Shadows of Yalta and Hiroshima: The US Perspective on Potsdam 1945

Philipp Gassert

When his plane touched down at Berlin-Gatow airport on 15 July 1945, US President Harry S. Truman entered a political arena that was much changed since the last meeting of the Big Three, which had taken place five months earlier in Yalta. The new American head of state was not the only thing that was different. Wartime president Franklin D. Roosevelt had died on 12 April. This threw an ill-prepared Truman, Roosevelt's vice president, into a complicated set of negotiations with global powers. Most importantly, the war's end was now imminent. The German Reich had been defeated, and Japan was on the verge of collapse. On 16 July, the day before the conference was to begin, the United States carried out the first successful test of an atomic bomb—in Alamogordo, New Mexico, carefully hidden from the public eye. Truman learned of it the evening before discussions opened in Potsdam. Coming on the cusp of Allied victory, the test spurred his pessimism and strengthened his fears. He worried, he wrote in his journal, that "machines are ahead of morals by some centuries".[1]

Expectations for the future had also changed. The final communiqué from Yalta had asserted nothing but noble intent. Flashpoints such as the question of free elections in Poland were rhetorically bypassed with the "Declaration of Liberated Europe". In the same way, the potentially explosive fight over reparations payments from Germany was quelled with nominal compromises. The participants at Yalta pledged themselves to the "unity of purpose" that had made military victory possible; this unity was to be "strengthen[ed] in the peace to come".[2] The US media set lower expectations for the Potsdam Conference: it would simply hash out practical solutions for post-war cooperation.[3] This was well suited to the sober personality of the new American president, who sought to promote a stable partnership with the USSR on behalf of world peace and global prosperity. However, in contrast to his predecessor Woodrow Wilson's approach at Versailles in 1919, Truman did not see himself as an advocate for all humanity or for a global expansion of democracy. Instead, he saw himself foremost as an advocate for his country: "I am not working for any interest but the Republic of the United States. I [am] giving nothing away except to save starving people and even then I hope we can only help them to help themselves."[4]

Truman's journey to Potsdam was carefully staged to cool any overblown expectations of a "new world order". This offered a clear contrast to Wilson, who went on a triumphal procession throughout Europe prior to the Versailles Peace Conference of 1919, celebrating himself as a visionary of global peace. But Wilson could not deliver on his vision—he was thwarted by Congress.[5] The failures of the Versailles peacemakers, including Wilson's European tour, were a living memory for most US politicians in 1945. Truman was therefore careful about the manner of his arrival. After an eight-day ocean crossing, he landed at Antwerp "with little pomp and ceremony".[6] He was driven past the cheering crowds to Brussels, where he boarded a

← Normandy landing, Omaha Beach, June 1944

plane for the three-and-a-half-hour flight to Berlin. On the afternoon of 16 July he went for a ride through the destroyed city, where he saw amongst the ruins blank faces, mostly of women, children and the elderly. He thought of 'Carthage, Baalbek, Jerusalem', of Babylon and Nineveh, of Scipio, Genghis Khan, Alexander, Darius the Great.[7]

Newsreels of the ride through Berlin mainly depicted destroyed buildings, along with a military parade. Unlike Winston Churchill, Truman refused to disembark at Hitler's Reich Chancellery, a structure that still managed to come across as ostentatious. Stalin was also rumoured to be in Berlin; this fact put *New York Times* correspondent Anne O'Hare McCormick in mind of an image: "of three men walking in a graveyard."[8] The *Chicago Tribune*, an isolationist and pro-Polish newspaper normally critical of Truman, ran an article comparing Potsdam and Versailles, in which it claimed that Berlin's "smell of death" hung over the conference: "Potsdam starts with pessimism and cynicism."[9] This kind of speculation was only exacerbated by a gagging order—another contrast to Versailles. American media had to make do with very few pictures of the Big Three in Potsdam; most were just of them shaking hands and sitting at the conference table amongst their advisers.[10] The strictly functional nature of the meeting took centre stage. Truman put it succinctly, stating in an address in front of the US headquarters that the intent was to achieve "peace and prosperity for the world as a whole."[11]

The American public's idea of the Potsdam Conference was fairly vague at the time, due to the media blackout. While it would be wrong to describe the conference as a non-event from the US perspective, it is also true that Potsdam was not associated with any watershed moments, in contrast to Yalta and to the San Francisco Conference (25 April–26 June 1945), the latter of which gave rise to the United Nations and was heavily covered by the media. In Germany, on the other hand, Potsdam was well known then and remains common knowledge to this day, since it resulted in the US map for the occupied zones, the relinquishing of the Reich's eastern provinces, the drafting of policies for occupation, and the Allied assumption of international legal responsibility for "Germany as a whole".[12] Potsdam left fewer traces in the US collective memory than did Yalta, which came to symbolise the divided world during the Cold War. Even as the Potsdam Conference proceeded, it was overshadowed by bitter fighting on the peripheries of Japan's main islands, and then by the atomic bombing of Hiroshima (6 August) and Nagasaki (9 August) shortly after the conference ended. Since the 1960s, "Hiroshima" has clearly demarcated the end of the Second World War in American popular understanding, while "Potsdam" has become the purview of historians and specialists.

Truman and Stalin with Gromyko, Byrnes, Molotov, Vaughan, Bohlen, Vardaman and Ross in Potsdam

An unfathomable victory:
American global power in 1945

Only in hindsight can we appreciate the unique position the United
States occupied on the world stage in summer 1945. By war's end,
America had gained the most, despite the low cost it paid in human
life. The tenures of Germany, Italy, and Japan as global powers were
over. The Soviet Union, Great Britain, France and China were just
as battered and drained as their former enemies and were now reli-
ant on US support. And America's casualties in the war were negligi-
ble. Compare the 400,000 US dead and 700,000 wounded to the
15 million residents of the Soviet Union who perished, the 6 million
dead Poles, 4 million dead Germans, 2 million dead Japanese.
Or compare it to losses in the US Civil War (620,000 soldiers dead).

All told, 60 million people were killed in the Second World War—less than one per cent of them American.[13]

The United States were also economically more robust by the time the fighting stopped, in contrast to almost all other countries. With the minor exceptions of Hawaii, the Aleutian Islands and its colonies in the Philippines, America was neither a theatre of war nor a victim of bombing campaigns. Its infrastructure was untouched —expanded, even—and its economy was in top gear. Its citizens enjoyed the highest standard of living in the world. In 1945, America was responsible for more than half of global industrial production. It led all other countries in imports *and* exports. The Bretton Woods Conference (1944) had already made the United States the anchor of the global economy during the war, a role they claimed from Great Britain for good. Most Americans were also convinced that their country had borne the greatest burden in the conflict. Many Brits, in contrast, thought that distinction belonged to the Soviet Union.[14]

Americans could also boast in 1945 that their political system, based on the Constitution of 1787, had made it through the Second World War unscathed. It is true that Americans of Japanese descent were unconstitutionally interned after the attack on Pearl Harbor. However, this time it remained relatively quiet on the "home front", in contrast to the turmoil of 1917/1918, which saw the widespread persecution of German Americans. No elections were cancelled due to the war. Roosevelt was re-elected to unprecedented third (1940) and fourth (1944) terms as president. The American republic glowed with confidence on the world stage and saw itself as a model for democratisation in occupied Europe and East Asia. Even its military was in a league of its own. The United States had one of the largest and most modernised armies in the world, along with the most powerful air force and navy. It was also the only country to possess the atomic bomb.

But this palmy view of America's position is by no means representative of the country's mood in 1945. Many Americans, recalling the pitfalls of the last post-war period (1919/20), checked their optimism this time around. Images of cheering crowds such as in New York's Times Square—so often shown in documentaries and printed in history books—can leave a false impression. While many people truly did break out in spontaneous celebration after the German ("V-E Day") and Japanese ("V-J Day") capitulations in May and August 1945, these joyous images conceal people's more decidedly ambiguous expectations for the future.[15] America fluctuated between optimism, anxious hope, disappointment and fear. Would internal division, mistrust and trepidation spoil the peace in 1945, just like they did in 1919?

But America in 1945 was a nation transformed. The Second World War had changed the relationship of the United States to the world and had revolutionised its foreign policy. Even though 7.5 million US soldiers were to be brought home on the double, as the public

Harry S. Truman, James F. Byrnes und William D. Leahy (from left to right), taking a ride through the ruins of Berlin, 16 July 1945 demanded, most political decision makers now understood that, as Secretary of War Henry L. Stimson said, America could "never again be an island to itself".[16] It was now *nolens volens* part of a global system that affected every aspect of its politics, economy and society. The isolationist mood in US foreign policy, which had long been influential, was intellectually and politically attenuated.[17] This isolationism had appeared to help enable the rise of Hitler's Germany during the inter-war years. One "lesson of 1919" that America learned was to honour its global commitments, even if the debate over the exact nature of American interests was not yet settled.[18]

America was not the only country with a new place in the world; the Soviet Union's position had changed, too. "Russia", as Truman called it, had not been at the negotiating table in 1919, and, like the United States, it stood outside the Eurocentric world order until 1939/1941. In 1945, the geopolitical situation changed drastically. From now on, Moscow would direct world events alongside Washington. Though Churchill, who could be called Hitler's "first enemy", participated in the council of the great powers, he did so mostly as a monument to bygone imperial grandeur; in reality, the United Kingdom was largely dependent on the United States and did not even speak for its own oversees dominions.[19] It was widely accepted among politicians that there was no getting around Stalin and that the relationship with the USSR, which America first officially established in 1933, would be the new pivot of world politics.[20]

Hope and anxiety: America 1945

Despite their moment of triumph, many Americans in 1945 anxiously wondered how they would deal with the upheavals that the Second World War brought in its wake. Essayist, literature critic and historian Bernard DeVoto used his monthly column in the liberal *Harper's Magazine*, titled "The Easy Chair", to muse about post-war developments. As bad as the war was, he wrote, the problems of peace might be worse. Though the conflict may have damaged America, it had at least held the country together. Without that external discipline, the United States risked collapsing into disorder, disunion and social displacement: "That whereas war has brought us hope, or at least courage, the coming peace may bring despair."[21] He foresaw problems for the economy; for reintegrating millions of veterans; and for restoring "normal" gender roles, which had broken down alongside sexual mores and family structures during the war. He clairvoyantly predicted a retrenchment of racial hatred—not only of "Jim Crow" (as apartheid was called in the southern United States), but of anti-semitism as well.

Many Americans worried about the economy. The mass unemployment of the 1930s was still a living memory. True, that problem had been fixed by the wartime boom, but what would happen when

American war poster

We CAN'T win this war
without sacrifice on
the home front, too.

A black American soldier
of the 12th Armoured
Division standing guard
over a group of German
soldiers

8 million veterans came flooding back into the job market? Would prosperity last, or would the transition to a peacetime economy revive the Great Depression of the inter-war years? Would the labour struggles of the 1930s break out anew?[22] Strikes had been on the uptick during the last phase of the war, particularly in mining. This resulted in a spectacular political reaction. In order to protect the war effort, Congress gave the president sweeping authorisation to commandeer factories and to restrict union activities in industries necessary for military production. As the war ended, would economic chaos ensue? Would the spectre of socialism menace America?

What did the future have in store for the American family? The war seemed to have fundamentally changed the relationship between men and women. Six million women had found work in war-time industries, earning their own keep. Few of them longed to return to cooking and childrearing. On the contrary, 61 per cent wanted to keep working outside of the home, according to surveys.[23] While some politicians, including Truman, wanted women to have the chance to work for a living, traditionalists saw a grave danger to the American family. They thought that children were neglected by mothers who worked during the war, that the home had to reclaim its place as the central American institution, and that a return to patriarchy was essential. As the sociologist Willard Waller put it, "women must bear and rear children; husbands must support them."[24]

The future condition of African Americans in society proved disquieting for many whites, and not just in the South. Black soldiers had served loyally in the war. Many of them died for America, while others returned wounded or maimed. They expected, rightly so, to finally be treated as equal citizens.[25] The Swedish sociologist Gunnar Myrdal wrote in 1944 of an 'American dilemma': many white Americans supported and celebrated democracy, but at the same time they had no qualms about treating their African American brothers and sisters unequally.[26] Most whites approved of legalised discrimination, in which blacks were treated as second-class citizens. However, the war increased the confidence and political consciousness of many African Americans. Black political and intellectual leaders sensed that the collapse of European empires heralded the arrival in America of a theretofore denied moment, when the "benefits of freedom and prosperity" could be mutually enjoyed.[27]

The war changed many Americans' views of the world. Millions of men and women had seen far-flung theatres of combat in strange lands. They brought back these often unique perspectives to their living rooms, farms and factories in the United States. However, their experiences "over there" created a desire to return to "normalcy" at home. Many Americans were now connected by the shared experience of military service, which created a superficial commonality in such a heterogenous nation. The war also prepared the US populace for a future in which America would continuously require a strong, if not the strongest, military—although the isolationist reflex still lingered, particularly in the Midwest, from whence Truman hailed. The US government therefore made it a point to school its citizens in internationalism.

The atomic bombing of Hiroshima and Nagasaki exacerbated the sense of cultural anxiety, despite the fact that the United States, by sacrificing the two cities, was able to end the war with Japan in a fell swoop and spare millions of people additional suffering and death. The "nuclear apocalypse" was quickly worked into novels and movies with dreary tones, such as Aldous Huxley's *Ape and Essence* (1948).[28] Cultural historians regard the early post-war years as an "age of anxiety", a name borrowed from W. H. Auden's Pulitzer-Prize-winning poem. For the United States in particular, the bomb meant that geographical isolation was no longer a reliable protection from attack. This was now largely apparent to American politicians.[29]

From Roosevelt to Truman: America's path to Potsdam

These were the ambivalent emotions that shaped the world view —and subsequent actions—of America's representatives in Potsdam in 1945. Truman and his Secretary of State James F. Byrnes, who had also recently been sworn into office, were all too aware of the social challenges on the home front. As democratically elected politicians in a land with a free press, and as trustees for the American people, they had to factor such challenges into their work in Potsdam. The economic revitalisation of Europe was therefore a priority, since American prosperity and jobs depended on it. And no one had forgotten Wilson's failure to unify the US public in support of the Paris peace agreement, which the Senate ultimately refused to ratify.[30] As a result, Truman tempered expectations and sought to "bring along" the American people this time.

By 7 July 1945, when Truman boarded the cruiser *Augusta* in Newport News to set off for Europe and the Potsdam Conference, Roosevelt had been dead for almost three months. Truman was not as unversed in foreign policy as he is often portrayed. He had served as a soldier in World War I; representing Missouri in the Senate since 1935, he was often confronted with foreign policy questions; and he had fought against waste in defence spending. However, he shared the isolationism of his midwestern constituents, who had no desire to be sucked into Europe's wars and who possessed only a superficial understanding of the world. Truman was truly intent on achieving a lasting peace, cooperating with Stalin (whom he regarded positively) and finding a viable compromise in Potsdam. However, like many of his fellow Americans, he also tended toward "a simplistic black-and-white view" of Moscow and the USSR.[31]

Truman inherited from Roosevelt a pile of unfinished business, the most important item of which was to find a way to deal with defeated Germany in its European context. It is difficult to identify a single American approach to this question. Plans for the post-war period were shaped by conflicts among executive departments, a typical occurrence in Washington. On the complex issue of reparations—which had put a lasting strain on the relationship with the Soviet Union—the Departments of State, War and the Treasury all took different tacks. Interpretations of the Yalta resolutions were internally disputed, and the question of reparations remained open: Yalta produced "a decision ... that was no [decision]".[32] Truman helped clarify policy immediately before the Potsdam Conference by forcing out Treasury Secretary Henry Morgenthau Jr., the most prominent advocate of hamstringing the German economy.[33]

Roosevelt considered it centrally important that Moscow approve of his United Nations plan; he had therefore conceded on the issue of reparations, despite British objections. Soviet reparations proposals were thus accepted at Yalta as the basis for discussion. But neither the Americans nor the British had been willing to discuss concrete numbers, so the debate was tabled for a yet-to-be-formed committee. For a long time it remained unclear what US policy should be: either restrict German potential through economic dismantling, as the Treasury Department and military proposed, or put Germany in a position to not only feed itself but also, through renewed industrial activity, to contribute to Europe's recovery and meet Soviet demands for reparations. "If the goal was the destruction or at least a considerable reduction of German economic potential, one could not simultaneously use that potential to generate reparations."[34]

Roosevelt's post-war vision—an invigorated United States cooperating successfully with the USSR in a new world order that ensured peace, in front of the backdrop of a non-violent decolonisation—was already crumbling by the time he died.[35] His plan "bore utopian traits in its own day", admitting as it did the necessity of working with the Soviet Union. But Roosevelt was aware of the domestic political risks, so he avoided coming clean with the US public: it was already clear at Yalta that Eastern Europe would be unable to democratise as long as the Red Army was present, especially since America's "boys" were to be brought home quickly. Roosevelt thereby spurred a set of expectations among the American people in early 1945 "that could only be let down by the reality in Europe."[36]

Truman entered office during this time of thorough ambivalence on the national and international stage, one shot through with mercurial and unrealistic expectations. As hostilities wound down, the US public longed for a lasting peace; meanwhile, the country's foreign policy elite heatedly debated the future relationship to the USSR. Aside from the internal dispute over German reparations (on which Americans expected severity), it was Stalin's treatment of Poland that proved most contentious. Polish Americans commanded a lobby with a powerful media arm, and the president had to take this fact into account. For instance, when the decision was made at Yalta to push Poland's borders westward, it led to a flurry of protest from congressional delegates of Polish descent, who saw it as a "second Munich".[37]

Even if Truman had been more privy to Roosevelt's plans for the future relationship to the Soviet Union, and even if he had been able to rely on a team of devoted foreign policy experts, he still would have found it difficult to handle the conflicts that broke out before and after Potsdam. For their part, the Soviets resented the abrupt termination of the American lend-lease programme the moment hostilities ceased in Europe, while the Americans were outraged over Moscow's intransigence during the inaugural meeting of the UN in San Francisco. Truman wanted to take a hard line with the USSR, but he also held on to the hope of a continued and productive cooperation that could bring about a peaceful post-war order. Though he oscillated between these two poles, he always struck a conciliatory note.

Truman travelled to Potsdam with the "kindliest feelings in the world toward Russia", as he later noted in a retrospective interview.[38] He worked to find a *modus vivendi* with Stalin in the weeks leading up to the conference. In spite of Churchill's frantic reactions, he kept to the European demarcation line agreed on at Yalta. He ordered the withdrawal of US troops from Thuringia as well as from the northern German and Austrian provinces, which lay in the agreed Soviet zone. Churchill wanted to hold on to these "bargaining chips" in order to force Stalin into concessions on the "Polish question". Harry Hopkins, a former associate of Roosevelt, was sent to Moscow in early June. There he accepted communist hegemony over the provisional government in Warsaw, which subsequently received diplomatic recognition despite protests from the Polish American community. Given the facts on the ground, Truman considered further delays to be a pointless and unnecessary strain on the relationship with Stalin. Thus Poland's freedom was sacrificed as a down payment for the Potsdam Conference.[39]

"… as a well known Missouri horse trader, the American people expect you to bring something home to them": this is the quintessence of a July 4 conversation between Truman and his advisers in preparation for Potsdam.[40] Truman approached the conference just like Byrnes. Both were former senators who knew how to serve as hard-nosed advocates for their constituents and their states. They understood international relations as a rarefied form of horse trading, one whose results could likewise be measured in dollars and cents. Truman therefore did not give much thought to an ideal world order in a Wilsonian sense while on the way to Potsdam. After all, the United Nations had just been formed. Truman was much more concerned with hashing out concrete results, ending the war and then pivoting to domestic politics. And to achieve this, he would require a stable partnership with the USSR that was as free of conflict as possible.

The negotiations:
pragmatism tempers expectations

Truman had not been looking forward to his journey to Potsdam. "How I hate this trip", he wrote in his journal.[41] Nevertheless, he dutifully sailed across the Atlantic for the first time since his deployment in the First World War. At the time, his top negotiating priority was to reaffirm Russia's entry into the war against Japan, a result most Americans expected and wanted.[42] Secondly, Europe needed long-term economic stabilisation; this point was material for US taxpayers, since it would check the runaway financial costs of occupation. The third priority was to secure Great Britain's full participation in the Pacific theatre of war; the fourth was to clarify the specifics of the policy toward Germany. Truman's two other, minor goals were to set a US location for the war's final peace conference and to acquire overseas military bases.[43]

This grouping of set pieces for the negotiation was quickly whittled down to the "German question", elections in Eastern Europe and reparations. Stalin agreed to join the fight against Japan during his first meeting with Truman, before the conference even started, though that participation would depend on the outcome of Russian-Chinese negotiations regarding Manchuria.[44] Truman wrote in his memoirs that he had many reasons for travelling to Potsdam: "But the most urgent, to my mind, was to get from Stalin a personal reaffirmation of Russia's entry into the war against Japan." He noted that this was the only secret deal struck at the conference, a clear jab at Wilson.[45] Yet the agreement with Stalin, which had been so important for America, was ultimately rendered obsolete by technological developments. In the following days, the atom bomb's potential became clear: "Japs will fold up before Russia comes in. I am sure they will when Manhattan appears over their homeland."[46]

Negotiations began on the afternoon of 17 July at five o'clock. A nervous Truman was called on by Stalin to lead the meeting.[47] Truman's nerves remained hidden from US media, however, which only got glimpses of the new president in photos, smiling with Churchill and Stalin, or sitting at the conference table in Cecilienhof Palace amid his advisers.[48] The *Christian Science Monitor* did make note of the fact that Truman was the "unknown quantity" of the negotiations, but it also pointed out that his shrewd bargaining skills and his open and honest manner more than made up for his limited experience on the international stage.[49] The American press noted with approval that their president led the negotiations, while simultaneously complaining that they themselves were reduced to reporting on official dinner menus and the exchange of diplomatic gifts.[50]

The Potsdam negotiations quickly pivoted to the question of a standing Council of Foreign Ministers, as well as to the specifics of German occupation[51]; meanwhile, the US press speculated about whether Stalin would honour his agreement from Yalta to declare war on Japan.[52] This laser focus on Japan was unavoidable, since the relatively sleepy conference in Potsdam had to share the media spotlight with the Pacific campaign. The American public was understandably captivated by the massive bombing runs on Tokyo and other cities, as well as by the imminent invasion of Japan's main islands, which was expected to prove a bitter fight. By the third day of the Potsdam Conference, US newspaper stories about the negotiations were already being bumped below the front-page fold, or even placed in inside sections, while the war in Asia dominated the banner headlines. Stories about Potsdam remained on front pages for a time, nestled among other topics, but these stories mostly offered conjecture on the plans of the Big Three for Japan.[53]

On 20 July, the conference produced its first concrete result with the founding of the Council of Foreign Ministers. (The American public, fixated on Japan, took little notice.) The Big Three also agreed to allow France and China to participate in the council on a case-by-case basis, and they set plans for an initial meeting in London.[54] This represented the achievement of another important goal on Truman's part: the establishment of a standing process for international consultation. Already at Potsdam it was the foreign ministers who were drafting most of the decisions, which would be presented to the Big Three sometime in late afternoon in Cecilienhof's grand conference room.[55] The plenary meetings, on the other hand, kept getting bogged down on the issues of reparations and Poland's western border. Churchill made a point of defying Soviet aims on a range of topics—on Yugoslavia and the Balkans, on the former Italian colonies, on a Russian military presence in the Dardanelles. He also clashed with Stalin over the Polish question and the Oder-Neisse line, while the "Americans were passive".[56]

Two major events brought the negotiations at Potsdam back into the spotlight of the US media. The first was the Potsdam Declaration issued by the United States, Great Britain and China, which once again called on Japan to learn from Germany's mistakes and to surrender immediately, or face "prompt and utter destruction."[57] The second was the shocking news of 26 July that Winston Churchill, the towering leader of the Allies throughout the Second World War, had been ousted as prime minister by UK voters. (Members of the American delegation in Potsdam learned of this development at the same time as the American public.) In contrast, the role of mediator assumed in Potsdam by the United States, its president and its secretary of state was not visible to the American (nor, for that matter, to the Soviet or British) public—just as the wealth of issues raised in the negotiations, their geographical scope and the complexity of their content completely eluded US newspaper readers.

These events—the ultimatum for Japan and Churchill's electoral defeat—put some sensational pep back into the Potsdam Conference from 26 July on. The Potsdam Declaration got the press speculating that Japan had sent out feelers to the Allies regarding a

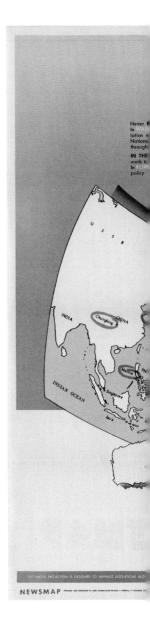

Newsmap, vol. 4, no. 35

U. S. ROLE IN WORLD AFFAIRS

...tates been so active in world affairs. ...as passed and sent to the House legis... ...res to participate fully in the United ... States diplomacy already is engaged ...solutions to complex postwar problems.

...es occupy JAPAN for the Allies and ...one that will not be a threat to peace. ...cupation tasks with the Russians. U. S. ...y Secretary of State Byrnes, calls for

support of the Nationalist Government and includes the desire that the Chinese build a "strong, united and democratic" nation. In the PHILIP-PINES, the U. S. prepares to grant full independence.

IN EUROPE AND THE MIDDLE EAST: In Germany, the U. S. shares the responsibilities of occupation and denazification, and is participating in the trial of Germany's war leaders at NUREMBERG. In eastern Europe, the U. S. desires free and democratic governments. In RUSSIA it seeks to achieve understanding and cooperation. The U. S., with Russia and

Britain, is pledged by the Teheran Declaration to maintain the inde-pendence of IRAN, from which American troops are scheduled to be withdrawn on 1 January. An American-British committee will make recommendations concerning Jewish immigration into PALESTINE. At LONDON, the U. S. joins in preparations for the first UNO meeting.

IN LATIN AMERICA: The U. S. pursues the good neighbor policy. Secretary Byrnes has approved a proposal by URUGUAY for collective intervention against any Western Hemisphere nation that denies its citizens essential rights or does not fulfill international obligations.

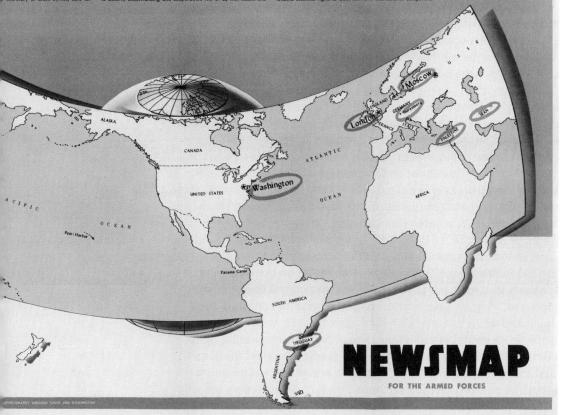

NEWJMAP

FOR THE ARMED FORCES

possible peace deal.[58] News outlets in America tried to outdo each other with arresting headlines about how the "Japs" had been given their final warning: "Yield now, or die".[59] If Japan thought that British elections could weaken the Allied resolve to force unconditional surrender, they would be sorely disappointed—so editorialised the press. The fact that the declaration was issued in Potsdam lent more credence to popular rumours that the conference revolved around East Asia.[60] In reality, the negotiations had long been hung up on Poland and reparations. In his last meeting as part of the Big Three, right before flying back to London to await election results, Churchill had sparred heatedly with Stalin over Poland and the Ruhr.[61]

The transition from Churchill to Clement Attlee, who was already a member of the British delegation at Potsdam, generated new interest in the negotiations.[62] Neither the American nor the Soviet delegation had expected that Churchill, a war hero, would be defeated.[63] From the US perspective, this development was surprising, sensational and also inscrutable. It required explanation. During the break in negotiations, Truman had travelled to the area around Darmstadt and Mannheim to visit American troops. He now hurried back to Potsdam to debrief on the implications of the British election.[64] (The US press was not expecting Attlee to return immediately, but Truman still wanted to beat him there.) By the time Attlee arrived in Germany two days later, Potsdam had vanished from the front pages. It was replaced (once again) by the bombing campaign against Japan and also by the US Senate's ratification of the UN charter.[65]

The American press continued to report on the world and on the war's progress, but Potsdam would take centre stage only once more. On 3 August 1945, numerous headlines and editorials were dedicated to the conference's final communiqué, which was reproduced in its entirety in all major newspapers. The focus was on Germany's place in the agreement; the US media conveyed the sense that the Reich was to be turned into a "farm state" whose entire industrial capacity would be stripped away.[66] Almost every newspaper printed some kind of map depicting the eastern territories that were being transferred to Poland. This highlighted in a readily visible manner the extent of Germany's "humiliation".[67] Many commentators praised the newly created process for hashing out peace deals, which was shaped by the Council of Foreign Ministers and the terms settled on for the occupation. On the other hand, the absence of a Soviet promise to enter the war against Japan produced much disappointment and rampant speculation.[68]

The agreement found general support in Congress, though few members could foresee its far-reaching consequences. They, too, were primarily concerned with the desired Russian offensive against Japan.[69] Harsh criticism emanated from the former isolationist camp in the Midwest. These voices were spearheaded by the Chicago Tribune, which ran an editorial calling the agreement "folly". The Tribune warned that stripping out Germany's industry would drive millions into hunger; furthermore, there was no clear vision for reconstructing Europe's economy, and Poland still was not free. According to the paper, Stalin was the conference's big winner, since he had achieved his goals without having to commit to the fight against Japan. The loser was Truman: "Mr. Truman got nothing, or rather less than nothing, for he assented to unlivable arrangements in Europe that only can prevent recovery and sow the seed of a new war."[70]

Though the Potsdam Agreement was published in full, and though Truman clearly stated that there were no additional arrangements made in secret at the conference, the actual results from Potsdam remained shrouded in ambiguity for most observers. Many perceptions of the agreement were erroneous, as we can see today. In this errant vein, Anne O'Hare McCormick of the *New York Times* questioned whether taking permanent imperial control of the second most important industrialised nation on Earth and destroying its economy was really the ticket to a prosperous and peaceful Europe. But, she wrote, this question did not bother the "Big Three": "The trouble is that the full result of today's decisions will not be felt in the lifetime of the men who make them."[71] In early August, the American public simply could not predict what the long-term effects of the Potsdam negotiations would be.

In the shadow of the bomb and the Cold War: the US memory of Potsdam

When Americans opened their newspapers on the morning of 7 August 1945, they were greeted with sensational front-page stories of the atomic bombing of Hiroshima. From that point on, the Potsdam resolutions would hold interest only for a specialised audience, no longer for a general one. They soon became "history", fast falling out of the American collective memory. This can be seen in the precipitous drop in the number of articles written about Potsdam. The conference reclaimed media attention only once more, on 9 August, while events in Nagasaki were still fresh. The Soviet Union had declared war on Japan the day before. The press now claimed in approving terms that Truman's real objective at Potsdam—bringing the Soviets into the war—had become clear. Even the *Chicago Tribune* showed Truman respect.[72] The *Boston Globe* cut to the chase: "Truman Made Parley Trip to Bring Reds In".[73] In this view, however, the conference's only purpose was to secure Russian military support against Japan.

By mid-August, Potsdam was through for US media outlets. Emperor Hirohito's radio address of 15 August had marked the end of hostilities with Japan. The instrument of surrender was signed on board the *USS Missouri* on 2 September. During this time, the foreign ministers of the Big Three nations were busy preparing for their first council meeting, which took place in London from 12 September to 21 October 1945. The meeting did not concern Germany, but rather its former allies: Finland, Italy, Hungary, Bulgaria and Romania. During the council meeting, the United States blocked the Red Army from participating in the occupation of Japan; meanwhile, the Soviets pressed to exclude China and France from the council. This produced references to Potsdam, since the Council of Foreign Ministers was initiated there, as Secretary of State Byrnes explained in a radio address.[74]

When the Council of Foreign Ministers met in Moscow a year and a half later, in March/April 1947, the divisions among the Allies were on full display—and so, too, was the unsustainable nature of the institutional mechanisms created in Potsdam. The second London meeting of the foreign ministers, in November/December 1947, saw the end of Allied cooperation in Germany. By that time, Byrnes had been replaced by George C. Marshall as secretary of state. Marshall's appointment signalled a new policy towards the Soviet Union, one which was historically marked by the promulgations of the Truman Doctrine (March 1947) and the Marshall Plan (June 1947). The transition to a policy of containment was complete. Due to Moscow's intransigence on the question of reparations, the United States began pursuing the formation of a West German state. The expansion of the Bizone to the Trizone in 1947/1948 was an early step in this process. The USSR, on the other hand, held on to the unrealistic goal of German unity.[75]

In December of 1947, in London, the Council of Foreign Ministers effectively came to an end. This prompted journalist Walter Lippmann to reflect on the mechanism born in Potsdam. Lippmann—who was responsible for popularising (though not inventing) the idea of the "Cold War"[76]—took a critical view of Truman and Marshall's increasingly aggressive approach. He also saw fundamental flaws in the Council of Foreign Ministers. The close cooperation of the ministers dated back to Yalta, he thought. However, at the conferences in Yalta and Potsdam the negotiations had been carried out under the watchful gaze of the Big Three. The system that came out of Potsdam, on the other hand, lacked a direct connection to the heads of government, and it operated in a public spotlight that zeroed in on every triviality. This, according to Lippmann, made the system not just unproductive but "an inconceivably bad diplomatic system". Moscow and Washington had to find a new way to interact.[77]

If Potsdam represented, from the American perspective, the gradual breakdown of cooperation among the Big Three, then Yalta was seen one of two ways. Either it was celebrated as the apex of Allied wartime comradery—a chance for the great powers to collaborate on behalf of world peace, foolishly thrown away by Roosevelt's successor. Or it was pilloried as a symbol of American naivety vis-à-vis Stalin and the USSR.[78] Critics such as French President Charles de Gaulle pointed to Yalta as the place where the West breached its faith with Poland and Eastern Europe; supporters romanticised it as an opportunity of world-historical import. In contrast to "the betrayal

US troops entering Nagasaki, September 1945

54

Japanese Foreign Minister
Mamoru Shigemitsu and
Chief of Staff General
Yoshijiro Umezu during the
surrender ceremonies on
board the USS Missouri,
2 September 1945

of Yalta", Potsdam conjures few emotional reactions.[79] Even historiographers regard it less as a turning point and more as a step, though an important one, on the way to the Cold War. This is precisely why many historical surveys of the early Cold War begin at Yalta, rather than at Potsdam or Tehran.

The fact that "Potsdam" faded from US memory faster than "Yalta" and "Hiroshima" has less to do with the Potsdam Conference itself and more to do with a set of political interests and a culture of remembrance that ascribed higher symbolic value to these two "places" than they did to "Potsdam". A search of the *Proquest Historical Newspapers* database for "Potsdam Conference 1945" and "Yalta Conference 1945" returns more hits for Yalta from the 1940s, though results evened out by the 1960s (Table 1). In the 1980s, as the world prepared to overturn the Cold War order, Yalta (rather than Potsdam) re-emerged as the most common historical reference point for the divvying up of the globe; it stood for the division of Europe between East and West. This can be seen in established concepts like "Yalta", which was said to be supplanted in 1990. Yet the transition from Roosevelt to Truman, the first Cold War president, occurred before Potsdam. The post-war order could rightly be called the "Potsdam order", but this formulation does not seem to hold the same sway over the public memory as does the idea of "Yalta".

Then again, since the 1960s both "Potsdam" *and* "Yalta" have easily been overshadowed in the US collective memory by "Hiroshima". An analysis of the same database reveals this trend (Table 1).

Table 1:
Number of References in American Newspapers, 1945–2016

	"Potsdam"	"Yalta"	"Hiroshima"
Only 1945	1.588	2.310	810
1940–49	2.163	2.803	1.284
1950–59	829	1.090	819
1960–69	282	295	901
1970–79	183	219	948
1980–89	180	248	1.816
1990–99	192	239	2.090
2000–09	15	15	330
Total	**3.913**	**4.921**	**8.392**

Source: Proquest Historical Newspapers (Atlanta Constitution, Boston Globe, Chicago Tribune, Christian Science Monitor, Los Angeles Times, New York Times, Wall Street Journal, Washington Post). Search terms used were: "Potsdam Conference 1945", "Yalta Conference 1945", "Hiroshima 1945".

Here, too, the discrepancy is explained less by contemporary perception and more by latter-day imputation: in 1945, Hiroshima was referenced half as often as Potsdam and barely a third as often as Yalta. It lagged behind both conferences for the entire 1940s. By the late 1950s, however, it had surpassed them both. This change may have been prompted by the US-Soviet nuclear arms race, which saw its high-water mark in the 1962 Cuban Missile Crisis. Many people had become preoccupied by the spectre of nuclear death— and Hiroshima, in retrospect, appeared to be the beginning of the nuclear age. Since then, "Hiroshima" has become a twofold cipher, laying bare both the apocalyptic capabilities of modern civilisation and the unimaginable extent of military violence.[80] Yalta and Pots- dam were not entirely forgotten, but neither could they be recalled in America's cultural memory the same way the atomic bomb could. This may now be true for Germany as well. The farther the Cold War recedes into the grey mists of the past, the more imposing Hiroshima becomes in contrast.

Throughout the decades, Hiroshima was increasingly seen as a historical turning point, while Yalta and Potsdam faded from memory. At least this is what a quantitative analysis of the news coverage suggests. Hiroshima was not simply a symbol of the destructiveness of nuclear weapons, either. It also served as the natural starting point for a debate, which raged during the Ameri- can culture wars of the 1990s, about the decision to drop the bomb in the first place. This, too, kept the public interested in Hiroshima. Ironically, the generation that dropped the bomb ascribed less importance to it than we do today. Meanwhile, the events that they considered more historically meaningful—the conferences at Yalta and Potsdam—continue to lose perceived relevance. They are topics for historians and experts. "Hiroshima" and the decision to drop the bomb, on the other hand, still provoke strong emotions; they have served as a kind of patriotic litmus test in the United States since the 1990s.[81]

Of course, Potsdam has not been entirely forgotten in Amer- ica. This is thanks in no small part to the presence of a physical place of remembrance in Cecilienhof, which attracts many US tourists. The Lonely Planet travel guide describes Cecilienhof as a location with significant historical import: "Where Stalin, Truman and Church- ill (and later his successor Clement Attlee) hammered out Germany's post-war fate and incidentally laid the foundation for the Cold War."[82] In the New York Times travel section, articles about Berlin and its surrounding areas rarely fail to mention the setting of the Potsdam Conference.[83] The meeting of the Big Three even provides the backdrop for the occasional crime novel.[84] And as members of the "greatest generation" began passing away in larger numbers in the 1990s and 2000s, the obituaries of former war heroes, Truman's companions among them, offered yet more opportunities to reflect on Potsdam.

The US historian Michael Neiberg has criticised the fact that "Potsdam" no longer stands for the Second World War's last chapter, either in American memory or in academic research.[85] Since the 1960s, it has been treated instead as part of Cold War history. This can be seen in the lingering enigma of "atomic diplomacy": did Truman take a harder line in the Potsdam negotiations because he knew the nuclear test at Alamogordo had been successful, and did he intend the destruction of Hiroshima and Nagasaki to send a message to the USSR about the future of US-Soviet relations? (Such an interpretation is not supported by the conference protocols, only by apocryphal sources.) This debate drowns out the historiographical interest in Potsdam.[86] In reality, the politicians assembled at Cecilienhof had much on their plate: Germany, Poland, reparations, rebuilding Europe, ending the war in the Pacific. No one in 1945 expected that the Grand Alliance would collapse within a few short years. Quite the opposite. The Big Three hoped to meet again in Washington, as Truman suggested at the end of negotiations. "God willing" was Stalin's reply to the suggestion. Attlee seconded him: "I hope that it will be a milestone on the road to peace between our countries and in the world."[87] | JP

Notes

1 Ferrell 1980, 52; journal entry from 16 July 1945. / **2** Communiqué Issued at the End of the Conference, 11 February 1945, FRUS 1945, The Conferences at Malta and Yalta, Nr. 500, 975. / **3** "Potsdam Meeting: Big Three Confer", New York Times, 15 July 1945, 1. / **4** Ferrell 1980, 52; journal entry from 7 July 1945. / **5** Berg 2017, 187–212. / **6** Universal Newsreel, July 1945, footage available through Footage Farm, 250081, www.youtube.com/watch?v=YqosWmpjQvA [accessed 4 December 2019]. / **7** Ferrell 1980, 52; journal entry from 16 July 1945. / **8** "Abroad: Man From Missouri, Meets Man from Georgia", New York Times, 18 July 1945, 26. / **9** "From Paris 1918 to Potsdam 1945", Chicago Tribune, 20 July 1945. / **10** "Potsdam Secrecy", New York Times, 17 July 1945, 12; "Abroad: Unfortunate Aspects of the Potsdam News Blackout", New York Times, 21 July 1945, 10; "Potsdam Blackout", Wall Street Journal, 25 July 1945, 8. / **11** "Let us not forget that we are fighting for peace, and for the welfare of mankind. We are not fighting for conquest. There is not one piece of territory, or one thing of a monetary nature that we want out of this war. We want peace and prosperity for the world as a whole." Harry S. Truman, 20 July 1945, "Remarks at the Raising of the Flag Over the U.S. Group Control Council Headquarters in Berlin", Truman Library, Public Papers of Harry S. Truman, www.trumanlibrary.gov/library/public-papers/86/remarks-raising-flag-over-us-group-control-council-headquarters-berlin [accessed 1 November 2019]. / **12** This can also be seen in US academic research, which rarely focuses on the Potsdam Conference in and of itself, with the exception of Feis 1960; it is overwhelmingly treated as a part of early Cold War history, or as "atomic diplomacy", the latter being argued by Miscamble 2007; Neiberg 2015 presents it as multilateral diplomatic history, without a particular focus on the United States; German research focuses on legal questions, such as in Koch 2017. / **13** Emmerich and Gassert 2014, 171–72. / **14** See Wittner 1984, 103. / **15** For a description of the victory celebrations, see Dallas 2005, 505–06. / **16** "Can never again be an island to itself", quoted in Patterson 1996, 82. / **17** On the isolationism debate, see McDougall 1997, 39 et seq. / **18** In 1937, 55 per cent of Americans opposed membership in a "world organization"; in early 1945, 81 per cent supported such membership; this according to a survey from 9 April 1945, Public Opinion Quarterly 9, no. 2 (Summer 1945), 253; "Prevention of War", survey from 15 July 1945, ibid., no. 3 (Fall 1945), 384. A publication meant to inform returning soldiers about developments on the home front highlighted precisely this transformation in its chapter on foreign policy perspectives; it also included a text contribution from a

US senator; see Ball 1946, 552–72. / **19** Briefing Book Paper: Britain as a Member of the Big Three, FRUS 1945, The Conference of Berlin (The Potsdam Conference), vol. 1, no. 223, 253. / **20** Briefing Book Paper: British Plan for a Western European Bloc, FRUS 1945, The Conference of Berlin (The Potsdam Conference), vol. 1, no. 224, Attachment, Excerpts from a Letter from the Joint Chiefs of Staff to the Secretary of State, 16 May 1944, 265: " … as regards Britain several developments have combined to lessen her relative military and economic strength … " / **21** DeVoto 1944, 345. / **22** Chafe 2003, 27. / **23** "Postwar Employment", *Public Opinion Quarterly* 9, no. 1 (Spring 1945), 103. / **24** Chafe 1991, 156. / **25** See Höhn and Klimke 2010, 21–38. / **26** Myrdal 1944. / **27** According to NAACP Executive Secretary Walter White, quoted in Berg 2005, 116. / **28** See Gassert 2012, 126–41. / **29** A majority of Americans expected that another country, likely the USSR, would develop an atomic bomb within five years without US help; survey from 30 November 1945, *Public Opinion Quarterly* 9, no. 4 (Winter 1945–46), 531; on the post-war period as an age of anxiety, see Levering 1978, 91–104. / **30** Bailey 1980, 767 et seq. / **31** Shell 1998, 57. / **32** Mausbach 1996, 90 et seq. / **33** See McCullough 1992, 404. / **34** Fisch 2004, 273. / **35** See Byrnes 1947, 49; Lamberton Harper 1996, 131. / **36** Schwabe 2006, 150. / **37** Quoted in Bailey 1980, 764; the quote refers to the Munich Agreement of 1938 and the policy of appeasing Hitler. / **38** Miscamble 2007, 187. / **39** See Truman 1955, 355 et seq. / **40** Memorandum for the President, 6 July 1945, FRUS 1945, The Conference of Berlin (The Potsdam Conference), vol. 1, no. 192, 228. / **41** Ferrell 1980, 49; journal entry from 7 July 1945. / **42** "Russia's role in the war against Japan", *Public Opinion Quarterly* 9, no. 2 (Summer 1945), 249; "Opinion on Russia", ibid., no. 3 (Fall 1945), 386. / **43** Memorandum for the President, 6 July 1945, FRUS 1945, The Conference of Berlin (The Potsdam Conference), vol. 1, no. 192, 228. / **44** Truman-Stalin Meeting, 12 July 1945, Bohlen Notes, FRUS 1945, The Conference of Berlin (The Potsdam Conference, vol. 2, 43–47. / **45** Truman 1955, 454. / **46** Ferrell 1980, 54; journal entry from 18 July 1945. / **47** Miscamble 2007, 196. / **48** For an example of such a photo story, see "Big Three Conference Under Way", *Chicago Daily Tribune*, 18 July 1945, 2. / **49** "Truman Test", *Christian Science Monitor*, 17 July 1945, 16. / **50** "News About 'Potsdam Area' Confined to Food and Gifts", *Christian Science Monitor*, 18 July 1945, 11. / **51** See Feis 1960, 26 et seq. and 117 et seq.; Gormley 1990, 36. / **52** "Stalin Prepared to Stand on Pacific War?", *Christian Science Monitor*, 18 July 1945, 1; "Potsdam: Key to the Pacific War", *Atlanta Constitution*, 20 July 1945, 8. / **53** Pars pro toto: "Potsdam May Draft Terms To Japanese", as a sub-header underneath the headline "U.S. Tells Japs: Quit Or Be Destroyed", *Los Angeles Times*, 22 July 1945, 1; almost identical to *Boston Sunday Globe*, 22 July 1945, 1. A headline in the *Washington Post,* 23 July 1945, "12 Jap Ships Sunk in Joint Fleet Attack", underneath which are ten more sub-headers on different topics, mostly covering the war, one of which reads "Big 3 Discuss Peace Tangles in Sunday Talk", 1; the article reports that Truman wants to speed up the negotiations, that he attended church service on Sunday and that he and Churchill were invited to dinner by Stalin. It also contains the normal complaints about the lack of information. / **54** Fourth Plenary Meeting, 20 July 1945, Cohen Notes, FRUS 1945, The Conference of Berlin (The Potsdam Conference), vol. 2, 178; Miscamble 2007, 198. / **55** See Byrnes 1947, 70–87. / **56** According to Trachtenberg 1999, 13; Miscamble 2007, 200. / **57** Proclamation by the Heads of Government, United States, China, and the United Kingdom, 26 July 1945, FRUS 1945, The Conference of Berlin (The Potsdam Conference), vol. 2, doc. no. 1382, 1474–75. / **58** "Say Allies Got Feeler at Potsdam", *Atlanta Constitution*, 27 July 1945, 1. / **59** "Yield Now, Or Die, Japs Told: Inevitable Destruction Promised at Potsdam", *Atlanta Constitution*, 27 July 1945, 1; "Surrender or be Destroyed", *Los Angeles Times*, 27 July 1945, A4; the US press regularly used terminology with racist connotations, such as "Japs". / **60** This kind of speculation was exacerbated by the fact that Admiral Lord Louis Mountbatten, Supreme Allied Commander for South East Asia, was flown to Berlin directly following discussions with General Douglas MacArthur, and that he met with Stalin while in Berlin; see "Stalin Talks With Mountbatten As Chief in Far East Meets Big 3", *New York Times*, 26 July 1945, 1. / **61** Ninth Plenary Meeting, 25 July 1945, Cohen Notes, FRUS 1945, The Conference of Berlin (The Potsdam Conference), vol. 2, 388–91. / **62** This can be seen in the sudden increase in reporting on the conference, even though negotiations had been put on hold. / **63** See Byrnes 1947, 78; Gormley 1990, 52; Neiberg 2015, 173–74. / **64** "Truman Hears News, Hurries to Conference", *Chicago Daily Tribune*, 27 July 1945, 1. / **65** For instance, *New York Times*, 29 July 1945, 1, which references Attlee and contains headlines on the ratification of the UN Charter; the *Chicago Daily Tribune* on 29 July 1945 printed the story "Big 3 Take Up Final Tasks As Attlee Arrives" only on page 4, while page 1 was devoted to the Senate decision and East Asia. / **66** "How Big 3 Lays Foundation for European Peace: Germany Farm State", *Boston Daily Globe*, 3 August 1945, 1; "Germany Stripped of Industry by Big 3", *New York*

Times, 3 August 1945, 1; "'Big Three' Carve Up Germany and Order Severe Reparations", *Atlanta Constitution*, 3 August 1945, 1; "Big Three Set Hard Peace for Germany. Germans to Pay for Crimes", *Los Angeles Times*, 3 August 1945, 1; "Reich 'Humiliation' Without Parallel", *Christian Science Monitor*, 3 August 1945, 5; ibid., "Potsdam Gulped, Versailles Sipped".
/ **67** Poland is Granted Big Bite of Germany", *Atlanta Constitution*, 3 August 1945, 7; "Text of Potsdam Parley Agreement", *Los Angeles Times*, 3 August 1945, 6; "Centuries of German Expansion End", *Christian Science Monitor*, 3 August 1945, 10. / **68** "The Potsdam Communique", *Atlanta Constitution*, 3 August 1945, 8; "Russia Silent on Japan as Powers Tell Plan to Reduce Reich Industry", *Los Angeles Times*, 3 August 1945, 1; "Continuing Teamwork", *Christian Science Monitor*, 3 August 1945, 16; "No Word On Japan", *New York Times*, 3 August 1945, 1. / **69** "Capital Comment on Pact Cautious: Congressmen See Advance For Peace but Regret Soviet Stand on Japan", *New York Times*, 3 August 1945, 9. / **70** "The Potsdam Folly", *Chicago Daily Tribune*, 4 August 1945, 6. / **71** "Potsdam Inaugurates a Great Experiment", *New York Times*, 4 August 1945, 10. / **72** "Truman's Aim At Berlin: Get Reds Into War", *Chicago Daily Tribune*, 9 August 1945, 1. / **73** "Truman Made Parley Trip To Bring Reds In", *Boston Daily Globe*, 9 August 1945, 11; "Russian Entry Into War Revealed As Truman's Chief Aim at Berlin", *New York Times*, 9 August 1945, 5. / **74** "Russia Complains: Potsdam and the London Failures", *Washington Post*, 6 October 1945, 8; "Byrnes Radio Address on the Results of London", *New York Times*, 6 October 1945, 8. / **75** See Spevack 2004, 47–48; Dülffer 1998, 201–24.
/ **76** See Stöver 2007, 11. / **77** Walter Lippmann, "Today and Tomorrow: The Breakdown At London", *Washington Post*, 12 December 1947, 15. / **78** See Marcowitz 1999, 115–28.
/ **79** Borodziej 2019, 104–13. / **80** The first deployments of the atomic bomb were not initially seen as turning points in world history; on this topic, see Gassert 2012, 130–31. / **81** For more on the heated debate surrounding the fiftieth anniversary of Hiroshima, see Nobile 1996. / **82** Lonely Planet (online version), 2019, www.lonelyplanet.com/germany/potsdam/attractions/schloss-cecilienhof/a/poi-sig/488864/359368 [accessed 1 November 2019].
/ **83** "Where Leaders Waged War and Sought Peace", *New York Times*, 17 September 2000, TR28; "Where the Bargains Keep Rolling", *New York Times*, 25 May 2008, TR7. / **84** "Bookshelf: The Good Old Days Were Dangerous", *Wall Street Journal*, 13 March 2000, A44.
/ **85** Neiberg 2015, 247–56; see also Roberts 2017, 215–33. / **86** According to Alperowitz 1965; in contrast, see Dülffer 1998, 153–60. / **87** Thirteenth Plenary Meeting, 1 August 1945, Cohen Notes, FRUS 1945, The Conference of Berlin (The Potsdam Conference), vol. 2, 601.

The Soviet Interests at the Potsdam Conference

Jacob Riemer

Destroyed cities and ruined landscapes pulled past the windows of the heavily guarded special train, in which Joseph Stalin, in mid-July 1945, travelled from Moscow to the Potsdam Conference, where he met his negotiating partners from the USA and Great Britain for the anti-Hitler coalition's last major summit.[1] It had only been two months since the Second World War had come to an end in Europe. Large parts of the continent, especially in the East, lay in ruins. In Western Europe, the violence of war, largely due to the German occupation there, had remained comparatively limited, despite the many victims and the devastation. Eastern Europe, on the other hand, from the beginning of the war in 1939 and the German invasion of the Soviet Union in 1941, had experienced the bloodiest and most extensive land war in history.[2] The number of casualties was enormous. In the course of the brutal battles and the escalating violence against the civilian population and, not least, as a result of the pervasive hunger and poverty, around 40 million people had lost their lives in Europe—25 to 27 million of these, around 70 per cent of all European war deaths,[3] in the Soviet Union alone (by comparison: USA 400,000, United Kingdom 350,000 deaths).[4] Moreover, the economic and demographic heartland in the west of the Soviet Union had been devastated.[5]

Politically, the Soviet Union advanced in the course of the war from being a regional power excluded from world politics to a new great power with global power projection. It was the aim of the Soviet leadership at the Potsdam Conference to secure this great power status by permanently disempowering Germany and delimiting its own sphere of power from those of the other victorious powers. Further, the Soviet Union strove to enforce an exclusive sphere of power and influence, with Eastern and Southeastern Europe as its core but extending to parts of the Middle-East, Mongolia and parts of China and Korea. On the whole, Stalin was not interested in unduly binding resolutions that might limit the Soviets' freedom of action, especially in their zone of occupation in Germany or in Eastern Europe.

← The centre of the city of Stalingrad after the surrender of the German 6th army, 2 February 1943

The aggressor's permanent disarmament: political dealings with Germany and the question of reparations

From the Soviet perspective, the Second World War had essentially been fought to defend the country and to push back Nazi Germany. Hence, the question of how to deal with Germany after its surrender was of greatest significance to Stalin and the Soviet leadership. The strategic goal after two bloody world wars was to eliminate Germany as a European power and to protect the Soviet Union against a renewed threat of German aggression.[6] For this purpose, Germany was to be divided into zones of occupation, as had already been agreed by the Allies at the Yalta Conference in February 1945. When the Americans took the initiative to negotiate common political principles for the treatment of Germany, Stalin opted for a formula compromise to guarantee the Soviet Union full sovereignty within its zone of occupation. The Allied Control Council, jointly formed by the victorious powers, was to enforce the principles of demilitarisation, denazification, democratisation and decentralisation enshrined in this context. At the same time, the formula gave all those involved sufficient scope for interpretation to achieve their own strategic goals in their respective occupation zones.[7] Stalin, in any case, had already created facts on the ground in the Soviet occupation zone before the beginning of the conference by installing an extensive military administration, admitting political parties and securing the primacy of the re-founded Communist Party of Germany—thus setting the course for a political and economic Sovietisation early on.[8]

The question of how to deal politically with the former Reich was closely connected to the issue of German reparation payments to the allies. Since the Soviet Union had by far suffered the most significant losses among the powers represented at the conference, Stalin aimed for the most far-reaching solution. Finally, reparations were not to be made in foreign exchange but in benefits in kind—to an extent that would substantially contribute to the expected reconstruction costs. At the same time, a de facto economic "disarmament" of Germany was to be achieved by the extensive dismantling of industrial plants and the extraction of raw materials.[9] In the end, the Allies in Potsdam agreed that each of the powers should satisfy its reparation claims from its own occupation zone in Germany.[10]

Soviet war poster:
"Soldier, of the Red Army,
Help!"

The Polish question and its regional context as the vanishing point of Soviet geopolitics

The future of Poland and the associated question of the Soviet western border were of crucial geopolitical importance to Stalin and the Soviet leadership. From a Russian perspective, Poland had since the nineteenth century been the front-line state to the west that was essential for national security.[11] Poland lost its statehood between 1772 and 1917–18, when its territory was divided between the major regional powers of Russia, Prussia and Austria.[12] Since Russia's withdrawal from the First World War in 1917 and the ensuing loss of its western periphery, Poland, which was re-established in 1918, had become an important point of reference for a Soviet policy aimed at regaining territories and powers lost during the war. In addition to the East Slavic areas in Eastern Poland, these territories included the Baltic States and Finland in the north as well as Bessarabia and Bukovina in the south. Competing Polish and Soviet expansionary interests had first been fought out in the Polish-Soviet war (1920–21). As a result, Ukraine and Belarus were effectively divided between the two states after a series of Polish military successes.[13] Joseph Stalin, who was directly involved in the conflict as Soviet Party Secretary for Nationalities, had taken the outcome of this war as a personal defeat.[14] Some twenty years later, in the dramtic political situation of Europe teetering on the brink of the Second World War, Stalin once again attempted to settle the Polish question on his terms. When the Anglo-French settlement with Germany in the 1938 Munich Agreement dashed Moscow's hopes for a reliable European alliance against the increasingly aggressive German Reich, he decided to pursue a policy of rapprochement towards Germany.[15]

The deeper reasons for the German-Soviet rapprochement in 1939 do not lie in any political proximity to Germany.[16] At that time, Nazi Germany was steeped in an anti-Communism imbued with connotations of anti-Semitism and in the ideology of the country's belligerent expansion to the East.[17] From a Soviet perspective, the actions undertaken by the Moscow leadership in the heated situation of 1939 resulted from a fundamental lack of trust in potential Western European allies.[18] In the British establishment, the clearly articulated will to isolate or even destroy the Soviet Union had been a political commonplace since the end of the First World War, most prominently championed by figures such as Neville Chamberlain and Winston Churchill.[19] As negotiations with Britain, France and Poland on a collective security pact against the German threat dragged on—not only because the Soviets demanded free hand against the Baltic States and the right of passage through Poland in the event of war, but also because of a general distrust between the partners[20]—contact was made with Berlin.[21] On 24 August 1939, the Treaty of Non-Aggression between Germany and the USSR was signed in Moscow. For the Soviet Union, which in 1939 saw itself threatened by German expansion plans in the west and Japanese expansion efforts in the east,[22] the Treaty offered the opportunity to consolidate its own state territory and to secure its western flank against the German aggression expected in the future. Moreover, Stalin thus gained time for further armament.[23]

In the Secret Additional Protocol to the Treaty, Germany and the Soviet Union divided the countries of Eastern Europe into spheres of influence.[24] In the wake of German agression after the outbreak of the Second Wold War in Europe, the Soviet Union in 1939 and 1940 therefore implemented an expansionary and security policy in Eastern Europe that was based on the outline of the Tsarist Empire's erstwhile western borders which the Soviets claimed as a security zone.[25] In this context, the first territories to be annexed were Poland's eastern provinces, predominantly populated by Ukrainians and Belarusians, and the Romanian regions of Bessarabia and northern Bukovina.[26] The Soviet Union also waged war against its northern neighbour, Finland, whose government had approached Nazi Germany.[27] As a further step, the Baltic states of Estonia, Latvia and Lithuania were forcibly incorporated into the Soviet Union in the summer of 1940. Moscow feared that, if war with the Reich broke out, these states would become part of the German deployment zone against the Soviet Union.[28] Viewed in this context, the Soviet expansion policy of the years 1939–40 was carried out as an advance safeguard against the expected German deployment along its national borders.[29] Generally speaking, the crucial political initiative for the Non-Aggression Treaty as well as the military will for escalation in the autumn of 1939 were clearly on the German side[30] As far as the Soviet Union's interests at the Potsdam Conference are concerned, however, its territorial gains around 1940 are an important point of reference.

Already in December of 1941, half a year after the German attack of 22 June had confirmed Soviet forebodings and the loose cooperation of convenience concluded in August 1939 had collapsed, Stalin told British Foreign Secretary Anthony Eden that the retention of territorial gains made in Northern and Eastern Europe in 1939 and 1940 was a major strategic goal in the war against Germany.[31] The Soviet Union enforced this goal against the Western powers at the Allied conference in Yalta in early 1945, when it was decided that the future Polish-Soviet border would roughly run along the so-called Curzon Line.[32] In addition, the Soviet Union was also granted to annex the northeast of Prussia around Königsberg.[33] The Curzon Line was a demarcation drawn in 1919 in the context of the Versailles peace negotiations and roughly running along ethnic settlement borders.[34] At the time, Poland had temporarily accepted this line, but a little later, in the course of the Polish-Soviet war, revoked its approval from a position of military strength—a circumstance from which the Soviets drew legitimation for their territorial claims. In order to

Ruined houses on what
was to become the Square
of Fallen Fighters in
Stalingrad, 15 January 1943

compensate for the loss of territory suffered in the east, Poland at Potsdam was to be compensated with former German territories in the west.[35]

The question of how much German territory should be ceded to Poland after the end of the war remained highly controversial between the Soviet Union and the Western powers and had a considerable impact on the negotiations at Potsdam. According to the Soviets, Poland was to receive the German provinces of Silesia, Neumark, Pomerania and the southern part of East Prussia, which conflicted with the American and British wish of allowing Germany to retain parts of Lower Silesia.[36] After tough bargaining, the Americans and British eventually accepted the Soviet demand for a substantial westward shift of the German-Polish border to the Oder-Lusatian Neisse line and the associated resettlement of the German population from Silesia, Pomerania and East Prussia.[37] Already before the conference, the Soviets had created a fait accompli by installing Polish administrations and expelling or relocating large parts of the Polish population from pre-war Poland's eastern provinces, and of the German population from Silesia, Neumark, Pomerania and East Prussia.[38]

From Moscow's perspective, both Poland's shift to the west and the integration of Western Ukraine and Western Belarus into the Soviet Union, which was concluded in the same context, amounted to a de facto reunification with the rest of these countries after years of Polish "interregnum".[39] The recognition of Poland's new borders, however, had far-reaching consequences in that it politically substantiated the annexation of the Baltic States, Bukovina and Transcarpathia, which the Western powers considered highly controversial.[40] From the Soviet point of view, on the other hand, the international recognition of the new borders in Eastern Europe was a great geopolitical success.

A Soviet sphere of influence in Eastern Europe: a security zone against the Western powers

Poland was of central importance to the Soviet Union's post-war planning for a buffer and influence zone along its national borders, but Soviet goals extended to other countries in Central and Eastern Europe as well. The Balkans, a long-time object of the major European powers' competing interests, played an important role in this planning. As early as the nineteenth century, Russia had considered itself a protective power of Orthodox Christians in the Balkans, seeking to establish on its southwest flank a cordon sanitaire against other major powers and their interests. Already in October of 1944, Stalin had arranged with British Prime Minister Winston Churchill to divide the region into spheres of influence, with Bulgaria, Romania, Albania and Yugoslavia being included in the Soviet sphere. Greece, on the other hand, was assigned to British influence.[41] In addition to the Balkan countries, Hungary and Czechoslovakia also came under Soviet control.[42]

The Soviet aspirations to an exclusive zone of power and influence need to be seen in the context of the then not unusual phenomenon of superpower politics redolent with imperial overtones. The origins of such politics go back to the nineteenth century, when Great Britain, the United States and the Tsarist Empire defined extensive spheres of influence.[43] When designing the global post-war order, the British, too, were no strangers to thinking in terms of clearly defined spheres of influence.[44] What is striking when looking at the political situation in Soviet-controlled Eastern Europe immediately after the Potsdam Conference is that, with the exception of the Soviet zone of occupation in Germany, Stalin's ideas for the Soviet sphere of influence were relatively flexible at first. Initially, only few interventions in the domestic policies of the respective countries were undertaken to ensure Soviet primacy. It was only with the gradual intensification of the East-West conflict after 1947 that control became more restrictive and staunchly socialist one-party governments were installed.[45]

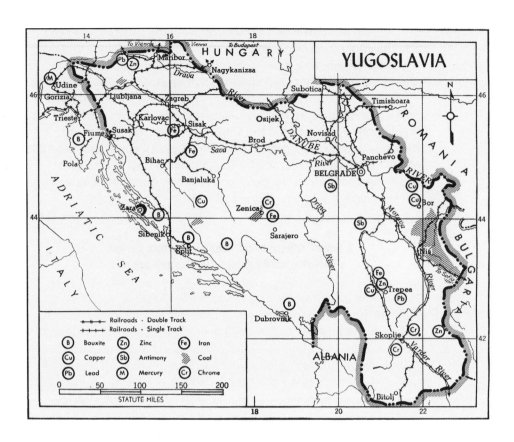

**Strategic competition with Great Britain
and the USA in the Middle East**

Another focus of Soviet geopolitics after the war was the Middle
East, above all Iran and Turkey. The Iranian question was discussed
at the Potsdam Conference on 21 July.[46] Since 1941, Iran had been
occupied by the Soviets, the British and later by the Americans;
it had been divided into occupation zones to protect the Soviet
southern flank and to thwart any cooperation between Iran and Nazi
Germany. In addition, the supply of western industrial goods and
food to the Soviet Union, granted as part of Allied economic aid from
the summer of 1941 on, had to circumvent the German Eastern Front.
The Soviet Union's geostrategic interest in Iran, however, went far
beyond the question of war supplies. Already in the course of the
nineteenth century, in the heyday of imperialism, the Russians and
the British competed for hegemony in the region—which resulted
in the de facto division of Iran into a Russian and a British sphere of
influence in 1907. In the 1920s and 1930s, also the Soviet Union, in
the tradition of the Tsarist Empire, saw Iran as a buffer state.[47]

Map detailing the Soviet
interest in the Balkans
and Yugoslavia, excerpt
from US pamphlet
The Soviet Union

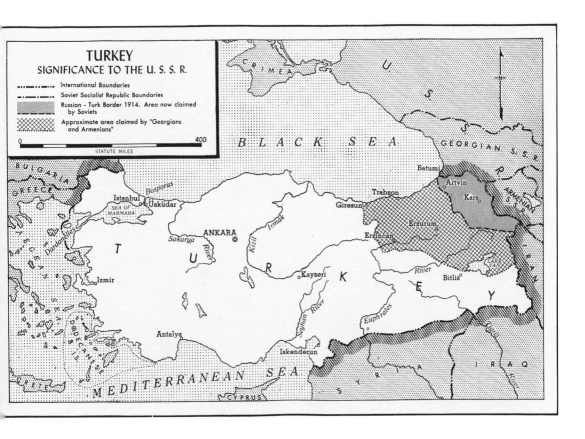

TURKEY
SIGNIFICANCE TO THE U. S. S. R.

International Boundaries
Soviet Socialist Republic Boundaries
Russian - Turk Border 1914. Area now claimed by Soviets
Approximate area claimed by "Georgians and Armenians"

0 | 400
STATUTE MILES

Map of Turkey with the strategically important Black Sea Straits, excerpt from US pamphlet *The Soviet Union*

Towards the end of the war, despite joint efforts against Germany, tensions between Soviet and Anglo-American interests in Iran increased noticeably. As a result, the Soviet Union sought to maintain its traditional power position in Iran against both the strong British and the expanding geopolitical influence of the USA.[48] Particularly the north of the country, which the Soviets claimed as their hereditary sphere of influence, was affected. Also, there were Soviet efforts to exploit, much like the British and Americans, Iran's rich oil reserves.[49] At Potsdam, the British Foreign Secretary, Anthony Eden, raised the question, already discussed at Yalta, of Allied troop withdrawal from Iran. Stalin flatly refused, invoking concerns about being displaced by the Western powers.[50] Only after massive American pressure and a sensational Iranian complaint to the recently established UN Security Council did the Soviets withdraw their troops in early 1946. Their endeavour to instigate secessions in Northern Iran in 1945–46 triggered the first serious crisis of the emerging East-West conflict.[51] For Iran, however, foreign influence did not end after the withdrawal of Allied troops.[52] Western influence in Iran continued until the Islamic Revolution in 1979.[53]

ARMS FOR RUSSIA . . . A great convoy of British
ships escorted by Soviet fighter planes sails into Murmansk
harbour with vital supplies for the Red Army.

...British

Printed in England

Next to Iran, Soviet interests also focused on Turkey. At Potsdam, Stalin demanded the return of the Kars plateau in Northeast Turkey (controlled by Russia between 1878 and 1917) and de facto control of the access to the Black Sea near Istanbul.[54] Turkey, however, had remained largely neutral during the war; it was not a war party proper and enjoyed strong political backing from Britain and the USA.[55] The Soviet Union therefore failed to enforce its demands regarding Turkey. This notwithstanding, Soviet pressure did not subside even after the Potsdam Conference and continued until Stalin's death in 1953—a key factor in Turkey's turn to the West and its accession to NATO in 1952.[56]

Soviet post-war geopolitics in East Asia

Alongside questions about the future of Europe and the Middle East, the Big Three at Potsdam also discussed further Allied action in East Asia, where the war against Japan, the other aggressor of the war, still continued. Following a decision of principle taken at Yalta, Stalin confirmed that the Soviet Union would enter the war against Japan on 8 August, three months to a day after Germany's surrender.[57] The strategic rivalry between the two countries in Northeast Asia dates back to around 1900 but intensified following the Japanese expansion into parts of China during the 1930s.[58] After Japanese border violations in Mongolia, then under Soviet influence, and in the Soviet Far East in 1937–38, which Moscow had successfully fended off,[59] both sides had maintained mutual neutrality during the war.[60] Nevertheless, after pressure from the Americans, Stalin had already agreed at Yalta that the Soviet Union would enter the war against Japan. In return, he demanded the restoration of "historical rights" that Russia claimed to have had in the region before its defeat in the Russo-Japanese War (1904–05). Both the Americans and the British granted his demand,[61] acknowledging the return of South Sakhalin and the Kurile Islands from Japan, the maintenance of the existing Soviet protectorate over Mongolia and the restitution of Russian or Soviet rights to use the Chinese warm-water port of Dalian/Port Arthur. Further, Soviet rights to use the Manchurian railway in northern China were to be renewed.[62]

Compared to the issues surrounding the restructuring of Europe after the war, however, Stalin and those close to him were far less interested in China and East Asia and rather sought to maintain a balance within the complex power structure in the region.[63] Nevertheless, a competition for influence and power in China arose in early August 1945 between the Soviets and Americans, in the course of which the Soviet Union occupied the industrially developed region of Manchuria.[64] This way, the Red Army put an end to the nearly 15 years of sometimes brutal foreign rule which the Japanese had exercised in

British war poster. A convoy of British ships with arms for the Red Army, escorted by Soviet bombers, on the way to Murmansk

the region.[65] Until the Red Army's withdrawal from Manchuria in 1946, the Soviet Union gave the Communist forces around Mao Zedong a crucial base of operations in the resurgent Chinese Civil War, which helped lay the foundations for Mao's subsequent victory and the proclamation of the Socialist People's Republic of China.[66]

Another topic on the Allied agenda for East Asia in Potsdam was the will to push back the Japanese from the Korean peninsula. Having thwarted Russian interests in Korea with its victory in the Russo-Japanese War in 1905, Japan annexed the country in 1910, subsequently expanding its economy and making it the second-most industrialised country in Asia after Japan in 1945.[67] As the Americans, at the time of the conference, concentrated their military potential on the Japanese islands, the Big Three agreed that the Soviet Union, after entering the war in Asia, should invade Korea alone to liberate the country from Japanese rule.[68] Shortly after the end of the conference, however, the dropping of the atomic bombs on Hiroshima and Nagasaki fundamentally changed the military situation. Washington's position of military strength found expression in a proposal, hastily drafted during the night of 10 August by the US Department of Defence, to divide Korea into two zones of occupation along the 38th parallel as the line of demarcation between Soviet and American forces. The Soviets responded to the unexpected American proposal and had their forces stop at this line on 28 August—even though the American Navy would not be able to land in the South Korean port of Pusan until 8 September.[69] The developments in August of 1945 laid the foundation for the division of Korea that continues to this day.

War poster, 1945

The breakthrough solution reached
at the end of the conference

What stands out when one looks at how Stalin and his entourage negotiated at Potsdam, was their tendency to prioritise geopolitical over economic interests. This was particularly evident in the conference's response to Soviet territorial demands in relation to Poland. The Polish question and the associated issue of redrawing borders in Eastern and Central Europe after the war defined the entire summit. Only on 29 July, three days before its end, Secretary of State James F. Byrnes proposed to his Soviet counterpart, Vyacheslav Mikhailovich Molotov, to reconcile American and Soviet interests: the Soviet Union was to waive part of its extensive claims to exact reparations from German territories, in return for which the US would accept the substantial westward shift of the German-Polish border favoured by the Soviets.[70] And, in fact, two days later, Stalin dropped Soviet reparation claims regarding the western zones in exchange for American recognition of the new borders in Eastern Europe.[71] This way, Stalin enforced the key Soviet interest in the restitution of territories and claims to power lost in the First World War, but also the creation of a Soviet sphere of influence and security in Europe and East Asia, which would protect the Soviet Union from future aggression.

Emperor Puyi, the former puppet ruler of Manchukuo, in the Krasnogorsk POW camp no. 27. USSR, Krasnogorsk, 1946

Conclusion: an attempt at classification

Despite the existential threat that the German war of extermination posed to its statehood, the Soviet Union managed to preserve and even expand its territory. At the same time, it gained a global power position unprecedented in the country's history, thus sealing its rise from a Eurasian regional power to a global superpower on par with the US. It is therefore no wonder that the Soviet leadership hailed the Potsdam Conference as a great achievement—according to Foreign Minister Molotov, it had successfully enforced its key strategic demands.[72] This perception corresponded to the feeling of the majority of Soviet citizens, even though it was not shared by all population groups, particularly in the territories of Western Ukraine and the Baltic States that had been (re)integrated into the Soviet Union in 1939–40 and 1944–45. Here, anti-Soviet national guerrilla groups operated in the western border regions until the 1950s. Similar to what had happened in the Baltic States in 1940–41, hundreds of thousands of people were, after liberation from the Nazi occupation in 1944, deported to Central Asia and other remote regions of the USSR as potential critics of the new regime.[73] In most other regions of the Soviet Union, however, the experience of war had a strong consolidating effect and helped forge a patriotic Soviet identity—an identity which, based on the common bond of pride in the nation's victory in the Great Patriotic War and the memory of suffering and deprivation,[74] was to become typical of the decades to come.

The position of the Soviet Union as a hegemonic power in Eastern Europe and a global superpower—a status internationally recognised at the Potsdam Conference—lasted for around 45 years. Only with its collapse in 1990–91 and the end of its domination in Eastern Europe did the post-war order that had been sanctioned at the conference come to its historic end.[75] The debate over the nature of the Soviet role after the Second World War continues, with differing interpretations between supporters and opponents of the socialist system and its dominance in Eastern Europe—which repeatedly leads to conflicts over the legitimacy of the Soviet post-war order. What is undisputed, however, is the fact that the Red Army and the entire Soviet population with unprecedented effort managed to stop and push back Adolf Hitler's imperial dreams and the murder and oppression politics associated with them in Eastern Europe. This historical achievement and the awareness that the moral right to victory in the Second World War clearly lay with the Soviets fills many people in the states of the former Soviet Union to this day with great pride.[76] |CN

Notes

1 Beevor 2014, 869. / **2** Kershaw 2016, 473–74. / **3** Ibid., 473. / **4** Barber and Harrison 2015, 225. / **5** Kershaw 2016, 481. / **6** Laufer 2009, 80 and 87. / **7** Amtsblatt 1946, 13–20. / **8** Laufer 2009, 566. / **9** Laufer 2009, 540. / **10** Ibid., 588. / **11** Darwin 2017, 307. / **12** Heyde 2008, 54–91. / **13** Borodziej 2010, 118. / **14** See Kappeler 2017, 167–68, also Leonhard 2018, 1191. / **15** See Weber 2019, 47 and 59. / **16** See Hartmann 2012, 20. / **17** See ibid., 14 et seq. / **18** Ibid., 18–19. / **19** Beevor 2014, 28. / **20** Kotkin 2017, 647–48. / **21** Beevor 2014, 28–29; Kotkin 2017, 648. Stalin was suspicious that Britain, then the dominant imperial power across a quarter of the globe, did not want to allow the Soviet Union to pursue a ramp-up policy within its "own" former imperial periphery. / **22** See Beevor 2014, 24–27. / **23** Weber 2019, 70. / **24** Weber 2019, 69–72. / **25** Ibid., 70. / **26** Borodziej 2010, 191 and 195–98; Kershaw 2016, 477. / **27** See Hoesch 2009, 129–32; Kotkin 2017, 647. / **28** Barber and Harrison 2018, 239. The fear that the Baltic States might turn against the Soviet Union in war was fuelled by non-aggression pacts which Estonia and Latvia, on 7 June 1939, had concluded with Nazi Germany to prevent a Soviet invasion, see Kotkin 2017, 647. / **29** Angermann and Brüggemann 2018, 280. / **30** See Beevor 2014, 30; Hartmann 2012, 19. / **31** Quoted after Laufer 2009, Soviet draft of a Soviet-British agreement of 15 December 1941, source: Personal Archive of the Soviet Foreign Minister V. Molotov (RGASPI f. 82, op. 2, d. 1141, 133–36.), 94–99; see also Beevor 2014, 259–60. / **32** Laufer 2009, 198–99, also Borodziej 2010, 254.; Beevor 2014, 810. / **33** See Laufer 2009, 440. / **34** Leonhard 2018, 1191–92. / **35** Ibid., 1192; Borodziej 2010, 256. / **36** Laufer, 204. / **37** Borodziej 2010, 256. / **38** Ibid., 258–60; Laufer 2009, 203. / **39** See Yekelchyk 2015, 537. / **40** For this topic, see Angermann and Brüggemann 2018, 293; Yekelchyk 2015, 537. / **41** Calic 2016, 503. / **42** See Beevor 2014, 863–64. / **43** Osterhammel 2009, 646–54 (Great Britain); 679, 686–87 (US); 521–31 (Russia). / **44** See Calic 2016, 503. / **45** Kivelson and Suny 2017, 315–16. / **46** Blake 2009, 22. / **47** Ibid., 9–12. / **48** Darwin 2017, 404. / **49** Blake 2009, 19–20. / **50** Forsmann 2009, 235–36. / **51** See Blake 2009, 22–38. / **52** Gronke 2016, 102. / **53** Ibid, 102–05. / **54** Kreiser 2012, 76. / **55** Ibid., 68–70, 76. / **56** Ibid., 76–77. / **57** Coulmas 2010, 20. / **58** Darwin 2017, 337–41; Quested 1984, 98–100. / **59** Quested 1984, 103. / **60** Darwin 2017, 397. / **61** Laufer 2009, 580. / **62** See Quested 1984, 106. / **63** Quested 1984, 113. / **64** Ibid., 100–13. / **65** Vogelsang 2013, 523–24. / **66** Ibid., 534. / **67** Eggert and Plasen 2018, 135–36. / **68** Ibid., 151. / **69** Ibid. / **70** Laufer 2009, 587. / **71** Ibid., 596–97. / **72** Laufer 2009, 599. / **73** Kivelson and Suny 2017, 319. / **74** Ibid. / **75** Kivelson and Suny 2017, 354–63. / **76** On this topic, see Jahn 2005, 10–21, among others.

Great Britain and the Potsdam Conference

Victor Mauer

For more than a fortnight in the second half of July 1945, hundreds of journalists had endured at the gates of the "forbidden Big Three city"[1] before they could finally put out to the world the results of the Potsdam Conference on 3 August. The only written statement published eight days previously was the Potsdam Declaration. Worded by US President Harry S. Truman and British Prime Minister Winston Churchill and telegraphically signed by Chiang Kai-shek, Chairman of the National Government of the Republic of China, it laid down the conditions for Japan's surrender.[2] Otherwise, the gagging order imposed at the start of the conference had held.

It was against this background that Lord Beaverbrook's *Daily Express* on 3 August made the sensational announcement: "What a tremendous, forward-looking programme has been hammered out in the Cecilienhof near Potsdam in the last fortnight and two days! Make no mistake, the Big Three Powers have done a good job of work. There has been give and take—wisely. Europe has made the first step forward to lasting peace. And it is the first step that counts. Germans get a chance to become civilised again—when they have paid the price of their barbarity. This great historical triumph of collaboration is important for its positive achievements, under conditions of maximum difficulty."[3] Britain's highest-circulation mass newspaper—it was selling more than 3 million copies every day—by no means stood alone in its verdict. Both quality and popular press hailed the "Work of Peace" wrought at Potsdam, celebrating the supposed closing of ranks between the Second World War's three major victorious powers.[4]

Little had been left of the sceptical assessments which prior to the conference had cautioned against the consequences of a division of Germany and Europe.[5] Prime Minister Clement Attlee, Britain's chief negotiator for the last five days of the conference, expressed his satisfaction to his cabinet, his predecessor as well as Commonwealth leaders.[6] Permanent Under-Secretary for Foreign Affairs Alexander Cadogan wrote to his wife Theodosia: "We have not done too badly, I think."[7] (At Potsdam, as so often before, he had pulled the strings of the British delegation, even beyond the change of government.)

Only Churchill himself, now a retired war hero, immediately slipped back into the prime role he had already played in the 1930s. Cassandra-like, he warned the Commons in mid-August 1945 of a "tragedy on a prodigious scale … unfolding itself behind the iron curtain".[8] He thus created the tenaciously-upheld legend that, had he still been in office at the end of the conference, he would have engaged in a trial of strength with the Soviets. Little wonder he consistently distanced himself from the Big Three's final communiqué in front of anyone who would listen: "I am not responsible for Potsdam after I left."[9] The key decisions, even if only temporary in some cases, were in fact not taken until the end of July, when following the most devastating Conservative defeat since 1906, Churchill

← Churchill arriving at
Gatow Airfield

left Downing Street to let his long-time deputy shape the future of the United Kingdom.

After the conferences in Tehran (28 November to 1 December 1943) and Yalta (4 to 11 February 1945), the Potsdam Conference (17 July to 2 August 1945) was the Big Three's last meeting. Hence Churchill's suggestion to use "Terminal" as code word for the conference hosted on the banks of Jungfernsee in the New Garden. "Terminal" was, however, an appropriate attribute also in that the parties involved—as though "floundering through the corridors of chaos"[10]—were looking for clues for a new world order.

The simultaneity of opposites: Great Britain in 1945

International framework conditions had begun to change. With Germany's unconditional military surrender, signed at the American and Soviet headquarters in Reims and Berlin-Karlshorst on 7 and 9 May 1945, respectively, the informal temporary alliance had reached the goal which the Western Allies had set themselves in Casablanca in January 1943. The Reich's political surrender, upon which the European Advisory Commission had agreed in July 1944, followed on 5 June 1945 by a unilateral legal act.[11] Germany was occupied as a conquered enemy state, and the main victorious powers assumed supreme authority.

The achievements of the past, however, said little about the new challenge of jointly shaping a European peace order. Yesterday's coalition partners had not been able to forge a lasting consensus—neither about the structure of future peace, nor about the future shape of the occupied country. Even those in the corridors of power were far more aware of what they wanted to prevent than of what was to become of the vanquished. In the absence of a classic cease-fire agreement, they understood the combination of unconditional surrender and the Allied takeover as a kind of preliminary peace[12] that would allow them to clarify the procedural options for a final peace settlement in the course of time.

Britain's policy was influenced, first, by the uncertainty about the general conditions—specifically, Moscow's and Washington's intentions, the catastrophic economic situation at home, the unpredictability of the upcoming elections to the Commons as well as powerful historical narratives such as "Versailles 1919" and "Munich 1938"—and, second, by its self-image.

In February 1945, Churchill had returned confidently from Yalta to London. "Poor Neville Chamberlain believed he could trust Hitler", he told some of his advisers. "He was wrong. But I don't think I'm wrong about Stalin."[13] A few weeks later, this was no longer the case. On the contrary, when during the last weeks of the war, Central Europe's historic capitals fell one after the other, the question of the

87

goals pursued by the Soviet Union in Europe once again became the centre of London's concern. And once again, the succinct, yet far from reassuring, answer was: "a riddle wrapped in a mystery inside an enigma"[14]. To his dismay, Churchill had to acknowledge that the need for foreign policy action was inversely proportional to his individual room to maneuvre. While the need for action increased, his scope was shrinking from month to month, from week to week, and, ultimately, even from day to day. Two things need to be seen against this background: Churchill's proposal, made to Stalin in October 1944, for a division of Southeastern Europe into spheres of influence as well as his equally erratic and unsuccessful appeal to the new American President for delaying the Anglo-American forces' withdrawal from the areas agreed with Moscow so that the Western Allies would be able to extort concessions from Stalin at the conference table.

More than ever, Britain had to rely on the support of the American government. Churchill's warnings, however, were ignored in Washington, first by President Franklin D. Roosevelt (who seemed eager to closely cooperate with Stalin at any cost), and then with his successor Truman (who, at least for the time being, was opposed not only to a showdown with Moscow but also to immediately scheduling a peace conference).[15] Since Roosevelt had not revoked his announcement made at the Crimea Conference of withdrawing American forces from Europe within two years at the latest, London had no choice but to play wait-and-see. Orme Sargent, Alexander Cadogan's designated successor, was not alone in finding as little attraction in the role of Lepidus (in the triumvirate with Octavian and Antony) as in the prospect of eventually facing Stalin alone.[16]

Since the end of 1940, only American loans had prevented Britain's early economic collapse. After the victory, British war debt totalled £4.7 billion, and the trade deficit, £1 billion. Overseas markets had collapsed, and British export volume reached a mere 31 per cent of its value in the last year before the war. Gold and dollar reserves were largely exhausted; there was an acute shortage of foreign exchange; more than a quarter of national wealth, more than double that of the First World War, was lost. A considerable part of the assets located abroad had to be sold. Balance-of-payments crises occurred with great frequency.[17] No wonder that John Maynard Keynes warned his government against a "financial Dunkirk" and even sketched out the prospect of accepting "for the time being ... the position of a second-class power, rather like the present position of France".[18]

What also contributed to the general uncertainty in the run-up to the Potsdam Conference were the elections to the House of Commons on 5 July 1945. "I shall be only half a man until the result of the poll", Churchill told his personal physician.[19] As the soldiers' votes were only counted three weeks later, election results were not known until 26 July. In the meantime, a heap of unfinished business had piled up at the conference table in Potsdam. To prevent any

eventualities, Churchill had invited his opponent Attlee to join the
British delegation there.

Ultimately, Britain's policy was based on its inter-war experiences. On the one hand, the focus was on the structural errors of the
1919 Treaty of Versailles, which, according to widespread perception,
had facilitated the rise of National Socialism. The fear of a reinvigorated expansionist and revanchist German nationalism spawned
the fear that a peace agreement would remain an isolated event. For
this reason, the Potsdam Conference, in the eyes of its participants,
was not to be a classic peace conference but rather the start of a
permanent peace conference embodied by the Council of Foreign
Ministers.[20] On the other hand, "Munich 1938" was turned into an
increasingly stylised shibboleth and conjured up as a political-peda-
gogical narrative. The more this pre-war memory was exaggerated,
the more powerful its impact became in a country where an anti-
appeasement stance was mandatory. Since past ties change when
the perspective is oriented to the future, memory assumed agenda-
setting power and was to prove the ability and willingness to learn.
It was impossible, however, to overlook the potential conflict
between the various historical narratives.

Despite all the uncertainty, Churchill wanted to preserve Britain's fragile world power status in the face of his ostensibly overpowering Allies in East and West, codifying it in a future peace order.[21] Britain, after all, had not just won the war; it was part of the Big Three and, as a member of the United Nations Security Council, not only trusted in the continued cooperation of the victorious super-powers, but had also secured its influence on the major founding goal of the world organisation: the maintenance of world peace. The Empire had survived the war largely intact, at least superficially. The British presence around the world was still overwhelming. Iraq, with its rich oil fields, was still the cornerstone of British power in the Middle East. The "winds of change"[22] proclaimed by Harold Macmillan did not blow through Africa until the early 1960s. And the global tasks financed by the defence budget (in 1947, it devoured around 18 per cent of Britain's gross national product) ranged from Hong Kong to Honduras. The British thought of themselves as a superpower and intended to act accordingly: "We must not be afraid of having a policy independent of our two great partners and not submit to a line of action dictated to us by either Russia or the United States, just because of their superior power or because it is the line of least resistance."[23]

Half a superpower:
Great Britain and the Potsdam negotiations

On 7 July 1945, the Foreign Office was alarmed to find that prepara-tions for the Potsdam Conference were progressing slowly at best. A "policy for Germany", let alone for the reorganisation of the world, was only vaguely emerging. The "Berlin Declaration", the European Advisory Commission's decisions and the Yalta agreements, equally provisional and in need of interpretation, may have defined guide-lines for a future order, but certainly not more than that.[24]

Right after the election, Churchill went to Saint-Jean-de-Luz for a week's vacation. On 15 July, he arrived in Potsdam via Berlin. In the meantime, the Anglo-American troops had moved into their respective Berlin sectors. With great media impact, Churchill used the late arrival of Stalin for a visit to the old capital of the Reich. He and his delegation encountered a "staggering sight" of Berlin in ruins.[25] Few believed the city would ever return to its former glory. Like the ghostly "preview of the collapse of civilization ... to have occurred in a pre-atomic age"[26], the "city seemed dead—a ghost of its former self. ... every one of those dim architectural forms spelled a broken dream, spelled one more bit of frustration for people who had once felt the call of hope and initiative."[27] The ruins of the soot-blackened spire of the *Gedächtniskirche* resembled the "stump of a dirty old cigar", helpless life in the ruins was like "living in a dugout".[28] Such pity, however, was inexpensive. The actual price was to be determined at the conference table.

Already in the first few days, there was growing concern among the Foreign Secretary's advisory staff. Terrified, Permanent Under-Secretary for Foreign Affairs Alexander Cadogan wrote to his wife: "The P.M., since he left London, has refused to do any work or read anything. That is probably quite right, but then he can't have it both ways: if he knows nothing about the subject under discussion, he should keep quiet, or ask that his Foreign Secretary be heard. Instead of that, he butts in on every occasion and talks the most irrelevant rubbish, and risks giving away our case at every point."[29]

Truman's primary objective at the beginning of the conference, like Roosevelt's in Yalta, was to urge the Soviets to enter the war against Japan. The main British interest, on the other hand, were the European issues already negotiated yet not decided at Yalta: the question of a democratic Eastern Europe, in particular Poland; the Polish western border; the immediate transfer—the term "expulsion" was avoided—of the German population from Poland; the reparations question and, finally, the German question as the starting and ending point of the whole conference.

"Joe", noted Alexander Cadogan with reference to Stalin at the end of the conference, "has got most of what he wants, but then the cards were mostly in his hands, and we *have* got something, mainly in the matter of the treatment of Germany. "[30] In fact, the British delegation had consistently invoked the Declaration on Liberated Europe adopted in Yalta, which, like the Atlantic Charter before, codified the right to free elections and the formation of a government. Already on the sidelines of the Crimea Conference, Stalin, shrewd calculator that he was, had instructed his concerned People's Commissar for Foreign Affairs as follows: "We can deal with it in our own way later. The point is the correlation of forces."[31] Against the background of the Soviet's military power, Stalin succeeded in enthroning a communist government in Poland—he had already done so in Bulgaria and Romania—and waived the prospect of free elections while keeping intact the façade of people's democracy in the form of a mock coalition.

The factor which, with regard to the Polish western border, ultimately proved decisive was military calculation. While Churchill, on power-political and economic rather than moral grounds, remained opposed to shifting the border to the Western Neisse until his departure from Potsdam,[32] the provisional Polish government, in view of the border question, was no longer the Soviet government's hostage but also—and understandably so—its partner. When Attlee and Bevin arrived in Potsdam on 28 July after the Labour landslide, the border issue had been settled bilaterally between the American and Soviet delegations, as had the reparations issue.[33] Alexander Cadogan sarcastically remarked that the Big Three had become the "Big ... 2½!"[34]

The Agreement on Control Machinery in Germany, signed on 14 November 1944, remained the decisive political instrument. According to it, supreme authority in Germany was exercised on instructions from their respective governments, by the Commanders-in-Chief, "each in his own zone of occupation, and also jointly, in matters affecting Germany as a whole, in their capacity as members of the Control Council."[35] The result was a dualism between the administrative bodies of the zones of occupation, on the one hand, and the Allied Control Council, on the other. This dualism "corresponded with the wish of all powers to combine a maximum of zonal autonomy with a maximum of influence on the other zones with the help of the Control Council".[36] Only in this way could the essential contradiction between the chapters on "economic principles" and those on "reparations from Germany" persist. The intention of considering Germany during the period of occupation "as a single economic unit" sorted ill with the decision to divvy up the reparations area according to the zonal principle. Such a construct could have worked only if the Allies had reached a basic consensus on how to fashion a new international order, and if the unanimity principle governing the Control Council had sustainably tamed the centrifugal forces set loose in the zones by the unrestrained pursuit of national interests according to each government's requirements. However, as a consequence of the American proposal to give each military governor, in the absence of agreed decisions, the right to act independently, the former principle of "uniformity of action by the Commanders-in-Chief in their respective zones of occupation"[37] degenerated into a non-binding recommendation. By using its veto in the Control Council, which never managed to perform any formative tasks, each of the occupying powers was given free rein in its respective zone. Thus, the consensus-based dualism, even in its fundamental principles, soon began to mutate into potential conflict.

From Potsdam 1945 to Berlin 1989–90

The bomb went off four days after the end of the conference. Upon their arrival in Potsdam, President Truman and Secretary of War Henry L. Stimson had immediately informed Churchill and Attlee of the successful nuclear test carried out at the White Sands Proving Grounds in southern New Mexico on 16 July. Both the War Premier and his successor had made it absolutely clear that, with a view to ending the war in the Pacific as quickly as possible without Soviet help and not to endanger the lives of hundreds of thousands of their soldiers, they were in favour of dropping the bomb on Japan.[38]

When time stopped in Hiroshima and Nagasaki, the world entered a new era. In the face of the Apocalypse, it looked as though the promise of a lasting peace between the superpowers might find a new home. Little Boy and Fat Man, however, did not merely epitomise the horrors of a rapidly changing world; they also fundamentally changed the hierarchy of the international state system. "Britain has had its day", Churchill said to White House legal adviser Clark Clifford.[39] And Stalin told his closest advisors, "Hiroshima has shaken the whole world. The balance has been broken."[40] Consequently, he forged ahead with his own nuclear programme, whatever the cost, until the first successful test in August 1949.

The spectre of a modern Armageddon entailed the obligation to exercise self-restraint. Unmistakably, however, it also meant that things had been taken to a new rung on the escalation ladder of mutual distrust. Formed in the days of the National Socialist threat as an anti-Hitler coalition, the alliance of unnatural partners eventually disintegrated, as participants to the London Council of Foreign Ministers in December 1947 failed to agree on questions concerning Germany without even negotiating the future of the country in the proper sense.

"Potsdam 1945" disappeared from the history books and the collective memory of an entire nation as a misunderstood cipher for a short summer of cooperation. Whitehall and Westminster learned to live with the division of Germany, as they had learned to live with the bomb. From this perspective, the Big Three, when meeting just outside of Berlin in July – August 1945, may have created the conditions for the possibility of a new post-war order. But the Potsdam Conference neither fixed the post-war order of the Cold War, nor did it establish the division of Germany, Europe and the world.[41] Both were the result of the intensifying East-West confrontation since 1947.

It cannot be gainsaid that, in this context, the division of Germany was at times of outstanding importance for the British government. Churchill and Eden, Attlee and Bevin, however, already knew in Potsdam that it would not provide a *solution*. It would persist "for a long time", but it would not last.[42] It was, and remained, a means to an end, a station on the way to the goal—and the goal was a democratic Germany: united, integrated and firmly anchored in the West.

The goal of a reunified Germany with a liberal-democratic constitution, to which the new Churchill government, together with its American and French counterparts, committed itself in the 1952 General Treaty (to come into effect as part of the Paris Treaties in 1955), perfectly tied in with the Attlee government's interpretation of the Potsdam Conference Proclamation. Since then, this formula, similar to an endless tape that could be played at every opportunity, was part of the British Prime Ministers' and Foreign Secretaries' basic stock: "[R]eal permanent stability in Europe will be difficult to achieve so long as the German nation is divided against its will."[43] Nobody really bothered when it turned into a ritual as the years went by. On the contrary, the more unrealistic the unification of the two German states seemed, the more easily the formula passed over the responsible actors' lips.

When world politics—overnight, as it were—started moving again in autumn 1989, Foreign Office officials realised that the conditions for the possibility of these events had been created in 1945—by obliging the Second World War's victorious powers to cooperate on the German question, the Potsdam Conference had thus for decades stood for an end without end. As if seen through inverted binoculars, different epochs of the past became small and merged into one another: "It was never the intention to divide Germany into two separate states after the War", Hilary Synnott, Head of the Foreign Office's Western European Department, wrote two weeks prior to the fall of the Berlin Wall on 9 November 1989. "The Potsdam Agreements of 1945 envisaged a peace treaty with a unified Germany after a period of unification."[44] The Potsdam Conference, to use a phrase coined by Achim Landwehr in a very different context, had thus for decades been "the absent presence of the past"[45]—a past that only had a chance to come to an end when the major victorious powers, in the late summer of 1990, managed to bring about a consensual solution to the German question. | CN

Notes

1 "Stalin Is There: It's a Secret", *Daily Express*, 16 July 1945, 1. / **2** See Proclamation by the Heads of Government United States, United Kingdom and China, 26 July 1945, DBPO 1984, no. 281, 709–10. / **3** "The Hope of the World", *Daily Express*, 3 August 1945, 2. / **4** See "Wide Welcome for Potsdam Declaration. Allied Unity Maintained in Work of Peace", *The Times*, 4 August 1945, 4. / **5** See "A Common Policy," *The Times*, 7 July 1945, 5; "Planning for Potsdam. Security in a Much Changed Europe", *The Times*, 13 July 1945, 5. / **6** See Burridge 1985, 223; Gilbert 1988, 116; Dilks 1971, 779. / **7** Sir Alexander Cadogan (Potsdam) to Lady Theodosia Cadogan, 31 July 1945, in Dilks 1971, 778. / **8** "The Iron Curtain Begins to Fall," 16 August 1945, in James 1974, here 7213. / **9** Winston Churchill to publisher Victor Gollancz, 28 December 1946, quoted after Gilbert 1988, 117. See also Moran 2006, 6; Churchill 1953, 671–72. / **10** Thus, with reference to diplomacy in the heyday of imperialism, American historian Henry Adams in his autobiography *The Education of Henry Adams* (Adams 1995, 381). / **11** See Declaration regarding the defeat of Germany and the assumption of supreme authority with respect to Germany from 5 June 1945, in Münch 1968, 19–24. / **12** See Küsters 2000, 234 et seq. / **13** Quoted after Pimlott 1986, 836. / **14** From Churchill's broadcast on 1 October 1939, in James 1974, 6161. / **15** See Reynolds 2006, 235–48 and 267–87; Roberts 1996, 55–62; Charmley 2004, 145–63. / **16** Minute Orme Sargent, 1 October 1945, The National Archives, FO 371/44557 (AN 2560/22/45). / **17** See Addison 2010, 7–41; Reynolds 1991, 159–60; Sked and Cook 1993, 26. / **18** Our Overseas Financial Prospects. Memorandum by John M. Keynes, 13 August 1945, in Bullen and Pelly 1986, Annex to no. 6, 28–37, here 37; John Maynard Keynes in a letter to Robert Brand, 11 July 1945, in Moggridge 1979, 374. / **19** Quoted after Dilks 1996, 81. / **20** See Küsters 2000, 213–14, 881, 895. / **21** See Kettenacker 1989 and Tyrell 1987. / **22** Macmillan 1972, 156–57. / **23** Stocktaking after VE-Day. Memorandum by Sir Orme Sargent, 11 July 1945, DBPO 1984, no. 102, 181–187, here 187. / **24** See Troutbeck Memorandum, 7 July 1945, DBPO 1984, no. 30, 46–48. / **25** Sir Alexander Cadogan to his wife Theodosia, 16 July 1945, in Dilks 1971, 762; Attlee 1954, 147. / **26** Hayter 1974, 74. / **27** Kennan 1989, 119–20. See also Kennan 1968, 430–31. / **28** Harold Nicolson to his wife Victoria Sackville-West, in Nicolson 1968, 150. / **29** Sir Alexander Cadogan (Potsdam) to Lady Theodosia Cadogan, 18 July 1945, in Dilks 1971, 765. See also Colville 1986, 592, 599; Dutton 1997, 213; James 1987, 307–08. / **30** Sir Alexander Cadogan (Potsdam) to Lady Theodosia Cadogan, 31 July 1945, in Dilks 1971, 778 (emphasis in original). / **31** Resis 1993, 51. / **32** See, for instance, Fifth Plenary Meeting, 21 July 1945, DBPO 1984, no. 219, 499–519. / **33** See Bevin to Morrison, 31 July 1945, DBPO 1984, no. 500, 1094–95. / **34** Sir Alexander Cadogan (Potsdam) to Lady Theodosia Cadogan, 31 July 1945, in Dilks 1971, 778. / **35** Protocol of the Proceedings of the Berlin Conference, https://history.state.gov/historicaldocuments/frus1945Berlinv02/d1383 [accessed 24 January 2020]. / **36** Mai 1999, 229. See also Deighton, 33–35, 62; Görtemaker 1999a, 214–17. / **37** "Agreement on Control Machinery in Germany, Adopted by the European Advisory Commission, November 14, 1944", in *Documents on Germany 1971*, here 5. For the division of the reparations area see "Minutes of Byrnes-Molotov Meeting, July 23, 1945," FRUS 1945, The Conference of Berlin (The Potsdam Conference), vol. 2, 274–75; Minutes of Informal Meeting of the Foreign Ministers, July 23, 1945, FRUS, 295 et seq.; Laufer and Kynin 2004, LXXXII. / **38** See Reynolds 2004, 481–84; Rosenberg 1999, 171–93; Churchill 1953, 637–39; Attlee 1954, 149; Williams 1961, 72, 95; Harris 1995, 278. / **39** On the train journey to Fulton, Missouri in March 1946, quoted in Addison 2004, 24. See also Hennessy 2003, 46. / **40** Quoted in Gaddis 1997, 96; Craig and Radchenko 2008, 90, 94, 110; Holloway 1994. / **41** Thus Manfred Görtemaker and Wolfgang Benz, quoted in Georg Gruber: Deutschland in engeren Grenzen, Deutschlandfunk broadcast, 20 July 2005, www.deutschlandfunkkultur.de/deutschland-in-engeren-grenzen.984.de.html?dram:article_id=153280 [accessed 22 November 2019]. / **42** "Revised Draft of Memorandum setting out present position in Germany and giving possible Russian reactions to United Kingdom policy (Top Secret)", n. d. [March 1949], The National Archives, FO 371/76577 (C 2721/23/18G). / **43** Thus Sir Geoffrey Howe, Margaret Thatcher's Secretary of State from 1983 to 1989, on 8 February 1989 in front of the House of Commons; Parliamentary Debates (Hansard), House of Commons, Official Report, Sixth Series, vol. 146, col. 979. The identical wording can be found in a joint statement by the heads of government, Thatcher and Kohl, from May 1984; quoted in Synnott to Waldegrave, 6 October 1989, DBPO 2010, no. 15 (enclosure), 36. / **44** Synnott to Ratford, 25 October 1989, German Reunification, DBPO 2010, enclosure in no. 25, 68–78, here 69. See also Broomfield (East Berlin) to Major, 12 October 1989, DBPO 2010, no. 19, 51–56, here 51. / **45** Landwehr 2016.

The Potsdam Conference of 1945 and the Germans

John Zimmermann

By the time of the Potsdam Conference, Germany no longer existed as a body politic. Instead it was a country divided into four occupied zones. Even the population was fragmented in many respects. This fragmentation began with the Second World War's rolling end: for Germans in the region around Aachen, for instance, the war was already over in September 1944. In Berlin, on the other hand, hostilities did not cease until 2 May 1945. When the Wehrmacht leadership finally capitulated on behalf of the Third Reich, most Germans therefore took the news simply as official confirmation of an older (or perhaps newer) fact of life. We must keep this fundamental state of affairs in mind when discussing the situation of the German people after the Second World War. Over the intervening decades, the narrative of a supposed "zero hour" has all too often warped our perception of what German society was like in the wake of the war. In reality, a diverse range of local start-up conditions existed. Academic historians, for the record, have thoroughly refuted the existence of an actual "zero hour". But for many Germans at the time, the idea still rung true.[1]

One thing most people had in common was a feeling of relief at having survived the fighting. However, many were also united by a sense of apathy as well as by fears—both concrete and diffuse—of what was to come. Up until the bitter end, Nazi propagandists and many of the top military commanders had spurred on the populace with talk of "final victory" and with trumped-up warnings of Allied recrimination. At the same time, the last months of the war were by far the bloodiest even for Germans, who had previously subjected their neighbours to hardship, murder, death and destruction.[2]

The majority of the population perceived the end of the war as a defeat, one that would also end their way of life. (This of course does not apply to those who had been enslaved, tortured, displaced or otherwise disenfranchised by or on behalf of Germans.) They feared retaliation from the victors, particularly from those in Eastern Europe, and they feared an uncertain future. One immediate and positive change was the risk of violent death, which plummeted when hostilities ceased. Living conditions, however, did not change for the better. They continued to deteriorate rapidly, as they had during the last months of the conflict. The daily struggle to survive went on after the war ended: there was a shortage of everything necessary for living, from food to housing. Countless cities lay in ruins. The country's infrastructure was destroyed and its energy supply cut. Eleven million Germans were being held as prisoners of war, and millions of others had fled their homes. In the immediate aftermath of the war, the biggest concern for most Germans each day was survival. For these people, politics were happening in the background, or somewhere far over their heads. Many were also hesitant to take political positions in this context, since doing so could raise questions about one's own recent history and the personal responsibility borne for the crimes against humanity committed in the concentration

← Brandenburg Gate and
the Reichstag in ruins,
after 1945

Colonel General Alfred Jodl
signing the Instrument
of Unconditional Surrender
of the German Wehrmacht
at Reims, 7 May 1945

Cologne 1945 →

and extermination camps, or visited on the millions of forced labourers
who were now returning home following their liberation. Avoiding
these topics was another part of the daily struggle to survive.
Incidentally, this fact also refutes the "zero hour" theory:
the majority of Germans were looking out for themselves in highly
individualised ways, and not just since the war ended either.[3]

The Germans at the end of the war

In autumn 1944, the war made its way back to where it was first
unleashed. And it came not just by air, but by ground too. As the
Wehrmacht was forced to retreat on all fronts, including in Western
Europe, bombs began raining on German soil. This gave many
Germans their first true taste of war. On top of it all, the Nazi regime
intensified its reign of terror against anyone having second thoughts
or thinking of quitting. "My god, it is a terrible war! Now everyone
feels it", wrote Theo Paschmann on 19 February 1945. His hometown
of Erkelenz had recently been converted into a "fortress" and was
now in the crosshairs of the Allied forces.[4]

The erosion of the much-touted *Volksgemeinschaft* ("national
community") began in the watershed year of 1943, and it continued
apace throughout the series of defeats suffered over the next two
years by the Wehrmacht and its Axis confederates. When the ground

war reached the homeland, it confined all of German society to basements and reduced most else to rubble—a fate that had previously only been known in areas targeted by the bombing campaign. In such a setting, survival hinged more and more on the ability to improvise and organise. This required widespread individualisation. Surviving and "pulling through" were increasingly becoming the quintessential modes of existence during this period, on both the battlefield and the home front. Meanwhile, the trend toward individualisation was being spurred by the dissolution of existing social bonds, which were disrupted by military conscription, casualty rates, emigration and evacuation, including the evacuation of children into the countryside. As time passed, Germans began focusing exclusively on themselves and their immediate families.[5]

Because the moral support of the masses for the Third Reich depended on its successes, and because the reigning ideology was fixated on attaining success through brute strength, these developments thoroughly altered the nature and the role of the Nazi regime. The enormous fears of Soviet recrimination suggest that Germans were much more aware of Nazi crimes in Eastern Europe than most of them would admit. It is partially for this reason that many Germans in the last months of the conflict expressed hope that the Western Allies would occupy the country and end the war. France, the United Kingdom and the United States were viewed with a mixture of curiosity and uncertainty.[6]

As this situation unfolded, the general populace grew increasingly war-weary, but not rebellious. The social democrat Jupp Kappius wrote to a comrade in January 1945: "The people are by and large tired of the war. The long working hours, the great distances that they now have to travel by foot, the shortage of supplies, etc. etc. But they're simply tired of it, they only wish it away. Not just because no one wants to stick his neck out while there's still someone around to bludgeon him for it, but also because no one knows what he could do, how he could do it, with whom (sic!) could do it and with what. And most of all, he doesn't know why he should do something."[7]

External motivation was initially limited, since shelves were still stocked and hunger remained temporarily at bay. The Nazi regime ensured that bombed-out residents were well provided for; so well, in fact, that they kept their anger directed at those dropping the bombs. During the entire war, Germany's leaders were able to maintain a much stronger civilian supply chain for food and other provisions than they had during the First World War. They also had significantly more success in this regard than the other major belligerents, the United States excepted—though this distinction can be chalked up to the fact that the Wehrmacht utterly plundered the areas it invaded.[8] The church also did its part for the war. In a pastoral letter from 1 February 1945, Archbishop of Freiburg Conrad Gröber called on his flock to "not at all question or undermine the martial, heroic struggle for our existence and our future ... The raging world war does not just demand from a Christian populace its fighters, who are ready to suffer and die for the people. It also demands from those at home, in ever greater amounts, the greatest sacrifice that a people can possibly offer."[9]

In fact, most Germans did not rescind their allegiance to Hitler and the Nazi regime until the very last minute, which is to say, until it was a matter of their livelihoods. And even this occurred only in places where the state apparatus was no longer capable of enforcing orders and decrees.[10] Otherwise, the overwhelming majority still viewed the *Führer* as the only salvation— "the last bastion and the last hope", as it was worded in the final bulletin of the domestic intelligence agency.[11] Everyone bemoaned his or her own fate without bothering to take responsibility for it, placing all hope on Hitler instead. Meanwhile, those fates were beginning to look existentially threatened as the Third Reich haemorrhaged territory in the final months of the Second World War. During the war, Germany had systematically relocated its industries, including ones critical for producing civilian supplies, into conquered territory; as the fighting entered its end phase, this decision appeared increasingly disadvantageous.[12] Still, the widespread shortage of necessities that marked the final months of war was not a universal condition: though the regions that saw the most combat experienced gnawing hunger, there were other

German prisoners of war at Aachen, October 1944

regions where Germans were flabbergasted by the quantities of food and fuel that they found in storerooms.[13]

In areas conquered by the Western Allies, various factories and workshops were up and running again by spring 1945.[14] This was achieved in part by building on efforts already being made in Germany during the war's end phase. While Germany's state-sanctioned industry was ramping up activity to support the war effort—relying on temporary workers as well as brutally exploited forced labourers and POWs—large sections of the entrepreneurial class were going in the opposite direction. They had already started months earlier to plan for the transition from a war economy to a peace economy, and they created incipient working groups to this end.[15] Even government agencies were stipulating early on which economic sectors to preserve in order to shore up civilian supplies and infrastructure; this can be seen in a decree from Baden's interior ministry.[16]

However, these efforts cannot be explained by political concerns, nor by any desire to resist the regime. They sprung purely from the will to survive. Germans kept up appearances while necessary, but once enemy troops took firm control of an area, those same Germans would immediately begin cutting their line to the National Socialists and preparing for what was to come. Uniforms, flags and similar materials were burned, and valuables were buried. Even the potatoes wound up underground—planted unseasonably early in order to prevent confiscation by the occupiers. By at least going through the motions of their assumed duty, Germans were able to reconcile the reality of the war with their own personal desire to survive it. Saul Padover headed up a team of US interrogators working in the area around Krefeld. After a set of typical interviews with railwaymen in spring 1945, Padover wrote an exasperated letter to his supervisor in which he claimed that appeals to intrinsic motivation were worthless: "These people would work for Hitler until the last moment, and then for us with the same unquestioning obedience."[17]

Once the state apparatus and the regime collapsed for good, this kind of approach made it easier for many people to understand the transition to peace as a "zero hour". No one intended to claim responsibility for the crimes committed by or on the orders of Germans; when it came to the destruction of Europe's Jews, the most anyone would confess was having perhaps heard about it. After May 1945, Germans remained mum about the pervasive assent given by the majority of their countrymen to the goals of the Nazi regime. Norbert Frei has categorised this as a "company secret": everyone knew about it, but no one spoke of it, and very few questioned it.[18] In fact, far too many Germans maintained positive views of National Socialism even after the war ended. 41 per cent of those questioned by the Allies in 1945 answered *yes* when asked if National Socialism was a good idea that was simply executed poorly. Alarmingly, this number climbed to 55 per cent by 1948.[19]

Germans were therefore cautious in their early encounters with the occupying forces. These encounters were characterised by a mix of fear and anxiety about the future. Most Germans reserved their real dread for the Red Army. People in the western parts of Germany, on the other hand, were free of such misgivings, even when it came to the presence of black soldiers. This outcome could not have been assumed, given the race-obsessed ideology of National Socialism. But ultimately, seeing an end to the terrible final weeks of fighting proved more important for most people than Nazi convictions did. On top of that, the occupying powers in western Germany had generally shown more decency than the remaining hodgepodge force of Wehrmacht soldiers, SS members (including Waffen-SS), home guard and Hitler Youth. This band intended to carry on until the bitter end, and they brought the battle with them wherever they went. Their untimely actions caused the senseless destruction of numerous towns right before the fighting stopped for good.

Germans and the conference

It is difficult to know if Germans truly took an interest in the important political topics of this time, and if so, how much. Germany had ceased to exist as a body politic; it had turned instead into an "object of Allied politics".[20] Stalin, the self-assured host of the Potsdam Conference, controlled Eastern Europe. American President Harry S. Truman had only been in office since the death of Franklin Roosevelt in April 1945; British Prime Minister Winston Churchill was voted out of office during the conference and replaced by Clement Attlee. France's great war hero, Charles de Gaulle, was not even invited. The negotiations in Potsdam revealed the cracks that had developed in the anti-Hitler coalition; each country brought to the table its own political interest. However, the conference's central aim was still to find a common approach to the vanquished enemy. This was eventually settled with the four D's: demilitarisation, denazification, democratisation and decentralisation. The Soviet Union won major concessions on the question of reparations, including those involving Germany's eastern border: the Kremlin would annex the northern part of East Prussia, including Königsberg, while the formerly German lands east of the Oder and the Lusatian Neisse would transfer to Polish control. Germans in these regions who had not already fled during the end phase of the war were to be relocated in a "humane" manner, according to the Potsdam Agreement; in reality, they were driven out by force, often with reprehensible cruelty.[21]

For their part, an ever-growing number of Germans felt themselves to be victims too: they had been bombed to rubble, turned into refugees and displaced; they had lost their homes and farms, their livelihoods, their family members and their physical inviolability. Applying these attributes to themselves gave people the opportunity to reframe their condition as an affliction whose causes must be rooted out.[22] This was especially important, since the overwhelming majority of Germans had no political voice. Only a select few of them stood on Washington's "white lists", which noted those considered reliable enough to entrust with administrative tasks in the US-occupied zone. The Kremlin, on the other hand, had trained up a cadre of exiled German Communists who were to take over key positions.[23]

The plan forged at Potsdam to create a central German administrative division collapsed in the face of opposition from France, which was not even participating in the conference. This evinced the fact that the conference's battle lines were not drawn neatly between the Soviet Union and the Western Allies, at least when it came to the question of Germany. Paris's ideas on the subject were often entirely different from those harboured in London and Washington. De Gaulle's independent and occasionally obstinate policy pursuits furnished the Soviet Union time and again with a model for revising and relativising its own positions and commitments. By the time 1946 rolled around, Germany had turned "from a showcase of the Allies' ability to cooperate into a test case for the looming East-West conflict". Yet opinions differed even among the governments of the West. George F. Kennan, who had served since July 1944 as envoy to the US embassy in Moscow, had little regard for the Four Powers setup decided upon at Potsdam. In 1945, he began advocating for the United States to break off its cooperation with the Kremlin and instead simply divide Europe between America and the Soviet Union. This idea initially failed to gain traction with the US government.[24] However, it would eventually form the core of America's policy of containment, as expressed in 1947 with the announcement of the Truman Doctrine.

Global political affairs also determined the approach taken at the Potsdam Conference to the issue of Germany's domestic politics. This can be seen in the admittance of political parties. In June 1945, the Soviet Military Administration in Germany issued Order no. 2, which set the conditions for founding "antifascist-progressive parties" in the zone it occupied. Political parties were also founded in the Western occupation zones in summer 1945.[25] Yet it was not the parties that first "emerged as mandate holders for a reawakening political will" or that served as "liaison institutions to the military governments"; rather, these roles were filled by low- and mid-level administrative bodies.[26] In the Soviet occupation zone, knowledge was transferred among elites on the basis of ideology. Administrators in the Western occupation zones, on the other hand, underwent a gradual process of development, building their way up from the local to the regional and finally to the state level. By 1946, Germans were even given enough latitude to establish state parliaments— a fact that can be explained by the stark bipolarisation of the world order in that year, as well as by the dramatic economic situation in Germany.

Protest rally in Krefeld against the catastrophic food situation, 31 July 1947

After all, it was no easy feat for the occupying powers, who still had to deal with the effects of the war on their own countries, to also provide for millions of Germans. The average German was consuming a mere 800 to 1,000 calories a day—far less than the 3,000 required by normal working adults. Many resorted to the infamous black markets or to *Hamsterfahrten* (journeys into the agricultural countryside to barter for food). Without these options, living conditions would have been even worse. Hunger had already set in before winter 1946/1947, which proved to be one of the bitterest of the century. This was followed in turn by a long, hot summer. Admittedly, these climatic events affected not just Germany, but all of Europe. Still, Germans

German civilians being forced
by US troops to walk past
the exhumed bodies of Jewish
women, Volary (Wallern),
Czechoslovakia 1945

had been accustomed to living off plundered riches; they associated their new condition of hunger with military defeat and occupation.[27]

The German reaction to food shortages presents something of a foil to the highly optimistic media commentary on the Potsdam resolutions. For example, on 7 August 1945 the *Kölnischer Kurier* printed the following: "Germany will be able to take its place in the European family as soon as it has demonstrated its good will and begun to lift itself up ... Germans now have the possibility of securing their immediate necessities through their own labour. A series of immediate measures was initiated in Potsdam to this end. Potsdam has laid out the path and removed numerous barriers. The German people must lift themselves up."[28]

In contrast, the few recorded examples of everyday opinions reveal a different outlook, one nestled between a cognisance of global political developments and an apparent turning away from politics in general. As an anonymous administrative officer at the time stated, "[the] things are coming to a head because the opposition between East and West is too great. ... I don't give any thought to further developments, because we're busy day and night with everyday concerns. If there's a new war, then we're all done for anyway, and if there's no war, then we're lucky. It'll happen how it happens. The main thing is having enough to eat."[29] A shoemaker made a similar comment: "It's best not to bother with politics at all. ... My only hope is that another war doesn't start."[30]

This type of commentary even made its way into school essays. Winfried Schubarth, a ten-year-old student in Prenzlauer Berg (in the Soviet occupation zone), wrote the following in spring 1946: "Today we are pleased that everything is over and that the nasty war has ended. And we will have nothing more to do with that."[31] The memories Germans had of the war were often boiled down to the experience of the conflict's final months, in which people saw themselves as victims of violence. The early years—when Germany invaded neighbours, plundered the territories it occupied and enslaved or murdered the peoples to its east—receded into the background of their thoughts.[32] In this way, Germans set for themselves what Thomas Kühne calls a "victimisation trap", which would eventually hinder the country's attempt to come to terms with its past.[33] Even in the future German Democratic Republic, the experience of the occupation defined the experience of the war's end, which one was forbidden to speak openly of anyway.[34]

During this period, Germans were first and foremost faced with denazification measures, and a majority disapproved of them. However, given the fact that 95 per cent of the roughly 3.6 million denazification hearings carried out after the war produced a verdict of "follower" or "exonerated" (the two lowest categories), many questions remain about the success of these hearings.[35] Another important challenge at the time was the wave of refugees produced by the expulsion of Germans from areas now belonging to the Soviet

Union, Poland and Czechoslovakia. Their arrival exacerbated shortages of food, fuel and housing. Millions of people had to find their place in the occupied zones and then in the two new German states; they were accepted unwillingly, and without any spirit of generosity. In some regions, such as Schleswig-Holstein or Mecklenburg, the population doubled as a result of the new arrivals, which made existing problems exponentially worse.[36]

Conclusion

The German stance on the Potsdam Agreement could be described as bifurcated in a number of ways. On the one hand, there is a clear temporal dividing line between views on the agreement before 1949 (when the two German states were founded) and those after 1949. Then there is a clear geographic dividing line: East and West Germany saw the agreement in entirely different ways, largely for ideological reasons. Leaders in the Soviet occupation zone and later in the German Democratic Republic professed support for the agreement's stipulations from the very beginning. Those in the Allied occupation zones and the Federal Republic did quite the opposite: the stipulations were fundamentally rejected in West Germany until the introduction of the Neue Ostpolitik under the social-liberal coalition government in the late 1960s. Even then, hostility towards the agreement continued to colour much political discourse surrounding Germany's former eastern territories. This provision of the Potsdam Agreement was not fully accepted in the west until German reunification.

It took a long and tedious journey to get to that point, thanks to the peculiar historical memory that dominated public life in the Federal Republic well into the 1970s. This memory was shaped not by academic-historical insight, but rather by the political expediencies of the Cold War. In 1951, 80 per cent of (West) Germans surveyed on the topic stated that the years following 1945 were the worst ever for Germany. Revealingly, a plurality of respondents (44 per cent) claimed that the country's best years were during the Third Reich. Many people legitimised such views by referring to the Potsdam Conference in particular: they saw it as the place where Germany's fate was decided for it, without its input. A significant number of Germans held a similar view of the Nuremberg trials. They denied that the Allies—who firebombed Germany—had the moral authority to sit in judgement of others.[37]

These two instances blatantly exemplify the reluctance of mainstream German society to admit the individual responsibility borne for the crimes of the Third Reich. In another context, this perhaps could have been ascribed to understandable human frailty. But due to the widespread denials of any knowledge of the Holocaust, it is, in reality, nothing short of shameful.[38] |JP

Notes

1 Winkler 2014, 121; see also Görtemaker 1999 b, 159–60; Schieder 2000, 3–18. / **2** Bessel 2007, 259. / **3** Thießen 2012, 319–34; Steber and Gotto 2014. / **4** Erkelenz City Archive 14/1755, selection of the letters of Theo Paschmann from 17 September 1944 to 18 February 1945, letter from 19 February 1945, 22. / **5** See Reeken and Thießen 2013; Bajohr and Wildt 2009; for a discussion of the National Socialist conception of the *Volksgemeinschaft*, see Janka 1997, 172–216. / **6** Padover 2001, 87. / **7** Letter from Jupp Kappius on the situation in the Ruhr, 31 January 1945, printed in Rüther, Schütz and Dann 1998, 28–29; see also ibid., 24–34. / **8** Müller 1999, 478–98. / **9** Quoted from Jupp Kappius on the situation in the Ruhr, 31 January 1945, printed in Rüther, Schütz and Dann 1998, 222–225; see also the associated literature on ibid., 24–34. / **10** See also the numerous examples in Padover 2001. / **11** Steinert 1970, 572–73. / **12** ORR Dr. W. Tomberg/OKW/Fwi Amt of November 1944: Wehrwissenschaftliche Erkenntnisse von 5 Kriegsjahren; Bundesarchiv-Militärarchiv Freiburg (BArch) RW 19/1460, fol. 46–55 et seq. und fol. 74. / **13** See the corresponding passages in Rüther, Schütz and Dann 1998, 156–159, 490–91, as well as the literature cited on 492 et seq. and 277. VGD: Persönliches Tagebuch Leutnant Wingolf Scherer; BArch RH 26-277/11 or Erkelenz City Archive 14/1755, selection of the letters of Theo Paschmann from 17 September 1944 to 18 February 1945, letter from 11 October 1944, 4. / **14** Letter from Werner Hansen (in Cologne) to Werner Eichler (in Bonn), 27 March 1945, printed in Rüther, Schütz and Dann 1998, 159; see ibid., 156–59. / **15** See Herbst 1982 and Herbert 1988 for seminal discussions of the role played by industrialists as pillars of the Nazi regime. / **16** Schnabel 1985, 157; see ibid., 152–79. / **17** Padover 1946, 316; see ibid., 313–16. / **18** Frei 2001, 303. / **19** Kleßmann 1984, 91. / **20** Recker 2002, 11. / **21** Wolfrum 2007, 24–30. / **22** Dülffer 1996, 13–19; Bessel 2007, 254. / **23** Görtemaker 1999 b, 31. / **24** Görtemaker 1999 b, 35. / **25** Görtemaker 1999 b, 31–33. / **26** Foerster 1982, 405; for a broader discussion of the subject, see ibid., 403–575, particularly 405–07. / **27** Wolfrum 2007, 30–33. / **28** Article in the *Kölnischer Kurier*, no. 21, 7 August 1945, in Nübel 2019, 75, doc. 2. / **29** Statements from people in Treptow on the topic of the East-West conflict; written communication of the SED state leadership for Greater Berlin, 6 April 1945, in Nübel 2019, 78, doc. 4. / **30** Nübel 2019, 78–9. / **31** Quoted in Bessel 2007, 253. / **32** Bessel 2007, 260. / **33** Kühne 2000, 183–96. / **34** Wierling 2007, 238–9; see also ibid., 237–51; see Morina 2012, 179–98. / **35** See Winkler 2014, 119; for general discussions of the topic, see Biddiscombe 2007 and Frei 1996. / **36** Schildt 2007, 230–31; see also ibid., 223–36. / **37** Schildt 2007, 223–27. / **38** Longerich 2006.

1945 – The "Bitter Victory". Poland and its "Liberation"

Krzysztof
Ruchniewicz

Polish doctor Zygmunt Klukowski, a member of the Polish Underground and a historian during the Second World War, noted in his journal entry of 8 May 1945: "Germany has capitulated completely. We have been so used to this idea lately that the final annihilation of our deadly enemy has not impressed us deeply as one would have expected. But people are concerned with another problem; the possibility of a conflict between Russia, Great Britain and America. It is apparent that such a conflict is inevitable. How bad our situation is! But hopefully the end final result will be good for Poland."[1]

Similar statements on the final days of the war can be found in great numbers. Those who understood the ongoing events in this larger context were not really euphoric over the end of the Second World War, even if they surely felt a certain sense of relief at the end of the German occupation. This mood was still a long way off from the joy of attaining freedom. It was clear to Klukowski and many Poles that although the war with Germany was over, the situation in that part of Europe was still marked by conflict and violence.

The future was uncertain and practically unforeseeable. Klukowski expressed this dilemma in his journal entry of the following day, 9 May: "At two o'clock in the morning we were awakened by a tremendous fusillade; machine guns from various directions, then single shots, cannon fire etc. ... We did not know what this could mean. We supposed it was an attack on the airdromes and other targets. A call from the post office explained the entire thing. These were victory salutes to celebrate the end of the war against Germany ... Thus a new page in the book of history was turned over. It is difficult to realise that proud, powerful and apparently invincible Germany lies at the feet of conquerors begging for mercy to celebrate. We are entering a new period of history. We are going to meet the unknown. Perhaps it will be even more difficult than what is left behind us?!"[2]

How different is the tone of this entry from that of the unconditional, spontaneous joy of the population of Western Europe, who took to the streets during these days and exuberantly celebrated the victory with song. How do we explain this reserved impression of the Polish doctor? Where did these new fears come from?

Poland had suffered great losses by the end of the war and occupation and had uncertain prospects for the future. Approximately 6 million citizens lost their lives, and a great number of people remained mentally and/or physically disabled for the rest of their lives. The orphanages were overcrowded. Over 90 per cent of the Jewish population lost their lives, and the century-old co-existence between Poles and Polish Jews was no longer. Almost a third of the Polish intelligentsia were murdered. In the first years of the war, Poland was occupied by two powers, Nazi Germany and the USSR (1939–1941). Both imposed their social and economic regime on their occupied areas, each based on its own totalitarian ideology. Common elements included terror and forced labour.

← Polish fighter squadron in the Royal Air Force, around 1945

The greater part of the larger cities was destroyed. Poland's capital Warsaw was reduced to ash and rubble, its population murdered or displaced. When Soviet and Polish units marched into Warsaw in January of 1945, only silence and empty ruins remained to greet them. Only gradually did the inhabitants return. On 9 May 1945, the writer Zofia Nałkowska noted in her diary: "A peculiar, far-reaching image of the victory imprinted itself on my mind in these ruins; they were actually the city that Warsaw once was. As if it was a light, finely-drawn, black and white pencilled sketch of death by Utrillo. You can still recognise the streets. From a distant perspective, one might think that nothing had happened, that these buildings were still filled with life."[3]

The destruction of Warsaw was not the only loss that Poland suffered. Poland irretrievably lost two important cities in the east, Wilno/Vilnius and Lwów/Lviv, which were both highly important to Polish history since time immemorial. The loss of these important centres was the result of territorial changes caused by the Soviet invasion of Poland. Before the aggression of the USSR in September 1939, the area of Poland was 388,000 km², of which around 180,000 km² was occupied by the USSR. Poland's present national territory is owed to the "reparations" of approximately 108,000 km², which was taken from its defeated western neighbour Germany and given to Poland. The Polish border was thus moved 200 to 300 km westward.

Old Town Market Place, destroyed by German troops, after the Warsaw Uprising 1944

In order to illustrate the extent of these changes, the Polish contemporary historian Włodzimierz Borodziej proposed the following comparison: "An idea that would have been in no way abstract in 1945 may help. It is enough to imagine that Stalin decided to make Slovakia the seventeenth Soviet Republic. The Czechs would have to be compensated somehow with Franconian and Bavarian territory. Bamberg, Nuremberg or Regensburg would be Czech today—just as natural as Stettin and Breslau are now Polish."[4]

The loss of the areas in the east and moving the frontiers westward was not without consequences for the ethnic composition of the Polish population. Most Jews were murdered. Most Lithuanians, Belarussians and Ukrainians found themselves outside the new Polish frontiers and inside the Soviet Union. Some Poles were also caught there for various reasons. Others moved to the west and were the subjects of population exchange. The remaining ethnic minorities in Poland's new east, including 500,000 Ukrainians, were brought beyond the Bug and San rivers over the following the months.
A similar fate affected Germans relocated from the Polish territory and the so-called "recovered territories" of Poland. Almost 3.5 million Germans had to leave Poland.

For the first time in its history, Poland became a homogenous national state. Forced relocation was not new. The models were Nazi Germany and the USSR and their policies of "ethnic cleansing". After the experience of the Second World War, the page turned completely, and the forced displacement of unwelcomed minorities was deemed necessary. Contestation of these policies and their implementation are undocumented. Aversion and national enmity also celebrated victories after the war. Not only do the Germans look back at this time negatively, but also other nationalities such as the Ukrainians. Even in the west, Poles arriving from the former Polish eastern territories were confronted with violence and fear of Soviet power and of their new neighbours.

As a result of the Second World War, the position of Poland fundamentally changed in the international system of alliances. Although it was part of the anti-Hitler coalition from the very beginning, the German occupation and the entry of the USSR into the anti-Hitler coalition meant that Poland became a weak ally. The founding of a so-called "Underground State" as well as the deployment of its own armed forces on the Western Front was not able to prevent the country from becoming a plaything of foreign Allied interests. After 1943, Poland was no longer a politically independent actor. For the Western powers, it only remained an uncomfortable burden.

This situation became blatantly apparent in 1945 as the fate of Poland was being considered. Poland was not a participant in the great conferences, but already in Tehran went from being a protagonist to an object to be decided upon.

The disappearance of Poland from the political stage was the intention and consequence of Stalin's ruthless and targeted policy,

which began in 1943, to establish an alternative political centre in
glaring opposition to the existing, legal structure of the Polish
government-in-exile. The extended war facilitated the realisation of
Stalin's expansive plans. The West was prepared to accept a high
price to spare the blood of its own armies. The ever greater losses of
Poland in its struggle with the German occupiers weakened it in the
face of the approaching new hegemon in this part of Europe.

Already in July of 1944, Stalin succeeded in laying the cornerstone of future Communist power in Poland in Chełm. He did not care
much about the international recognition of his actions, he was more
interested in accomplished facts. A bitter event for the future of

Poland on the international level was the crackdown of the Warsaw Uprising and the death of almost 200,000 people including both soldiers and civilians in Warsaw. Military resistance, even before the arrival of the Red Army, was futile and doomed to failure. Collaborative military action was pointless as well, of which the divisions of the Home Army in Kresy, the Polish eastern regions, were quickly able to satisfy themselves.

The Polish Division of Kosciuszko, which was formed in the USSR, fought together with the Red Army. After the pre-war Polish-Soviet frontier was crossed, additional units were established. They were to demonstrate support for the USSR. They were involved in battles near Kolberg, Bautzen and finally Berlin. From a military standpoint, these units did not play a great role. However, it should be noted that ordinary soldiers fought bravely and selflessly without knowing for what political project their efforts and sacrifice would be abused.

"The Soviets did everything", concluded historian Jan Szkudlinski, "to show Poland and the world that they now govern the country and that the legitimate Polish government is conducting activities in the areas occupied by the Red Army and not in London. The participation of Polish units in the conquest of Berlin was an element of this campaign. But we have to differentiate this political issue from the fight of ordinary Polish soldiers against the Germans since 1939. To these ordinary soldiers, this was a great victory."[5]

From month to month, the group of Polish Communists, protected by the bayonets of the Red Army and the NKVD, began to consolidate their power in Poland. A terror apparatus was quickly created, and the first fundamental political reforms were implemented. Political enemies and the old elites were eliminated. The conferences of the Big Three in Yalta and later in Potsdam confirmed Stalin's policies in East Central Europe. Indeed, Poland lost its independence in Yalta ("The Tragedy of Yalta").[6] The USSR received the confirmation of Poland's eastern frontier, drawn mostly along the so-called Curzon line, which meant a loss of a third of Poland's pre-war territory. Even worse, the powers could not agree on a common position regarding Poland's western frontier; it was only vaguely established that Poland would receive "substantial accessions" in territory there.

At this time, the resettlement of Poland from the areas conceded to its eastern neighbours began. The USSR, whose armies now controlled large areas including the eastern territories of Germany, was the only guarantor for a new order in Eastern and Central Europe. The fate of Poland also depended on it. In the spring of 1945, Moscow officially handed over the territory to the Polish authorities.

However, the issue of Poland's western frontier required an international settlement. This question was discussed during the Potsdam Conference.[7] The Polish side provided a memorandum suggesting the establishment of the western frontier along the Oder and Lusatian Neisse.[8] The lack of unity between the Allies was the reason

Wehrmacht soldiers patrolling the city centre during the Warsaw Uprising

119

Polish boy scouts fighting
in the Warsaw Uprising,
2 September 1944

for inviting a Polish delegation to Potsdam under the leadership of
the President of the National Council, Bolesław Bierut. At the time,
there was already a government, which also included a representative in exile, Stanisław Mikołajczyk from the Polish People's Party
(PSL). The Polish delegation brought forth its arguments on 24 July
1945 and their presentation not only covered territorial issues but
also demographic, economic and security concerns.

Mr. Bierut said—according to the American protocol of the
foreign ministers' meeting of 24 July 1945 in Potsdam with the participation of the Polish delegation—that the war had begun in Poland
and Poland had suffered immense human and material losses.
Poland, he added, was losing 180,000 square kilometres in the east
through the establishment of a new Polish frontier; it believed that
the new eastern frontier that was established on the principle of
citizenship is correct, but was also of the opinion that territories in
the west should be given to it. The Poles approach the matter from
the perspective of security and the economy.[9]

A few days later, on 1 August, the Polish position was
accepted after several rounds of talks and the territory east of the
Oder and Lusatian Neisse as well as Stettin were officially handed
over to Warsaw. At the same time, it was established that the land
would remain under "Polish administration" until the final decision
of the peace conference. The German population living in these
areas should be re-located in the following years. Beyond that, it
was agreed that Poland should receive reparations from the part of
Germany conceded to the USSR.

The decisions of the Allies on Polish matters further strengthened Poland's dependency on the USSR. Since a concluding peace conference did not take place, the Kremlin appeared to be the only guarantor to safeguard the new territory. For the national existence of Poland, which suffered so much material and human loss during the war, the new territory was required to survive.

In the following decades, the western frontier was contested by the Soviet Zone/GDR (until 1950) [10] and the Federal Republic of Germany (until 1970).[11] Its permanent acceptance was connected to the development of the so-called German question. In 1990, unified Germany finally signed a border agreement with Poland and ended the decades-old dispute surrounding the establishment of the German-Polish frontier at the Oder and Lusatian Neisse. Beyond that, the expulsion and re-location of the German population and the fate of the German cultural legacy in North and West Poland were reasons hindering the normalisation of German-Polish relations after 1945. The question of reparation payments is contentious even today.

However, the legacy of Potsdam in the form of the new borders was and is generally accepted. This was already apparent in the late 1940s. Revisionism in connection with demands for restoring the eastern frontier was never of great importance in post-war Poland. There are many indications that the following view of an expert that worked together with the Polish leaders during the Potsdam Conference quickly became the generally accepted opinion. Andrzej Bolewski, member of the Polish delegation in Potsdam, mineralogist at the Academy of Mining and Metallurgy in Cracow, recorded the following analysis in his memoirs *Z drogi do Poczdamu* (The Way to Potsdam): "An optimal result was achieved. Although the area of our country will become smaller, it is accompanied by the transformation from the multi-national Republic of Poland to the People's Republic of Poland, whose inhabitants are almost exclusively Poles. A simple comparison of the number of Poles and the area of the People's Republic of Poland leads us to the conclusion that we as a nation have suffered no loss in territory. A part of our territory has been lost, but also ethnic minorities who lived in the eastern part of the Republic of Poland. However, we have received a better structure, with the Vistula and Oder valleys as backbones as well as the access to the sea. This creates favourable conditions to build up an inland waterway network as well as a better network of railways and motorways. Large east-west and north-south transport lines have to cross in our territory."[12]

Even though Poland was a nominal victor, it did not attend the UN Conference on International Organisation in San Francisco on 27 June 1945 (only several months later did the representatives of the Interim Government of National Unity sign the UN Charter). The absence of Polish representatives at this important international conference reflected the unclear situation in Poland.

The Polish government-in-exile lost the recognition of the Western powers. The new coalition government, which in accordance with the Yalta Agreement also included representatives of the government-in-exile—apart from the Communists and their satellites it comprised several important exiled politicians—was led by former Prime Minister Stanislaw Mikołajczyk and was founded one day after the signing of the UN Charter. But despite all appearances of a broad representation of political orientation, in practice it was quickly demonstrated that in Poland it was the Communists, supported by Moscow, who wielded unlimited power.

A symbolic expression of the loss of Poland's international position was the absence of representatives of the Polish Army during the victory parade in London in 1946.[13] Although the Western Allies had become more and more politically distant from the Soviet Union, they were still of the opinion that a public display of the Polish contribution to the war against Nazi Germany would be an unnecessary provocation to Stalin.

In the spring of 1945, Polish society was tired of war. The return to normal life was without doubt a great dream. However, there was often no way back to the good old days. Millions of people had lost their loved ones, their homes, flats had been destroyed, their livelihoods ran dry, and many had simply lost their homeland. It was necessary to find a new direction. On the street at the time, one could see many of those transferred or expelled, marauders, black marketers, but also average citizens looking for a better life. State institutions that could have guided the rebuilding were weak or corrupt.

The complexity of the situation in which Poland found itself in 1945 is appropriately reflected in the poem "Powotry" (Homecomings) by the writer and Auschwitz prisoner Tadeusz Borowski, whose language is far away the euphoria of victory: "While we – furtively, one by one, / cross borders on forbidden trails / to our country, in our dreams, / home, to the graves ... / We shall search and find no one / we will look, look into strange faces / we will keep silent: well, we all know ... / yes ... / softly someone whispers: KGB / fear ..."[14]

Marcin Zaremba, a historian from that generation, made the feeling of deep anxiety, even fear, a leitmotif of his new book.[15] He shows the attitudes of the Polish people during this turning point and the sprouting of a new world in a convincing and unsettling fashion. Only after many years did war and post-war fears abate. But other, new anxieties and fears replaced them, those connected to life in the so-called real socialism.

Although the Polish Communists had taken and enforced their power, they failed in establishing a well-functioning political and economic system and in fulfilling their promise of equality and justice. The model of Soviet Communism proved to be a union of political oppression and lamentable economic incompetence.

Despite the loss of sovereignty during the following decades, Polish society resisted oppressing powers, although military struggle

Allied Victory Parade, London 1946

was avoided.[16] The government, weakened by economic failures, felt compelled to liberalise its policies, but could use force to maintain them at any time; for this purpose, propaganda with anti-German and anti-fascist slogans was even used until the 1980s. The year 1945 thus lasted for many decades on various levels.

In this light, the year 1989 should be seen as a great success for Polish society, in which a great objective, fought for since 1939, was finally achieved—an independent country. The Poles succeeded in removing the Communist rule peacefully. Polish Communism was banned to the junk room of history, together with the entire post-war system. Poland obtained its independence and since then, its role in Europe has been growing continually. Thanks to the activities of innumerable people, for example the late Władysław Bartoszewski and institutions such as the Catholic Church, a constructive dialogue with former enemies could begin, even during the time of the People's Republic of Poland, as well as the search for paths towards reconciliation and understanding. Today, Poland has no pending border issues with its neighbours and works together amicably with most of them. The past 30 years have been, in spite of a few dark spots, the most successful time in the history of Poland in the past 200 years.

In summary, from a Polish perspective, the year 1945 can be regarded as a "bitter victory". But we must neither forget the condition in which Poland had found itself, nor the fact that the German occupation would have meant the biological and cultural annihilation of the country. According to Jerzy Holzer: "In light of the situation, the Polish victory can be regarded as the lesser evil, but in certain historical contexts, even achieving a lesser evil can be a success. Opinions are often heard which do not appreciate such success, but for the Polish nation, this was nothing less than the preservation of life and the liberation from physical oppression, partly from the occupiers and partly from the future they planned."[17]

It is not easy to answer the question of whether Poland came out of this conflict as a winner or a loser. Historians avoid an unequivocal answer. They usually, if possible, write a balanced opinion and consider both wins and losses. But without a doubt, the year 1945 has had an enormous effect on today's Poland: its territory, its people, but also its political policies and ideas. |DC

Notes

1 See Klukowski 1997, 71–72. / **2** See ibid. / **3** Nałkowska 2000, 53. / **4** Borodziej 2015, 37. / **5** "W rogatywkach z orłem bez korony. Polacy w operacji berlińskiej. Adam Leszczyński rozmawia z dr. Janem Szkudlińskim", Gazeta Wyborcza, 1 May 2015. / **6** See Ruchniewicz 2012, 89–101. / **7** For the Polish perspective on the Potsdam Conference, see Borodziej 2012, 360–80. / **8** See Rysiak 1970, 9–23. / **9** Rysiak 1970, 86–87. / **10** See also Ihme-Tuhel 1998 and Tomala 2000. / **11** See also Lehmann 1979 and Binden 1998. / **12** Bolewski 2004, 180–81. / **13** See Polityka 2018. / **14** Borowski 1990, 57–59. / **15** See Zaremba 2016. / **16** See also Borodziej 2010 and Krzoska 2015. / **17** Holzer 2010, 168.

Counting the Exiles: Potsdam 1945

Andreas Kossert

"Things can follow one after the other only for as long as you are alive in order to extract a splinter from a child's foot, to take the roast out of the oven before it burns or sew a dress from a potato sack, but with each step you take while fleeing, your baggage grows less, with more and more left behind, and sooner or later you just stop and sit there, and then all that is left of life is life itself, and everything else is lying in all the ditches beside all the roads…"[1]

Jenny Erpenbeck, *Visitation*

Potsdam, summer of 1945. Three older men meet in Cecilienhof Palace. They lead the nations that have just defeated Hitler's Germany. We are all familiar with the photo of the Big Three—Churchill, Truman and Stalin—sitting in comfortable wicker chairs in the garden of the Potsdam residence. They are not just deciding Germany's future; they are also deciding how to divvy up the world anew. It is a world torn at the seams by global conflict and by the utter barbarity of National Socialism. The decisions made at Potsdam are only possible because all pre-existing limitations have been smashed by the war of conquest and annihilation that Germany unleashed. But something else is clearly afoot here. The war in Europe has recently ended, and victory over Nazi Germany is not the only focal point of the conference. The old rivalry between the United States and the Soviet Union, which temporarily went dormant during the war, has reawakened and now looms over these summer days. Potsdam is serving as a prelude to a new conflict, one that will be known for decades to come as the Cold War. For some, this means being mired in a deep freeze between two ideologies; it means the Iron Curtain. For many other parts of the world, though, it means countless and bloody "hot" wars—a fact erased by the Cold War's insidious terminology. These gentlemen have therefore come to Cecilienhof to gain concrete advantages, not merely to sit in judgement of Germany. Each wants to claim a piece of the pie. They eye one another suspiciously, and their entire entourages follow suit. They become global masterminds of a sort, playing a never-ending game in which they enjoy cigars and whisky while dividing up the world along new lines of geopolitical, strategic and ideological interest. It is not a crucial point to these three men that millions of people are affected by their mapping exercises. The millions are all just pawns and collateral damage—terrible though that thought is—in the power politics of the Big Three. In this sense, Potsdam represents a coda. It is one of the last conferences in the modern world where superpowers hash out their spheres of interest. This tradition, which originated in the early modern period, reaches its peak during the age of imperialism and lasts well into the twentieth century. At these conferences, borders are arbitrarily drawn, corrected, and moved again and again. In the end, countless lives are disrupted. On account of the decisions made at Potsdam, at its music-laced soirees and festive dinners, millions of Europeans lose their homeland forever.

← Escaping from approaching Soviet troops by horse and cart, early 1945

"The events that transpired in this village on the Oder in the middle of the twentieth century are surely just a tiny drop in an unending ocean of history." So recalls Karlheinz Gleß of Brandenburg, who loses his home in Peetzig as a result of these decisions. His small village lies on the river Oder, in the middle of Brandenburg—and in the middle of Germany. No one expects that this village will become Polish by war's end, henceforth to be called Piasek. For the villagers, the new land survey drawn up at Potsdam means the irretrievable loss of their ancestral homes, their familiar environs, everything from yesterday that was important. The three statesmen conferring in Potsdam have never heard of Peetzig. For them, the fates of the villagers are just those tiny drops in the unending ocean of history. But for the villagers of Peetzig it is a total caesura, a life in which everything is divided into *before* and *after*. The decision handed down at Potsdam to displace the villagers means for them the end of "life, irretrievable and irreplaceable life", as Karlheinz Gleß says in retrospect.[2] Barely one hundred kilometres from Cecilienhof Palace flows the river Oder, on whose banks sits Peetzig, a village in Brandenburg.

People lose their homelands. The writer Christa Wolf is one such person. "The exodus from home calls forth a flow of tears", says Nelly, the protagonist of her autobiographical novel *Patterns of Childhood*.[3] Wolf likewise originates from a part of Brandenburg that has been lost to history. She was born in the town of Landsberg, on the Warthe River, in the Neumark. There is hardly a denizen of Brandenburg alive today who could point to it on a map. It now lies in Poland, where it is known as Gorzów Wielkopolski. Christa Wolf's biography also demonstrates the drastic changes wrought on Brandenburg by the unsparing course of events in the mid-twentieth century: war, social breakdown, eventual displacement. Borders are moved. Millions of Europeans lose their homeland. Among them are 14 million Germans.

One of those is Friedrich Biella. Early in the morning of 21 January 1945, he and his family board a couple of horse-drawn wagons and leave their little village in Masuria. The day is recorded in his notebook under a brief entry, "Order to leave my farm". Through the ham-fisted diction, we witness the very moment this farmer terminates an intergenerational contract with his ancestors. He must leave behind everything from yesterday that was important. Even the animals. "Our dog 'Senta' followed us a way. She became more uncomfortable the farther we got from the village. Eventually she took our advice and went back home." There follow weeks without any notebook entries, as the strain of exodus takes its toll. The log picks back up in March 1945, after Friedrich becomes stranded in the Duchy of Lauenburg following weeks of wandering. Every day he goes to the local British army headquarters and asks when he can return home. And every day they put the old man off. In his notebook he records their eternally repetitive answer: "Just wait a bit before making the journey back."

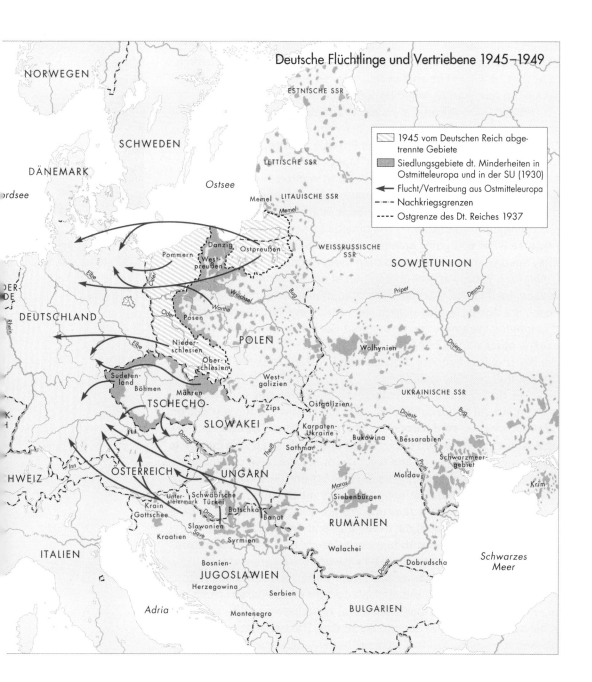

Deutsche Flüchtlinge und Vertriebene 1945–1949

NORWEGEN

SCHWEDEN

DÄNEMARK

Ostsee

Nordsee

ESTNISCHE SSR

LETTISCHE SSR

Memel

LITAUISCHE SSR

Memel

WEISSRUSSISCHE SSR

SOWJETUNION

	1945 vom Deutschen Reich abge-trennte Gebiete
	Siedlungsgebiete dt. Minderheiten in Ostmitteleuropa und in der SU (1930)
→	Flucht/Vertreibung aus Ostmitteleuropa
–·–·–	Nachkriegsgrenzen
– – –	Ostgrenze des Dt. Reiches 1937

ODER-
DE

DEUTSCHLAND

Rhein

Elbe

Oder

Pommern

Danzig
West-
preußen

Ostpreußen

Weichsel

Bug

Pripet

Desna

Warthe

Oder

Posen

Elbe

Nieder-
schlesien

POLEN

Ober-
schlesien

Wolhynien

Dnjepr

Sudeten-
land

Böhmen

Mähren

TSCHECHO-

SLOWAKEI

West-
galizien

Zips

Ostgalizien

UKRAINISCHE SSR

Dnjestr

Bug

K-

Donau

Karpaten-
Ukraine

Bukowina

Bessarabien

Schwarzmeer-
gebiet

SCHWEIZ

Inn

ÖSTERREICH

Theiß

Sathmar

UNGARN

Pruth

Moldau

Krim

Krain
Gottschee

Unter-
steiermark

Schwäbische
Türkei

Drau

Batschka

Banat

Maros

Siebenbürgen

RUMÄNIEN

Schwarzes
Meer

Slawonien

Save

Syrmien

Kroatien

Walachei

Donau

Dobrudscha

ITALIEN

Bosnien-

JUGOSLAWIEN

Herzegowina

Serbien

Montenegro

Adria

BULGARIEN

Map showing former German
settlement areas and streams
of German refugees and
displaced persons, 1945–1949

The erstwhile farmer finds his new life in the British zone difficult to bear, housed as he is among strangers. Friedrich learns a short time later that he will not be able to return to his Masurian home. He dies within the year, age 73, killed by homesickness.[4]

Some of those who are exiled never truly arrive anywhere; they become emigrants in their souls, mourning their lost homes. Older people in particular, such as Friedrich Biella, lack the strength to start anew after 1945. Many of them are unable to bear their loss. They begin to crack, both in mind and in body. Christa Wolf writes of homesickness as a cause of death: "For the old—for those who had babbled about death for years, just to hear the young contradict them—the time had come to keep silent; because what was going on now was their death, and they knew it. They aged years in weeks, and then died, not neatly one after the other, for a variety of reasons, but all at once, for one and the same reason, be it called typhoid, or hunger, or simply homesickness, which is a perfectly plausible pretext for dying."[5] Epitaphs announce this longing in cemeteries throughout Germany. Chiselled in stone are the place names of homes that were lost—Stettin, Schwerin an der Warthe, Reichenberg, Königsberg, Breslau. Thus the dead lament their worldly exile.

In 1945, Europe sees its largest wave of refugees since time out of mind. An entire continent lies in ruin, thanks to the war started by Hitler who elevated barbarism to a *raison d'état*. The crimes against humanity carried out by Hitler and the Nazis shake Europe to its very core. Persecution and displacement have been commonplace since the war began. As early as 1939, Poles and Jews are driven out of regions occupied by Germany. Arbitrary resettlements of undesired ethnic groups are a daily occurrence. Emigration and exile have been facts of life for political dissidents and racially persecuted people since 1933. Conventional wars used to be either local affairs or far-flung conflicts that could be viewed from a safe distance. By 1945, the latest world war has rendered this old verity obsolete.

Admittedly, the forcible displacement of undesired ethnic or religious groups has long been a tool for achieving political ends; it did not begin with the Second World War. The twentieth century marked the pinnacle of forced resettlement, as states tried to bring political boundaries into line with demographic ones. In this sense, the First World War served as a dress rehearsal for the population displacements that would follow. After 1918, democratic governments likewise sought ways to avoid conflict by reducing ethnic complexity. The "population exchange" between Greece and Turkey that followed the 1923 Treaty of Lausanne brought a huge influx of refugees to Greece, swelling the country's population by over a fourth and pushing it to the limits of its carrying capacity. The Soviet Union perfected its own idiosyncratic method of ethnic cleansing. Stalin would simply deport entire groups—including Poles, Germans, Finns, Balts and Koreans—as a form of collective punishment.

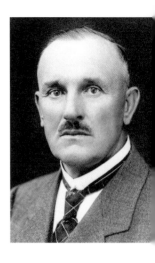

Friedrich Biella

Still, the Nazi's war of conquest and extermination displaces people on an unprecedented scale. Since the war began, massive expulsions have been part of daily life. The *Generalplan Ost* strategy for Central and Eastern Europe offers a glimpse into the long-term consequences of Nazi race policy. Mass murder is carried out on an industrial scale; millions perish; the ability to sustain human life is damaged across an entire continent. The number of people who are displaced, deported or turned into refugees during the Second World War is estimated between 50 and 60 million—one tenth of the European population. We must add to those another 25 million refugees and displaced persons after the war ends. The war puts all of Europe into massive flux. Countless people from all different backgrounds are in transit: soldiers, POWs, emigrants, civilians, evacuees, deportees, settlers, refugees, the displaced, the exiled. Götz Aly and Karl Schlögel call the first half of the twentieth century "Europe's marshalling yard".[6] "After 1945, Europe went from a marshalling yard under wartime conditions to a marshalling yard in the absence of war", according to historian Mathias Beer, but it still persisted "under the conditions bequeathed to it: existing borders, destruction, deracination, death".[7]

"Orderly transfer" is the term used in the Potsdam Agreement to describe the displacement of millions of Germans from Central Europe. Stalin, Truman and Attlee (who had replaced Churchill) agree on 2 August 1945 in Cecilienhof Palace to redraw the map of Central Europe. The goal of their post-war planning is to ensure greater ethnic homogeneity. To achieve this end, Germans must clear out of the east. Churchill had already given a speech in Parliament (15 December 1944) advocating the expulsion of the Germans, since this method would be "the most satisfactory and lasting". "A clean sweep will be made", he promised. The writer George Orwell admonishes these plans from the left wing of the spectrum: "This is equivalent to uprooting and transplanting the entire population of Australia, or the combined populations of Scotland and Ireland. ... I fancy ... that this enormous crime cannot actually be carried through, though it might be started, with confusion, suffering and the sowing of irreconcilable hatreds as a result. Meanwhile, the British people should be made to understand, with as much concrete detail as possible, what kind of policies their statesmen are committing them too."[8]

"Orderly transfer". That is the euphemism the Allies bestow on their decision of summer 1945. Yet no matter what name we use, there will never be anything "orderly and humane" about displacement, ethnic cleansing or forced migration. This is quite obvious. By ordering the removals, the Potsdam Agreement is trying to hold back a tide that has actually been rising for some time. In Poland and Czechoslovakia, so-called "wild expulsions" at the end of the war (but before the Potsdam Conference) were already setting brutal precedents. According to historian Raymond Douglas, these expulsions represented "the eruption of a massive state-sponsored carnival of violence, resulting in a death toll that on the most conservative of estimates must have reached six figures. As such it is unique in the peacetime history of twentieth-century Europe."[9]

After the war, German civilians in Czechoslovakia and parts of Poland are made to wear armbands or patches of white cloth marked with a letter N, which stands for "nemec/niemiec" ("German"). This is meant to identify them publicly. Dorothea Koch-Thalmann experiences first-hand the effects of this decree as a young girl in Silesia. "Someone also came with the message that a new announcement had been posted on the community bulletin board: 'All Germans have to wear a white armband and are not allowed to be out past eight o'clock in the evening. Anyone caught without an armband, or out after eight o'clock, will be shot!' Mother sewed armbands out of white handkerchiefs for everyone on the farm. They were fastened around the left arm with safety pins."[10] Finally, on 19 August 1946, Dorothea and her family are exiled from Wüstewaltersdorf, in the Owl Mountains. "During this commotion, two dark figures come down the lane and open the gate to the yard. We pause in a fright. In truth they look ragged, with crumpled hats on their heads. No militiamen these. 'What riff-raff', father hisses. 'Be quiet', mother says quietly. They have white sheets of paper in their hands. They call out our names in thick accents and check them off their list. Then they go in the house and lock up the doors. Good thing we already took all our stuff out." Dorothea recollects: "I threw on my bag and didn't look back. 'Get outta there!' they tell us. They've tacked up their white slips of paper all over. They wait until we've got everything out of the hallway, then they put a white slip on the front door too. They've taken the key out of the door. The words 'all shut' ring in my ears."[11] The family, just evicted, must watch as the door lock is sealed on behalf of future occupants.

Not far from the Owl Mountains, 16-year-old Katharina Elliger is forced to leave Wölfelsdorf, in the Grafschaft Glatz. "Sometime in mid-March 1946, while dawn was just beginning to break, rifle butts pounded on our front door", Katharina remembers. "Hoarse shouts bounced off the house wall, and heavy footsteps stomped through the snow. They're coming! Then they were in front of our window. 'Open up! Come out!' We threw on our gowns, tracked down a few possessions and a little bit to eat. A windowpane had already been smashed. Within barely ten minutes, we were on the path in front of the house. The bed I had just been sleeping in was still warm, yet they drove us before them, out into the street." Now they are on the street. "There was already a long line of sorry figures waiting there, with knapsacks and bags, back packs and suitcases. The line was four or five people wide, flanked by soldiers with their bayonets fixed. They kept yelling at people, striking anyone who wasn't tight enough in the line, kicking them, hitting them with their gun stocks. I crept into the middle of the line. My aunt, who wasn't familiar with this kind treatment, made a face of sheer horror and responded to a soldier's kicks with the words: 'A bit friendlier, please!' He struck her so hard that she fell into the snow slush, blood trickling down her face. Someone quickly helped her up and braced her. Then we were pushed on by those behind, who were driven by the lash of whips."[12]

Mieczysław Tankielun, from the village Daszyszki, also faces his moment of separation and departure. He is forced to leave his home on 14 April 1946, along with the rest of his Polish family. "The time came to say goodbye. My mother called us children to her side. We all wept from despair and melancholy. She took us out to the yard, to a large oaken cross with a picture of the crucified Christ. It had always been in that spot, where our family used to gather with the neighbours on evenings in May to say prayers. Father came to the cross too. There the whole family knelt down and said a prayer to God, asking him to watch over us and the house we were leaving behind. We all devoutly kissed the cross, and then mother put a couple of handfuls of earth into a little bag (she still has this today). Afterwards we went back to the flat, where we followed mother's instructions to kiss the two saints' pictures still hanging there, as well as the table, the threshold and the front door. From a distance of a few hundred metres, around where our farm road ended, I could still catch a glimpse of our farm—the tall crossbar of the well, and the old lime- and maple-lined lane in front of our house."[13]

The young Mieczysław Tankielun experiences a farwell for good. His home is now in Belarus. It is there because Stalin has got everything he wanted from Potsdam. Stalin's prize, as he understands it, is all of Eastern Europe. Besides the Germans who loose a fourth of their, it is Poland that is hit first and foremost. It was initially invaded in 1939 by Hitler and Stalin, who worked in tandem to occupy and annex its land. After six years of occupied rule, it again becomes a political football for international power brokers to kick around. No one bothers to ask Poland. Poland is allowed no control over its post-war fate. On Stalin's insistence, the country's borders are pushed far to the west; Stalin profits, since large swaths of Poland's pre-war territory are absorbed by the Soviet Union. Poland's Communist-led "Provisional Government of National Unity" eventually succumbs to the powers that be and supports the so-called westward shift. For Polish exiles, this moment is their parting farewell to a life they will lose forever. "We leave tomorrow. This is the last night in Lemberg. I am writing this in the dining room, sitting on a crate. A storm is brewing, you can hear the thunder in the distance. Today I saw the High Castle for the last time. It simply can't be true that I will never return. … I was born in the room where our daughter now sleeps. And now I have to leave this place. They are driving us from our native soil." Alma Heczko records these lines in her diary on 18 May 1945, right before she is forced from her home in Lemberg (now Lviv), never to return.[14]

At least 1.6 million people lose their homes in eastern Poland because of Stalin's power politics. As part of the "westward shift", Lviv, Grodno and Vilnius all go to the Soviet Union. The Kurowski family is exiled. Their old village, Dukszty Pijarskie, remains a mental anchor for many generations after their departure. For family elders Julian and Janina Kurowski, the village symbolises a very real loss; for the younger generation, it lives on in stories. Dukszty Pijarskie was part of the Second Polish Republic until 1939. Now it lies behind the Lithuanian border. Julian and Janina were married in Dukszty Pijarskie's parish church in 1937. They owned 20 hectares of farmland in the nearby village of Maluny. In autumn 1946, the Kurowskis must leave this home forever—it has been swallowed by the Soviet Union. They journey into the unknown, into a Poland that is foreign to them. After their expulsion, they live in Bartoszyce (formerly the German town of Bartenstein). Janina and Julian will straddle the border between these two worlds until they die. Their son Józef recalls how their voices would dance with the singsong cadence of Vilnian Polish whenever they spoke. "Although they spent most of their lives in Barten [an East Prussian territory], my parents always remained children of their beloved Vilnius, home of their forefathers, with all their hearts and souls. Every day that Julian and Janina spent in Bartoszyce on the Łyna River filled them with longing for their native ground and for the banks of the Duksztanka and the Neris, where they spent their youth."[15]

In her novel *Seven Springs*, Ulrike Draesner tells the story of a Silesian family across multiple generations. One of her characters —the Polish psychologist Boris Nienalt—represents the essential double bind of life as a displaced Pole. These people do not simply lose their homes; in most cases, they also have to resettle in what used to be Germany's eastern provinces. Boris explains how the mental landscape of one generation imprints itself on the next. He is the scion of a displaced family. The Soviets drive his mother, Halka, out of Lviv and into Wrocław, the former German city of Breslau that now lies in the western part of Poland. They live amid the ruins of a German past. "We were like pioneers", says Halka, "fallen into a vacuum full of corpses, muck, disrepute, garbage and danger, into what remained of cities and villages, into what remained of the lives and lies of our predecessors, a city not completely empty, but strewn with ashes and ugly dreams. In that place we would have turned into people without history, we weren't allowed to have any, and the place we were in didn't have a history anymore either, or if it did, it was battered and contrived, one thousand years in the past, just propa- ganda."[16] Existence in the west proves a tough balancing act for displaced Poles. Though they are victims of Stalin, who carried the day at the Potsdam Conference, they must remain silent about their own forced removal. According to official government doctrine they are "repatriates", a term meant to paper over the human catastrophe of displacement. Any public display of mourning is forbidden.

Janina and Julian
Kurowski, 1943

"Officially, our displacement didn't even happen", Halka remarks.
"We were brought home. What's there to complain about!"[17]

    Karelia, Istria, Transylvania, Bukovina, Galicia, Silesia, Bohemia,
Volhynia, Masuria, Gottschee: all places whose original inhabitants
fall victim to forced migration. Cities such as Rijeka, Grodno, Lviv,
Vilnius, and Wrocław change both on and under the surface. They
lose their ethnic and linguistic diversity. Hard numbers reveal a fate
shared by millions: 90,000 Magyars leave their homes in southern

Slovakia by 1949, heading for Hungary. By 1950, over 200,000 Czechs and Slovaks depart the former Habsburg territories for the newly forged Czechoslovakia; among them are 40,000 from Volhynia, which is now in the hands of the Soviets. They primarily settle in the corners of Bohemia from which the German population was recently expelled. The war and its backwash create countless streams of refugees, each with its own context and character. They present challenges for Europe for decades to come.

For millions of people, the Potsdam Agreement confirms with dramatic certainty that they will never be able to return to their homelands. They are cut off from the physical and social environments they knew so well. A feeling creeps over them: they are now strangers. This fate of being a stranger is not one which they themselves have chosen. Shared experiences still connect them, even after 1945. "There were no pictures, no blankets, no letters, no photos, no documents, no handed-down Christmas decorations, not a single old doll, no pots, no monogrammed handkerchief, to say nothing of furniture. No heirlooms, no legacy, no gifts passed down through generations."[18] On top of it all, the arrival that follows their forced departure is painful, for refugees are never a welcome sight.

Like a Biblical plague, 14 million expelled Germans show up after 1945. Returning whence they came is not an option. In Reinhard Jirgl's novel *The Unfinished*, a local from the Altmark objects to resettling a family of Sudeten Germans in January 1946: "*Refugees n the squits: you just can't hold them back*. Snapped the widow, removing the only bedstead."[19] Welcome they are not. A young refugee boy from East Prussia is greeted in Chiemgau with the words "Get lost, you stupid urchin!"[20] Some of the itinerants even have dogs set on them. They are alone in the world, so they must rely on the sympathy of strangers in a strange land. "The three greatest evils were the wild boars, the potato bugs and the refugees," according to a man in Emsland after the war.[21] The mandatory quartering of refugees in locals' homes, which Günter Grass experiences first-hand, undermines civil order itself in some places. Occupying soldiers routinely must brandish their machine guns to force locals to take in the homeless exiles. In 1946, Grass reunites with his parents and sister in the foothills of North-Rhine Westphalia. They had been apart for two years. Grass recalls them being forcibly housed with a farm family. "The people standing before me had been expelled from their homeland as individuals, but among millions they were of mere statistical value. I embraced survivors who, as the saying went, had got off with a scare. ... The officials in charge of relocation had moved my parents and sister in with a farmer. This kind of thing was usual at the time, because volunteers willing to take in refugees and those expelled were few and far between."[22]

"Those who flee drag the pathways of their escape behind them their entire lives."[23] Those who are always sure of their homeland never need to question their identity, while those who have lost their homeland must always question theirs. To be forced from home destroys the sense of certainty. It undermines feelings formed in earliest childhood: the sense of having a safe place, a family house, a native dialect, even a well-known smell in the kitchen. The experience of this loss has been recited millions of times; it is part of Europe's never-ending narrative of displacement. (This narrative seemed to reach its climax in the twentieth century, but it could always outdo itself.) Displacement was seen as a legitimate tool for ordering political affairs during much of the last century, from Lausanne to Yugoslavia. This first changed in Europe in the 1990s, when the international community finally decided to stop legitimising ethnic cleansing in the Balkans. The contours of Europe's history are defined by mass murder, tyranny, occupation and exile. The writer Olga Tokarczuk, born in 1962 to displaced Poles living in Lower Silesia, describes a general truth that is particularly relevant today: "A person who must abandon his locus loses an essential part of himself. He falls victim to a brutal amputation and will suffer phantom pains until he dies."[24] With its planned displacements, the Potsdam Conference sets in motion a human catastrophe that will change the long-term ethnic make-up of the continent. The Big Three make decisions at Cecilienhof that cast long summer shadows well into the twenty-first century. |JP

Notes

1 Erpenbeck 2010, 102–3. / 2 Gleß 2008, 83. / 3 Wolf 1976, 283. / 4 Biella 1946, journal entry from 21 December 1946. / 5 Wolf 1976, 297. / 6 Aly and Schlögel, *Süddeutsche Zeitung*, 23/24 March 2002, "Verschiebebahnhof Europa. Völker, die Geschichte leiden. Umsiedlung, Deportation und Vertreibung prägten das 20. Jahrhundert". / 7 Beer 2011, 9. / 8 Orwell 1968, 327–328. / 9 Douglas 2012, 129. / 10 Koch-Thalmann 2000, 158. / 11 Koch-Thalmann 2000, 294. / 12 Elliger 2006, 169–170. / 13 Tankielun 2006, 373–74. / 14 Kochanowski 2001, 104. / 15 Kurowski 2018, 78. The original Polish is: "Moi Rodzice, chociaż większość życia spędzili na terenie Barcji, nigdy nie przestali być sercem i duszą, całym swoim jestestwem dziećmi ukochanej Wileńszczyzny – ojczyzny ich antenatów. Każdy dzień życia Juliana i Janiny w Bartoszycach nad Łyną był przepełniony myślami o rodzinnej ziemi, dzieciństwie i młodości spędzonej nad Duksztanką i Wilią" (English translation after the German translation by the author). / 16 Draesner 2014, 453; translated from the original German. / 17 Draesner 2014, 486; translated from the original German. / 18 Draesner 2014, 17; translated from the original German. / 19 Jirgl 2020, 6. / 20 Ihlau 2014; Olaf Ihlau's recollections are of general interest here. The main narrative device in his autobiography is the hand wagon that attended him throughout his life, from the East Prussian city of Königsberg all the way to his ranch on Ibiza. / 21 Eiynck 1997, 495; interview with Manfred Meißner. / 22 Grass 2007, 241. / 23 Draesner 2014, 27; translated from the original German. / 24 Tokarczuk 2004, 9.

The Potsdam Conference and the Jewish Organisations

Thomas
Brechenmacher

The extermination of the larger part of European Jewry by Nazi Germany was by no means a key issue in the Big Three's negotiations at Potsdam; it was much more a footnote. At the end of the Second World War, "Jewish questions" had to be dovetailed with the respective Allied interests; only then was it decided whether they were even discussed. Beyond their own calculations, neither the United States, Britain nor the Soviet Union acted as advocates for the Jews, even though they sometimes claimed to be just that.

It was left up to Jewish organisations and groups to bring their people's catastrophe in Europe to attention when it came to the "reorganisation of the world" and to seek solutions for the related consequences.[1] Zionists, in this context, were setting the tone. In the years immediately preceding the establishment of the Jewish state, they played a central role in large diaspora organisations like the World Jewish Congress (WJC) and the American Jewish Committee (AJC). For the AJC, the founding of a Jewish state was part of the universalist perspective that aimed at granting Jews all over the world the comprehensive right to life and protection as a minority, as well as a guarantee of general human rights. There were sometimes fierce disputes between these "universalists" on the one hand and the Zionists (for example at the WJC) on the other, who saw the future of Judaism exclusively in a Jewish state.[2] The Jewish Claims Conference—a formation of twenty-three national and international Jewish associations, which, independently of the Zionists' goals, had set itself the task of negotiating Jewish restitution claims against the legal successor of the German Reich—was not established until 1951, when Chancellor Konrad Adenauer committed the young Federal Republic to making "moral and material reparations".[3]

Jewish institutions in 1945 faced three problem areas that overlapped in different ways. First, there was the question of the fate of Jews still alive in Europe, the Jewish displaced persons (DPs); second, the question of restitution or compensation payments and their addressees; third, the question of the reorganisation of Palestine and the establishment of a Jewish commonwealth or state (in the view of hardcore Zionists).

The refugee question concerned, above all, the survivors of the Holocaust, who primarily hailed from Eastern Europe and who had been scattered, exiled, displaced, or liberated from the concentration and extermination camps and now lived in the Western Allies' DP camps. Among the millions of displaced persons, the Jewish DP group was relatively small (totalling 50,000 to 75,000).[4] Since the end of 1945, separate camps for Jewish DPs were established in the American zone of occupation, where American Jewish aid organisations were active. The agreement concerning the repatriation of DPs, negotiated with the Soviet Union at Yalta, turned out to be difficult to execute and not applicable to the Jewish DPs. At the time of the Potsdam Conference, the future of this group had to be considered. The Zionists used the

← SS Exodus with illegal
Jewish immigrants at
Haifa port, 22 March 1947

143

issue to place additional pressure on Britain to revise its highly restrictive policy on immigration to the Palestine mandate. Since the so-called White Paper (1939), the British had virtually stopped allowing Jewish immigrants into Palestine. Zionist organisations were up in arms about this policy. The final declaration of the 1942 Extraordinary Zionist Conference, at the Biltmore Hotel in New York, directly addressed the misery of the "Jews in the Ghettos and concentration camps of Hitler-dominated Europe" and urged the British "that the gates of Palestine be opened" for Jewish immigration.[5]

Both the British (as mandatory power) and the political leaders of the Yishuv (the pre-state Jewish community in Palestine) were little interested in Jewish mass immigration during the war, despite the Zionist appeals usually made from outside Palestine.[6] From this perspective, the share of European Jews that survived the Shoah and that were living in the DP camps presented for the time being nothing more than material for arguments supporting the demand for a Jewish state or—a concept that was less clear and discursively more flexible—a "Jewish Commonwealth". Less than a year after the Potsdam Conference, the problem of Jewish DPs intensified when, after the Kielce pogrom on 4 July 1946, the majority of Jews who had remained there fled westward from Poland. By the summer of 1947, their number increased in Germany, especially in the American zone, to about 170,000.[7]

When it came to compensation, the Big Three were mainly concerned with reparations for the damage they had themselves suffered as a result of the war provoked by Nazi Germany. Awareness of compensation claims for Jewish victims had to be created and enforced by hard political lobbying. These efforts involved highly sensitive questions, such as the following: Who should be the bearer of these claims? Should there be individual or collective compensation? Which collective should succeed to the rights of the millions murdered?

The Palestine question held a huge potential for conflict—not just on a regional scale, but especially in the international political context between Great Britain and the United States. Both powers dithered; Britain was increasingly exhausted and lacked a clear vision for the future. The mandatory power, involved in both a war and civil war, had tried since the Arab uprising in 1936 (if not earlier) to manoeuvre between the Arabs' demands and the Zionists' claims without finding a consistent policy. The end of the war, which saw a reinvigorated United States and the emerging bipolar world order, also gave the Middle East a global political significance. As the British lost control of Palestine, the USA and the Soviet Union positioned themselves.

The Big Three and the interests of Jewish organisations
before the conference

The Palestine question had not been officially negotiated at Yalta.[8] President Roosevelt did not commit to a clear stance on the idea of a Jewish state. For both economic and geostrategic reasons, he considered it imperative not to burden his country's relationship with the Saudi kingdom. Roosevelt—"a master of ambiguity"[9]—was fairly flexible in meeting the objections of American Zionists. He preferred the region to be placed under trust administration, engaging the major ethnic groups and the three monotheistic religions, rather than allowing the establishment of a Jewish state.

After Roosevelt's death on 12 April 1945, the Zionist camp immediately approached the new president. On 20 April, a week after taking office, Truman received Rabbi Stephen S. Wise, WJC president and co-chair of the American Zionist Emergency Council.[10] Wise elaborated on the problem of Jewish DPs and pointed out the urgency of the demand for unlimited immigration and the establishment of a Jewish state in Palestine. Truman, however, had already been briefed by State Department experts and was committed to Roosevelt's line in foreign affairs: the highly complex Palestine question, to his mind, touched "vital interests" of the United States and involved issues far beyond the plight of the Jews in Europe.[11] Truman, according to his later recollections, recognised these larger contexts and acknowledged to Wise that he would continue his predecessor's policy. Of course, he admitted, he was sceptical of some of the views and attitudes assumed by the "striped-pants boys" in the State Department: "It was my feeling that it would be possible for us to watch out for the long-range interests of our country while at the same time helping these unfortunate victims of persecution to find a home. And before Rabbi Wise left, I believe I made this clear to him."[12]

As is known from his time as a senator for Missouri, Truman was not without sympathy for the Jewish concern in Palestine.[13] As president, however, there were other aspects he had to keep in mind, including US relations to the British mandate power. Prime Minister Churchill delayed acting. After the Yalta Conference, he informed Chaim Weizmann, president of the World Zionist Organization (WZO), that the Palestine affair could only be dealt with on an international scale in the context of a peace congress to take place after the end of the war.[14] Nevertheless, Churchill allowed in an internal memorandum of early July 1945 that the topic could be discussed at Potsdam. "I don't think we should take the responsibility upon ourselves of managing this very difficult place while the Americans sit back and criticise." Quite obviously, Churchill at this point was tired enough of the mandate. "I am not aware of the slightest advantage which has ever accrued to Great Britain from this painful and thankless task. Somebody else should have their turn now."[15]

The Soviet position, on the other hand, remained opaque. Stalin, of course, wanted to be involved, sensing that a British-American understanding in the Middle East was underway—and that it would be to his disadvantage. Like the US president, he was in favour of placing Palestine under a trust administration.[16] Roosevelt, in March 1945, believed that Stalin was neither pro- nor anti-Zionist, but not the Jew-hater he was sometimes considered to be.[17]

It was against the background of these dispositions of the Big Three—whether actual or assumed—that the Jewish interest organisations, with a view to the forthcoming negotiations, tried to make themselves heard. Externally (e. g. on the fringes of the San Francisco Conference hosted between April and June 1945 to prepare the UN Charter, and at numerous public rallies), these organisations demanded the swift establishment of a Jewish state and unhindered Jewish immigration to Palestine.[18] Yet in the crucial "inner circles", everything seemed to stagnate. The US ambassador to London told Secretary of State Stettinius in early July that Weizmann was so frustrated that he was about to resign from his post if progress was not made soon. "I am sure he did not say this as a threat. The man is tired and ill and completely discouraged because of the tragedies that have befallen his people."[19]

In addition to the WJC, the WZO, the AJC and the Jewish Agency for Palestine (JA)—the latter being the administrative body of the Yishuv and the mandatory power's Jewish contact—non-Jewish groups also campaigned for a solution to the Palestine question. The American Palestine Committee, consisting predominantly of non-Jewish US senators, collected signatures among the members of both houses of Congress from mid-May 1945. The petition to Truman, which was eventually signed by more than fifty senators and 250 representatives, urged the president to promptly exercise his influence on the British so that they would allow unhindered Jewish immigration to, and colonisation of, Palestine. They also wanted Truman to win other powers over to the idea of establishing a "Jewish Commonwealth at the earliest possible time"[20], namely at the upcoming Potsdam Conference. Truman received the petition in early July.

Even before that, the State Department had already recommended that the US president adopt a cautious approach to the negotiations at Potsdam. Palestine, so the argument went, was a British problem, and it was the Brits' responsibility to make a decision about what course of action to take there in the near future. Contrary to the Zionists' wishes, it was not up to the US president to go into detailed discussions with Churchill in Potsdam or to make any decisions by himself. The president should stick to the basic position that the issue of settlement in Palestine was to be resolved by the United Nations after the end of the war, in full cooperation with both the Arabs and the Jews.[21] Truman took a corresponding briefing paper with him to Potsdam.[22]

His situation, however, was by no means as relaxed as the
State Department had suggested. The American Jewish community
had a strong, high-profile lobby group; if nothing else, the support
received from the (non-Jewish) American Palestine Committee
shows what mobilisation effects it was capable of. The intelligence
agencies registered a growing "militancy" on the part of the Zionists
ahead of the Potsdam Conference, coupled with growing disappointment, even anger at the reticent policy of the US government.[23]
As the full extent of the annihilation of European Jewry became
apparent, the requests made of the victorious powers became more
and more urgent. Had they not done too little during the war to
prevent the Jewish catastrophe? Were they not now all the more
responsible to lend their strongest support to the survivors?[24]

Jewish considerations on the compensation issue
and the Palestine question

In addition to the demand for immigration, land, "commonwealth" or state, the large Jewish institutions internally formulated the question of restitution and compensation, even before the victorious powers had understood (or wanted to understand) that another difficult issue was arising. In April 1945, Nehemiah Robinson, an expert in international law at the WJC's Institute of Jewish Affairs, drafted a position paper on this issue. Himself a survivor of the Holocaust (he had fled Lithuania in 1940), Robinson went on to become one of the most prominent specialists in compensation and reparation issues at the WJC; he also served the Claims Conference as its main legal advisor in the subsequent negotiations with the Federal Republic of Germany on the Luxembourg Agreement.[25] His 1945 position paper and all other statements on the compensation issue were based on his book *Indemnification and Reparations: Jewish Aspects.*[26]

Between Yalta and Potsdam, Robinson first summarised the "present status of the problem" to then make recommendations on how the WJC should proceed. According to the statement at the Yalta Conference, he argued, the Allied Reparations Commission's meeting in Moscow was solely responsible for the Allied concerns. According to Robinson, the head of the US delegation to this meeting, Lubin, had "advised to request ... the Governments of the United States, Great Britain and Russia to allow the Reparations Commission to set aside certain reparation amounts for the benefit of the Jewish people". Lubin, he thought, believed that the Commission would readily implement such a decision. Accordingly, Robinson concluded, the WJC had to urge the governments "to do something about the return of Jewish property and satisfaction of Jewish claims. Where the measures taken are inadequate, proposals for better treatment could be presented. ... If nothing is done, no more or less uniform solution can be achieved".[27]

Deliberations intensified in the immediate run-up to the Potsdam Conference in mid-July. Time was short, as the reparations problem was expected to be "high on the agenda". Following a phone call, Robinson informed Nahum Goldmann on 17 July, the day the conference started, about the deliberations of a specially created working group. Its members, in concert with the Jewish Agency, had initially had the idea of cabling "on behalf of the Jewish people" to the heads of government convening in Potsdam, "without, how-ever, specifying the purpose for which the reparations, if granted, should be used".

On further reflection, however, Robinson abandoned the idea, on the grounds that the cable would very likely never arrive in Pots-dam. "But even if it is [recabled to the site of the meeting], it will hardly receive any consideration, because not one of those attending the meeting will be properly prepared to answer the numerous questions arising out of such a vague demand without any serious documentation." Unfortunately, the relevant bodies of the WJC had not shown much interest in the problem for more than half a year, "and a purely perfunctory cable can, at best, be ineffectual on the outcome of our struggle".[28]

Robinson probably sensed what strategy the State Department had recommended to President Truman. Also, his notes show that even a large organisation such as the WJC, in view of the complexity of the compensation issue, lacked purpose and preparation in approaching the victorious powers in their negotiations. The connection of compensation claims to the aim of establishing a state caused considerable headaches for, and disagreement among, the Jewish officials. Robinson vehemently rejected a proposal by Bernard Joseph, from the Jewish Agency's planning committee, that advocated global compensation for the Jewish people, to be paid to and administered by the JA in order to facilitate the establishment of a "commonwealth". Such a demand, according to Robinson, might have a highly counter-productive effect and only result in inciting the enemies of a state solution in Palestine—nothing, therefore, should be done that might add to the already existing difficulties. Incidentally, he argued that it was highly doubtful whether Palestine would even be on the agenda at Potsdam; at any rate, one should not take the second step before the first.[29]

The crucial point in this argument against the JA's proposal was the idea of compensating an "entire people". Robinson asked what justification there was for this idea, making it clear that apart from "Palestine", he saw none, especially none that was independent of territorial claims. What was therefore necessary was careful consideration as to whether claims for "reparations for a people" that did not yet have a state of its own were advisable. To Robinson's mind, the need for a state did not provide a legal title to compensation. "We have better titles than this."[30] Tactical considerations aside, what emerged from this opposition between the respective representatives of WJC and JA was a state of conflict between diaspora and Israeli Judaism; this conflict would also mark the "reparations settlement" with the Federal Republic later on.[31]

**"Jewish questions"–
not a topic of the conference**

Robinson reiterated his assessment of the situation in another memorandum for Goldmann on 24 July. Quite the expert on international law, he explained what claims international Jewish organisations were entitled to make on behalf of Jewish victims. Legitimately, he argued, this would only be the case for assets or property which, due to the mass murder carried out by the Axis powers, were now without heirs. As the mass murder had been aimed at the annihilation of the entire Jewish people, it was, consequently, the Jewish people that should inherit the rights to this "heirless property".[32] Again, Robinson warned against mixing up problems that, by their nature, should be kept apart. He advised restraint—no intervention in Potsdam, no coupling of the reparations issue to the Palestine question. Instead, a commission should be set up at the WJC with the task of exploring the whole topic in detail and preparing a careful plan before attempting a definitive solution.

While the issue of reparations for the victorious powers was indeed high on the Potsdam agenda, the question of compensation for Jewish victims remained unanswered, as did the Palestine question.[33] On 24 July, the date of Robinson's second memorandum for Goldmann, Truman sent a note to Churchill in Potsdam asking the British government to take steps "without delay" to lift the restrictive immigration regulations laid down in the White Paper,[34] arguing that there was great interest in this question in America. Truman's intervention came across as support for a Jewish "commonwealth" (if not necessarily a Jewish state). It also reflected the American pro-Zionist lobby organisations' campaigning activities. Although not entirely in line with the State Department, it certainly confirmed Churchill in his view that the "Americans sit back and criticise". In the final paragraph of his note, Truman affirmed that there was no time to adequately discuss the Palestine problem at the ongoing conference. The matter, however, should not be put on the back burner; he hoped that Churchill would soon submit his views on it so that they could be addressed "in concrete terms" sooner rather than later.[35]

In his capacity as prime minister, Churchill was no longer able to respond to Truman. Instead, his successor, Clement Attlee, confirmed receipt of the note on 31 July, asking for forgiveness that a response was not immediately available, but assuring that the new government would soon deal with Truman's proposals in detail.[36] The election victory of the Labour Party, which was considered to be pro-Zionist, was greeted with downright enthusiasm by the American Palestine Committee. Unlike Robinson, the thoughtful WJC representative, the non-Jewish lobbyists for a Jewish "commonwealth" in Palestine were very much in a position to directly intervene in Potsdam by cable. They appealed to Truman to immediately take advantage of the propitious moment and to urge the new British government to allow unrestricted immigration and to approve of the Jewish "commonwealth".[37]

The enthusiasm soon subsided. In particular, newly appointed Foreign Secretary Ernest Bevin came under criticism from Jewish politicians. Stephen Wise, just a few years later, remembered him bitterly. "Balfour brought Britain honor, Bevin brought Britain shame."[38] Such disappointment was, in some way had to, complementary to the excessive expectations initially harboured. Having taken on the responsibility of government, Labour politicians had to engage in different fields of policy than while in the opposition. In fact, Attlee and Bevin adapted to the Churchill line, especially in believing that the United States should take more responsibility in Palestine.

However, the Americans at first proffered little but talk—which had already angered Churchill. Truman, on his return from Potsdam, appeared before the press on 16 August to explain the US position: as many Jews as possible should be allowed to enter Palestine; the whole issue should be settled diplomatically on a peaceful basis, together with the British and the Arabs, because he—that is, Truman—had no need "to send half a million American soldiers to keep peace in Palestine".[39] Truman's rush towards the public delighted the Zionists and angered the British, who even under Labour remained a long way from opening Palestine for large-scale immigration of Jewish DPs from Europe.[40] An intricate coordination process between Britain and the United States, dealing with Truman's specified request to allow 100,000 Jews to immigrate led in late summer and autumn of 1945 to the establishment of a joint Anglo-American Committee of Inquiry (Truman-Bevin-Commission). Members of this group travelled to the Middle East and to Europe to get an idea of the respective situation of the Jews in both places.[41]

But what was the outcome of "Potsdam" for the Jewish reparation claims? Although these had been left out of the negotiations, Robinson thought he now noticed greater clarity. On 27 July, he had already worded an opinion for the Office Committee to the effect that the Jews, in all likelihood, had little to expect from the inter-Allied reparations commission: "The Russians", he noted, "behave everywhere as they please", and in the territories occupied by them were going their own way (which the Western Allies accepted). For this reason, Robinson considered the United States and, to a certain extent, Great Britain as the main contacts to which "the Jewish people will have to address their demands".[42] His impression was confirmed at the beginning of August by the Potsdam Protocol, now available.[43] The Jews would have to see to it that they were awarded part of the bulk of reparations to be generated from Germany—i.e., from its domestic and foreign assets, mobile and immobile. As the Soviet Union was following a special path and had effectively dropped out, only the United States and Great Britain remained available as addressees for claims.

"[T]heoretically", Robinson summarised, "the chances for reparations in favor of the Jewish people" had "somewhat improved" at the conference. On the other hand, he added, the available sums were considerably lower than had been originally assumed, because the special path granted to the Soviet Union limited the other two Allied powers to reparations from the West German occupation zones. Due to the deadline provided for in the protocol, it was advisable "to start the Jewish action" towards the United States government "at once".[44]

In a position paper in early February 1946, the AJC's Committee on Peace Problems summarised the considerations of its second session for the work of the upcoming Paris Peace Conference. In line with the AJC's "universalist" stance, the focus of the paper was on human rights.[45] Issues such as punishment of war criminals, compensation for individuals and free emigration were here seen less as specifically "Jewish problems" and more so as fundamental to the general pursuit of human rights, the disregard of which was to be sanctioned. In none of these points, according to the paper, were the "Allied declarations of policy at Moscow, Teheran, Yalta, and Potsdam" deemed satisfactory. Even though it admitted that much had been achieved, it also stated that "much remains to be done".[46]

On 9 December 1946, Chaim Weizmann opened the Twenty-second Zionist Congress, the first of the post-war era, with a blazing speech that was essentially an indictment levelled at the British. At the time of greatest need, Weizmann argued, the mandatory power, on which the greatest hopes had been placed since the Balfour Declaration, had closed the gates of immigration. With a few minor exceptions, he elaborated, the ignominy of the White Paper had not been eliminated: the pitiful remainder of European Jewry that had survived the Holocaust was still waiting for permission to enter Palestine, and the "Jewish National Home" had still not been set up, although the genocide required this most urgently of all. As much as he criticised Britain, he praised the efforts made by the United States and its president.[47] Of course, this comparison had more to do with political calculation than with the acknowledgement of effective steps already taken. Weizmann hoped, to no avail, that the United States would accomplish these long-desired goals.

From a Jewish perspective, the Potsdam Conference marks a rather meaningless step on the path towards the establishment of the Jewish state, the solution of the DP question and the regulation of the compensation issue. It was also a step that was far from satisfactory for the Jewish interest groups, whether radical, moderately Zionist or "universalist". Robert Weltsch, a German-Jewish emigrant, Zionist and temporary London correspondent for the Israeli newspaper *Ha'aretz*, considered "Potsdam", as early as 1946–47, as nothing more than a symptom of the failed Allied policy in Europe and especially towards Germany: "Potsdam" reinforced the division of the world into two halves without its consequences then (September 1946) being understood: "Potsdam has shown no way out and no possibility of rebuilding Europe."[48] The conference, Weltsch thought, had not had any significant results for "Jewish" questions.

Still, the gentle pressure that Truman had exercised on Churchill and Attlee during the conference as well as the press release he immediately published afterwards—both had undoubt-

edly been prompted by the activities of the pro-Zionist American lobbyists—indirectly led to the establishment of the Anglo-American Committee of Inquiry and, consequently, to the beginnings of a bilateral handling of the Palestine problem.[49] Things only started moving again in autumn 1947, when the British surrendered their mandate for Palestine to the UN, whose assembly finally adopted the famous partition plan in November.

The problem of the Jewish DPs remained unsolved under British mandate: Jewish immigration on a larger scale only became possible after the founding of the State of Israel and the Israeli War of Independence in 1948–49.[50] Robinson's cautious optimism on the compensation issue was not fulfilled immediately after the Potsdam Protocol. On the contrary, already at Potsdam, he had foreseen what he was going to sum up in 1952, following the conclusion of the Luxembourg Treaty: "By any stretch of imagination", he wrote, the agreement concluded with the young Federal Republic on compensation payments to the Claims Conference and the State of Israel "cannot be considered ... as having been either initiated or settled by orders or pressure from the Allied governments."[51] |CN

Notes

1 My thanks to Jürgen Matthäus (US Holocaust Memorial Museum) and Juliana Witt (The Jacob Rader Marcus Center of the American Jewish Archives) for their valuable help. / **2** Loeffler 2018, esp. 134–40. / **3** Adenauer before the Bundestag, 27 September 1951; for the Claims Conference, see Lillteicher 2011, 511–14. / **4** For a summary, with further literature, see Wetzel 2013. / **5** Timm 2017, 102–03; in the declaration, see mainly points 2 and 8. / **6** Segev 2018, 349, 353, 354, 362, 373. / **7** Gross 2012, 345–50; number according to Wetzel 2013. / **8** Hoskins to Alling, 5 March 1945, FRUS 1945, The Near East and Africa, 690–91; for a general discussion, see Ovendale 1989, 41–50. / **9** Ovendale 1989, 49. / **10** Truman 1955, 71–72; see also Ovendale 1989, 67. / **11** Stettinius to Truman, 18 April 1945, FRUS 1945, The Near East and Africa, 704–05. / **12** Truman 1955, 72. In September 1945, Truman complained to AJC President Blaustein that Rabbi Wise and his followers were "acting like fanatics" (quoted after Loeffler 2018, 134). / **13** Ovendale 1989, 66. / **14** Weizmann 1950, 539; US Ambassador Winant (UK) to Stettinius, 9 July 1945, FRUS 1945, The Conference of Berlin (The Potsdam Conference), vol. 1, 977–78; Ovendale 1989, 65–66. / **15** Churchill to Colonial Secretary and the Chiefs of Staff Committee, 6 July 1945, in Churchill 1953, 764. / **16** Ro'i 1974, 22. / **17** Hoskins to Alling, 5 March 1945, FRUS 1945, The Near East and Africa, 690–91. / **18** See Ovendale 1989, 67–75. / **19** Winant to Stettinius, 8 July 1945, FRUS 1945, The Conference of Berlin (The Potsdam Conference), vol. 1, 977–78. / **20** Ovendale 1989, 69–70. / **21** Memorandum Grews for Truman, 16 June 1945, FRUS 1945, The Near East and Africa, 709. / **22** Briefing Book Paper, Palestine, 22 June 1945, FRUS 1945, The Conference of Berlin (The Potsdam Conference), vol. 1, 972–74. / **23** Ovendale 1989, 72–75. / **24** Ibid., 73. / **25** On Nehemiah Robinson, see Perlzweig 2007, 356; see also Hansen 2004, 107 and 156. / **26** Robinson 1944. / **27** Memorandum Robinson for Goldmann, Problems of Indemnification and Reparations, 24 July 1945, 11 pages, typewritten. (AJA, WJC), Robinson 1945, 5 and 8. / **28** Memorandum Robinson for Goldmann, The Big Three and Reparations. The Recommendation of the World Jewish Congress Sub-Committee. Bernard Joseph's Memorandum on Reparations, 17 July 1945, 2 pages, typewritten (AJA, WJC), Robinson 1945, here 1. / **29** Robinson, The Big Three and Reparations, Robinson 1945, 2. / **30** Robinson, The Big Three an reparations, Robinson 1945, 2. / **31** See Zweig 2009, 235. / **32** Memorandum Robinson for Goldmann, Problems of Indemnification and Reparations, 24 July 1945, Robinson 1945, here 2. / **33** Byrnes to Pinkerton, 18 August 1945, FRUS 1945, The Conference of Berlin (The Potsdam Conference), vol. 2, 1407. / **34** Truman to Churchill, 24 July 1945, FRUS 1945, The Conference of Berlin (The Potsdam Conference), vol. 2, 1402. The Soviets were informed of the note on record. / **35** Truman to Churchill, 24 July 1945, FRUS 1945, The Conference of Berlin (The Potsdam Conference), vol. 2, 1402. / **36** Attlee to Truman, 31 July 1945, FRUS 1945, The Conference of Berlin (The Potsdam Conference), vol. 2, 1406. / **37** Telegram from the American Palestine Committee to Truman, 27 July 1945, quoted after Ovendale 1989, 81. / **38** Wise 1949, 301–02: "The leadership of the Foreign Office fell to a man whose lack of sympathy, imagination, and tact did grievous hurt to the Jews and Jewish Palestine, but even more and cureless hurt to the honor of Great Britain." See also Weizmann 1950, 540–41. / **39** Byrnes to Pinkerton, 18 August 1945, FRUS 1945, The Conference of Berlin (The Potsdam Conference), vol. 2, 1407. / **40** Thus, for instance, Bevin before the British Parliament on 14 November 1945: for the time being, the aim was merely to maintain "the current [low, ThB] rate of Jewish immigration" (*Der Kurier*, 14 November 1945, 1). / **41** See Weizmann 1950, 541–42; Crossman 1947; in detail Ovendale 1989, 77–105. / **42** Robinson to WJC Office Committee, 27 July 1945, 2 pages, typewritten (AJA, WJC), Robinson 1945. / **43** Minutes of the Potsdam Conference proceedings, 2 August 1945, in Biewer 1992, 2149–73. / **44** Memorandum Robinson, Implications for the Jewish People of the Decisions on Reparations from Germany reached at Potsdam, 6 August 1945, 5 pages, typewritten (AJA, WJC), Robinson 1945, here 5. – Deadlines according to Potsdam Protocol III.5. / **45** See Loeffler 2018. / **46** AJC, Committee on Peace Problems, 2nd Session, 31 January to 1 February 1946: Proposed Provisions for the Peace Treaties, here 16 and 21–22. / **47** Presidential Address by Dr. Chaim Weizmann, 9 December 1946, Twenty-second Zionist Congress, Basle, London 1946, reprint Frankfurt am Main 2001, especially 9 and 12. / **48** Robert Weltsch, London article manuscripts for *Ha'aretz*, in: LBI Archives, Robert Weltsch Collection 1770–1997, here Palestine Conference in the Balance, London September 17th [1946], and Bevin goes to Moscow, March 8th [1947]. / **49** This supposed "agreement", in turn, angered the Soviet Union, which felt it had been ignored on the Palestine question; see Ro'i 1974, 22. / **50** From 1946 until the founding of the state, only 48,451 Jews immigrated, most of them illegally, from Europe to the Yishuv; from the proclamation of independence (15 May) to the end of 1948, there were 76,554 legal immigrants; in 1949, 121,963; and in 1950–51 another 128,000 (see Wolffsohn and Grill 2016, 179). / **51** Robinson 1953, quoted after Balabkins 1971, 141.

Potsdam and Japan, around 1945

While Winston Churchill, Joseph Stalin and Harry S. Truman met at Cecilienhof Palace in Potsdam to discuss the post-war order, the Second World War was still raging in Asia and in the Pacific. The Allies were victorious over Nazi Germany and Fascist Italy, and hostilities had already ceased in Europe. The last Axis power, Japan, had not yet capitulated, however. In the Potsdam Declaration of 26 July 1945, the United States, Great Britain and China had affirmed their call for the Imperial Japanese Government to surrender unconditionally during the conference at Cecilienhof Palace; the declaration was read on the radio and leaflets were printed and dropped over Japan. However, they remained unanswered by the Japanese until the end of the conference; they were even ignored. Only eight days after the end of the conference, on 10 August, did the Japanese cabinet with Prime Minister Suzuki Kantarō at its head accept the Potsdam Declaration. The decision to surrender was made by Emperor Hirohito only on 14 August, just under two weeks after the meeting in Potsdam. It was publicly announced on 15 August in a radio broadcast.

With the end of this "war without mercy" in East Asia, Southeast Asia and the Pacific, the tragic history of mass killings and violence was over. According to estimates, over 50 million men, women and children died between 1937 and 1945. Hundreds of millions of people have suffered from Japan's war of aggression, its imperial expansion and colonial rule, and were affected by displacement, forced labour and sex slavery.[1]

Potsdam and the end of the war in Japan

There is great debate in Japan over the beginning, the course and the end of the Second World War in Asia as well as the importance of the Potsdam Conference and the Potsdam Declaration. This is because certain interpretations and mostly strongly held political opinions are attached to every single dating. A conservative interpretation of the war, also as promoted by Japan's post-war governments and thus politically established, sets the attack on Pearl Harbor on 7 December 1941 as allegedly clearly defined start of the war. This view of the Second World War mostly excludes Japan's aggressive imperial expansion in East Asia. And this is a very conscious omission, because the question of responsibility for hostilities, war crimes and atrocities of the Imperial Japanese Army, Japanese colonial officials and the infamous military police *Kenpeitai* in East and Southeast Asia before 1941 can be separated from their behaviour after the Japanese ambush on Pearl Harbor.

Critics of this periodisation thus have made an effort to use the term "Fifteen Years' War" (*jūgonen sensō*) to establish the actual beginning of the Second World War in East Asia as the Mukden incident and the invasion of Manchuria in 1931.[2] In the vicinity of the

← Japanese surrender aboard the USS Missouri, Tokyo Bay, 2 September 1945

city of Mukden (now Shenyang), Japanese officers of the Kwantung Army, stationed in Northern China since 1906 after Japan's victory over Russia, made a bomb attack on the South Manchurian Railway on the night of 18–19 September 1931, which they staged as a terrorist act by the Chinese military. The Japanese then used the attack as a pretext to invade Manchuria. In light of the subsequent aggressive expansion and the forced establishment of a Japanese Empire in East Asia, the events of 1931 could also be interpreted as the start of the Second World War in East Asia, which also puts the massive excess of physical and sexual violence by the Kwantung Army during the conquest of China in focus.[3]

However, these politically more progressive interpretations lose sight of historical developments between the early and late 1930s, which were decisive in evolving a culture of "total war". These include structural changes in Japan's politics and economy, affecting people of all social strata, such as the expansion of the Japanese police apparatus, the increasing influence of the military in politics and society, and the excessive focus of Japanese leaders on industrial production important to the invasion of China, all of which slowly replaced the consumer culture of the 1920s and 1930s. But this also includes the increased mass mobilisation and war propaganda on the home front, which insinuated the omnipresence of war. This also expressed itself very specifically in measures such as food rationing. Based on this view, historians have been increasingly arguing the establishment of 1937 as the beginning of the Second World War in East Asia, which excludes the beginning of the Japanese colonisation of Manchuria, but includes the violent conquest and occupation of China and thus the Nanjing Massacre committed by the Japanese Army in 1938.[4]

Emperor Hirohito, excerpt from ABCA map no. 71 (recto)

The end of the war is just as contentious. For a long time, scholars were predominantly of the opinion that mainly external influences such as the atomic bombs dropped on Hiroshima and Nagasaki on 6 and 9 August 1945, respectively, and the entry of the Soviet Union in the war against Japan on 8 August were decisive to the Japanese surrender.[5] However, this version neglects the actions, the expertise and the responsibility of the Japanese leadership elites. This is because several top leaders such as General Umezu Yoshijirō, commander-in-chief of the Japanese Army and former commander of the Kwantung Army, wanted to fight on until the end in order to put conditions on surrender and above all to preserve the institution of the emperor. According to the logic of high-ranking military leaders, the future of the Emperor (*tennō*) and the entire imperial system (*tennōsei*) appeared to be uncertain due to the Allied demand of unconditional surrender and subsequent military occupation of Japan as stated in the Potsdam Declaration.[6] The reluctance of the Emperor himself should also be taken into account, who despite the imminent defeat of Japan repeatedly missed several chances to end the war, even those that offered him

Attack on Pearl Harbor,
7 December 1941

"Little Boy", the atomic
bomb dropped on
Hiroshima

the opportunity to place conditions on the Allies—a failure that cost thousands of people their lives.

More recent critical analyses of the decision-making process in the last days of the war now argue that a combination of foreign policy events and domestic policy circumstances were decisive to the surrender. Based on documents in Japanese of the Japanese leadership, it is apparent that internal power struggles between the various factions of the Japanese political and military elites were at least as important to the decision as the atomic bomb drop and Soviet entry into the war.[8]

A combination of internal and external factors manifested itself not least in the alleged "specter of revolution", an imagined threat of a coming Communist infiltration and revolution put forward by the Japanese elites. Already since the beginning of the twentieth century, Japan's conservative leadership developed an almost obsessive fear of social revolution. This expressed itself in an abundance of accusations and slander in the media as well as police surveillance and persecution of predominantly socialist and anarchist groups, parties and unions. The climax of state repression was the mass imprisonment and show trials such as the Yokohama Incident of 1942 or, even more prominent, the High Treason Incident (*taigyaku jiken*) of 1910–11. In both cases, journalists, critics and activists were indicted and convicted of spying, distributing Communist propaganda or even planning political assassinations, sometimes with falsified evidence and with confessions made under torture— even innocent people were handed long jail sentences or even death sentences. These events and the subsequent media agitation and police persecution of leftist groups fuelled the purported ubiquity of a revolution, although such a scenario was not remotely within the realm of possibility and had absolutely nothing to do with reality. During the entire war, the Japanese Empire was never on the brink of being overthrown by organised, revolting masses or by a fifth column directed by Moscow. Nevertheless, Japan's elites were convinced that they absolutely had to prevent an imminent revolution. And because they thought that socialist and anarchist agitators could use the opportunity of an uncertain situation and weak state institutions at the end of the war, the fear of this "specter" was a significant factor in accelerating the decision to surrender.[9]

This "specter of revolution" did not haunt the highest echelons of the military command alone. After the announcement of Japan's surrender, which the Emperor described not as a defeat (*haissen*) but merely as the end of the war (*shūsen*), various Japanese authorities and administrators—predominantly men—took care to preserve the public order, which they saw threatened by a number of different forces. Although the majority of the Japanese population cooperated and came to terms with the increasingly militaristic or even fascist regime of the *tennō* system in the first half of the *Shōwa* era, and supported it by conviction or due to other motivations, some people increasingly expressed their discontent in graffiti that criticised the war or sometimes even denigrated the Emperor.[10]

The police unit *Tokubetsu Kōtō Keisatsu*, or for short *Tokkō*, also called the Thought Police (*shisō keisatsu*) due to their surveillance of political movements, made reports on a massive scale concerning incidents critical to the regime, which they evaluated to express the morale of the populace during the final days of the war. The main focus of the reports concerned above all socialist and anarcho-socialist groups who were accused of exploiting the uncertain situation to instigate a Communist revolution. This very clearly shows how closely the *Tokkō* was rooted in the logic of the Japanese imperial ideology which still resounded after the end of the war, and which classified every form of criticism and political activity as contaminant to the Japanese community and body politic (*kokutai*, literally: "national body") and wanted to eliminate it from the outset.[11]

As a result, the staff of the *Tokkō* also saw in the Allied occupation troops arriving in Japan a threat to the country's internal security and to the public order. Despite this, the *Tokkō* mobilised the greater part of the established propaganda apparatus to prepare for a smooth transition from wartime to the occupation, however with the goal of protecting, maintaining and securing existing authorities from the discontent of the Japanese population.[12] In order to save the regime from the prosecution of war crimes by the Allies, the *Tokkō* as well as other Japanese authorities destroyed tons of documents that could have been called upon as incriminating evidence before war crimes tribunals.[13]

Local police units and administrative officials also understood the coming arrival of occupation troops as a threat or a challenge to the population. The police and administrators were especially active in the two weeks between Japan's surrender and the arrival of the first Allied soldiers on 28 August and after the official start of the occupation on 2 September 1945. In a secret report of 20 August 1945, an official of the Tokyo Police Department (*keishichō*) noted that public opinion was rampant with "seditious uncertainty" (*fuan dōyō*), which above all was based on rumours of violent acts of revenge by the occupying forces. The terms that this police officer used in his description of acts of physical violence are *bōkō* and *ryōjoku*. Both Japanese words can also describe rape, in this way emphasising the threat to women.[14] Local officials in the neighbouring prefecture of Kanagawa, on whose Pacific coast it was assumed that the occupation troops would first land, evaluated the situation very similarly. Officials advised women and children to retreat to the interior. Municipal administrations and railway companies in Yokohama and Yokosuka even dismissed their female staff out of fear of them being raped by Allied soldiers.[15]

The public was informed of the instructions and actions of the authorities through a number of newspaper articles. The daily *Yomiuri Hōchi* recommended that women should no longer leave home alone

The destroyed city centre
of Hiroshima four weeks
after the atomic bombing,
6 September 1945

at night, wear "licentious cloths" and at most should only be seen in public in their *monpe* (wartime work clothes) with several layers of undergarments, so no body contours would be seen.[16] In a commentary in the same newspaper, however, Horikiri Zenjirō, the former Governor of Kanagawa Prefecture and Member of the House of Peers (*kizokuin*), called upon readers not to lapse into hysteria. On the contrary, he warned that the Japanese should not become the laughing-stock of the world with their fear of the occupation troops, arguing that they had nothing to fear, because the occupation was legitimised by the Potsdam Declaration.[17]

Horikiri's commentary was mostly lost in the surge of uncertainty. Reporting predominantly resounded with the fear of the occupation troops who would take revenge on the Japanese populace upon their arrival. In the most extreme scenarios, people imagined that the occupying soldiers would rape all of the women and make slaves of, castrate or kill all of the men. These kinds of rumours were particularly rampant in the *Kantō* Region around Tokyo, Yokohama, Kanagawa and Chiba, where the occupation forces were to land first. In hindsight, this fear of rape and murder proved to be unfounded. However, it caused people in the greater Tokyo area to flee to the countryside in August of 1945. Already starting on 16 August, the Tokyo and Ueno railway stations were completely overcrowded.[18]

With the surrender announced by the Emperor and the demands of the Potsdam Declaration, the end of the war triggered a multitude of reactions from the highest levels of command of the Japanese elites down to the many people of the lower political and social classes. The reactions reveal that people at the end of the war, at a time when daily life, above all in Japan's metropolitan areas, was characterised by destruction, deprivation and hunger, did not take the decisions dictated to their country in Cecilienhof Palace passively or as a given, but searched for ways to deal with them. Some people made an effort to shape the historical process; in most people's everyday experience, however, the Potsdam Declaration was too abstract and thus hardly had any importance.

The Potsdam Declaration from a post-colonial and world-historical perspective

The Potsdam Declaration defined, if very vaguely, the conditions for Japan's surrender. It also allows us insight into the way the Allied signatories of the declaration—the USA, Great Britain and their "junior partner" China—perceived their own position, and their concept of the post-war order.[19] The text of the Potsdam Declaration is characterised by a noticeably strong, practically solemn, almost apocalyptic language. Of course, the representatives of America, China and Great Britain had every reason to make a strong statement, if only, as they called it, to express their "determination" to "prosecute the war against Japan until she ceases to resist".[20] This is because they wanted to make it clear to the Japanese leadership that with the defeat of Nazi Germany, all military might would be brought to bear against Japan. This military superiority of the Allies, according to the threat, could not only destroy the Japanese military but if needed also devastate the whole of Japan. The kind of wording used in the language of the Potsdam Declaration leaves no doubt that the end of the war should be a world-historical event, because the only alternative to Japan's unconditional surrender would be Japan's "prompt and utter destruction".[21] Japan was being "given the opportunity to end this war". The Japanese leadership was to thoroughly consider the mistakes of the war years and to wrest control from "self-willed militaristic advisers". They had only brought Japan to the brink of destruction; now was the time to go down "the path of reason".[22]

Above all from the perspective of the victors, the USA and Great Britain, their vision of a new world order meant that only modern Western ideals would bring the necessary achievements, such as human rights—the Potsdam Declaration explicitly cites freedom of speech and religion—as pillars of a functioning democracy. In order to learn these and revive the "democratic tendencies among the Japanese people", which meant putting Japan and the Japanese on the supposedly right and only path of modernisation according to Western models to ultimately be "peacefully inclined" and "responsible"—meaning also mature enough—to govern themselves, a military occupation would be necessary after Japan's surrender.[23] Until then, Japan would have to persevere in the virtual "imaginary waiting-room of history", banned to a status of being "not yet" modern and mature enough for self-determination.[24]

The Potsdam Declaration demanded that the "Empire of Japan" surrender, a clear reference to Japan's imperial history, dominion and expansion. The Allied powers agreed that the Japanese Empire had to be deprived of power and its borders redrawn. The Potsdam Declaration thus stipulated that Japan "shall be limited to the islands of Honshu, Hokkaido, Kyushu and Shikoku, and such minor islands as we [the Allies] determine". Still today, this vague wording causes diplomatic tension between Japan and China (Diaoyu/Senkaku Islands), Japan and Korea (Dokdo/Takeshima/Liancourt Rocks), Japan and Russia (South Kurile Islands)— to mention nothing of the tension between Japan and the USA over Okinawa, once an independent kingdom (Ryūkyū). Annexed in 1879 by Japan, occupied by the US military after the war and only joined to Japan as a prefecture in 1972, Okinawa is still today often described as a US "military colony" because of the omnipresence of American armed forces.[25]

The experience of the people of Okinawa, who after 1945 suddenly stood between two powers—Japan and the United States— well illustrates that the Second World War in the Asia-Pacific was

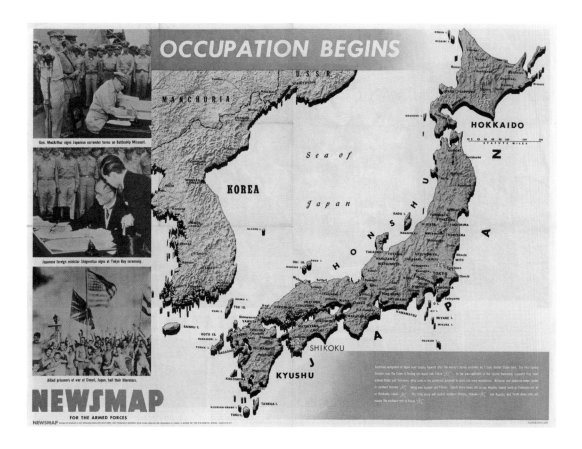

OCCUPATION BEGINS

NEWSMAP
FOR THE ARMED FORCES

Newsmap, vol. 4, no. 21,
10 September 1945

first and foremost a conflict between two empires. During the war, Japan's imperial expansion among other places fought against regional centres of Western colonial powers, such as Hong Kong and Singapore. There, the Japanese Empire also directly and explicitly attacked the "white supremacy" in the British Empire.[26] The re-conquest of the areas occupied by Japan in the Pacific and Southeast Asia during the war was also clearly motivated by the presumed claim of the Western colonial powers to control the areas lost at the beginning of the conflict. In this regard, with the end of the Second World War, the US empire reached its apex as the most important military, political, economic and cultural power in the region. Seen this way, the occupation of Japan was an integral component of America's global "empire of bases" to establish and assert itself as an international superpower.[27]

For this reason, the continued American military presence in Asia has been described an "extension of colonialism" to express the fact that the USA as the occupying power made use of the colonial structures of domination of the Japanese Empire.[28] This "extension of colonialism" manifested itself in the way the USA organised the

occupation of Japan, in America's uncritical handling of the existing Japanese political and industrial elites, in the security policies put in place by the USA as well as raging anti-Communism: Also, racist hierarchies and gender relations during the occupation period point to the fact that the occupying regime reproduced certain patterns of imperialism and colonialism. For example, this expressed itself in the occupier's ideas of white supremacy in approaching the Japanese population and the occupiers' ubiquitous benevolent paternalism, also present in the democratisation programme such as in introducing the enfranchisement of women.[29]

The experience of Pacific Islanders such as the people on Okinawa, but also in many other places in the Japanese Empire, demonstrate that the demands and perspectives as they were discussed and decided in Potsdam and set forth in the Potsdam Declaration did not have the same meaning to all people. From the conference rooms in Cecilienhof Palace, circumstances in Asia and in the Pacific seemed to be clearly definable. Yet this bird's eye view of the Allied military, political and diplomatic elites loses its

US Ssgt Robert M. Gongos presenting a parcel of sweets to a Japanese orphan at the Hiroshima Catholic Orphanage clarity if we look into the everyday life worlds of Japan's former colonies. Because what to the decision makers meant the end of the Second World War, was to most people in Asia, sometimes foremost, the end of colonial rule.

The resolutions of Potsdam resulted in a host of problems for the population of the countries of Asia. In many places, including the British crown colonies of Hong Kong and Singapore as well as Indonesia and Papua New Guinea, Japanese colonial rule was substituted with other foreign domination and/or authoritarian rule. Indeed, as studies of Taiwan show, the Potsdam Declaration, not least with its demand of an abrupt end to the Japanese Empire, significantly contributed to the fact that Japan could escape responsibility for the de-colonisation process. Since it was the Allied victors who declared the end of colonial rule in Taiwan and other places in the Japanese Empire and not Japan itself, the post-war governments of Japan and also Japanese society felt they were not obligated to conduct a comprehensive discussion of their colonial past. The societies of the former colonies seem to have had to bear the political, economic, social and cultural consequences of the sudden disappearance of colonial rule and its reminders and responsibilities themselves.[30] The remembrance of the atomic bomb dropped on Hiroshima is symbolic for the abrupt end and even the vanishing of Japan's colonial rule and imperial expansion. The memorial in Hiroshima merely tells the story of the first use of nuclear weapons in world history on 6 August 1945 as the climax and end to the Pacific War (1941–1945), which is embedded in the events of August 1945—Potsdam Declaration, Atomic bombing, Surrender—to name the seemingly unequivocal end of the war. This strongly nationalistic memory politics thus not only completely ignores Japan's past aggression in East Asia, but even enables Japan to portray itself as the victim of atomic warfare.[31]

However, for many people in Asia, the summer of 1945 did not necessarily mean the end of armed conflict or a peaceful order. In China, the civil war between the Kuomintang, whose leader Chiang Kai-shek was one of the signatories of the Potsdam Declaration, and the Communist Party of China under Mao Zedong still raged until 1949. In Vietnam, a new war began in December of 1946 which would last for the next 30 years, first against the colonial power of France, and then starting in 1964 against the United States. War also broke out on the Korean peninsula, during which at least 3 million people died by 1953.

Within the former Japanese Empire, 15 August 1945 thus did not mark the absolute end of the war, like a Japanese "Stunde Null". Rather, that date is one historical point in time among many, each having a different history with multiple trajectories, events, experiences and memories, but also perspectives, bundled together into an uncertain future.[32]

Conclusion

An investigation of the end of the Second World War in Japan that takes into account the behaviour and the experiences of the victims of the Japanese Empire should call into question established periodisation concepts. In doing so, it is essential that the surrender process and the importance of the Potsdam Conference and the Potsdam Declaration in Japan in 1945 is not only been narrated from the familiar European and American point of view. This history must also incorporate the many and diverse voices in Japan and in the former Japanese colonies. For this purpose, it should be recognised that the beginning of the Second World War in East Asia and in the Pacific does not correspond to the very clear dating of the European perspective. Even before the German attack on Poland on 1 September 1939, this war was well underway with Japan's aggression in China in 1937 at the latest, and it continued to be fought after the surrender of the German Reich.

The Second World War in East Asia was first and foremost part of a long imperial past. Japan's violent expansion overstepped political and moral boundaries and international law, and moreover, it also overstepped imperial boundaries constructed by the European countries and the United States. Japan's pan-Asian vision challenged the imperial world order and the supremacy of the "white man" that has dominated the world since the late fifteenth century. A closer look at the Potsdam Conference and the Potsdam Declaration and its effect on Japan allows us to highlight continuities, ruptures and changes of imperial power structures that continued in the Asia-Pacific and have been maintained to the present day. The defeat of Japan in the Second World War and the subsequent occupation of Japan were pivotal to the development of new forms of hegemony in Asia and the Pacific that still influence the post-1945 international order even today. |DC

Notes

1 The description "war without mercy" is taken from Dower 1985. For numbers and a classification of the mass murder committed during the Second World War in Asia, see Dower 1985, 3. Also see Tanaka 1996 and Yoshiaki 2000. / 2 The classic works by Japanese historians on the "Fifteen Years' War" include Keiichi 1986; Saburō 1985 and Yoshiaki 1987. / 3 Young 1998, 40–51. / 4 Uchiyama 2018, 5–9. / 5 Bernstein 2007, 9–64; Hasegawa 2005. / 6 Butow 1954, 132 and 231. / 7 Bix 1996, 80–115. / 8 Suzuki 2011; Furukawa 2012. / 9 Yellen 2013, 205–26. / 10 Dower 1993, 124–40. / 11 Umemori 2013, 63. / 12 Kushner 2006, 169–75. / 13 Dower 1999, 39. / 14 Keishichō, "Tōmen no mondai ni taisuru shominsō no dōkō", Awaya 1980, 149–51. / 15 Kanagawa-ken keisatsu, "Shinchū ni taisuru hankyō to taisaku", Awaya and Kawashima 1994, 170 and 174. / 16 "Hikaeyo fujoshi no hitori aruki: fushidarana fukusō wa tsutsushimō," Yomiuri Hōchi, 23 August 1945. / 17 Horikiri Zenjirō, "Dema ni odoru wa gu: Yatara ni konran sureba sekai no monowarai", Yomiuri Hōchi, 20 August 1945. / 18 Duus 1985, 19–20; Inoue 1995, 10. / 19 See article by Thoralf Klein in this volume. / 20 Quoted from Potsdam Declaration 1945, Article 2 of 26 July1945. / 21 Potsdam Declaration 1945, Article 13. / 22 Potsdam Declaration 1945, Article 4. / 23 Potsdam Declaration 1945, Article 10. / 24 . The phrase "imaginary waiting-room of history" was coined by Dipesh Chakrabarty and is a returning rhetoric figure of colonial discourse. Chakrabarty 2000, 8. / 25 Asato 2003, 299. / 26 Horne 2004. / 27 Lutz 2009. / 28 Shigematsu and Camacho 2010, xv. / 29 Cumings 1993 and Koikari 2008. / 30 Ching 2000, 769. / 31 Yoneyama 1999, 3. / 32 Dirlik 2001, 301–02.

The Potsdam Conference and China

Thoralf Klein

China was not represented at the Potsdam Conference. With the exception of the Potsdam Declaration, it was also not a topic on the official conference agenda. However, the results of the conference were important enough to have them made available to an interested Chinese audience in the form of a small brochure in the country's official language, which was sold for 200 Yuan or 40 US cents.[1] This undoubtedly had less to do with the immediate results achieved at Cecilienhof Palace and more with the global interest of Chinese elites and the changing international status of the Republic of China resulting from the Second World War. China, which was still under imperialist control, had won back its formal sovereignty during the war, albeit temporarily and with restrictions. Beyond that, the Big Three granted the country victor status, but at the same time treated it as a junior partner. In Potsdam, no decisive groundwork was made; essentially, the conference only confirmed previously drafted resolutions.

The initial position

When the Potsdam Conference began at Cecilienhof Palace, China had already been at war with Japan for fifteen years. The Japanese invasion of Manchuria in September of 1931 initially only worsened the long-standing political and military crisis, because after the overthrow of the monarchy in 1911, China had been at war almost without interruption, even if it was not raging in all areas of the country to the same degree. Although the Republican revolution was itself a short civil war between radical and conservative elites, the young republic decayed into feuding warlord dominions starting in 1916, which could only be curbed in the mid-1930s by the Nationalist regime formed in 1928 under Chiang Kai-shek. On the other hand, this new leader provoked a civil war against the Communist Party of China, the former ally of the National Party (Guomindang, GMD), in the spring of 1927. Despite massive anti-Japanese protests all across the country, Chiang initially made fighting Communist bases his priority, until a combination of domestic and foreign policy factors caused him to change tack in the mid-1930s, thus allowing a second, if loose, united Nationalist-Communist Front against Japan to form that lasted until 1941.[2]

China's external weaknesses contributed to its inner fragmentation. During the nineteenth century, imperialist states had taken away important areas of its national sovereignty, especially the exterritorial jurisdiction over Western foreigners and sovereignty regarding customs issues. At the end of the 1890s, several great powers leased coastal base colonies for 99 years under the threat of violence if their demands were not met. Beyond this, they pressed the Chinese government to grant concessions for the building of railway lines and mines. The First World War smashed the imperialist united front; the German Empire lost its privileges in China in the Treaty of Versailles

← Chinese soldier guarding a line of P-40 fighters of the "Flying Tigers"

175

Chiang Kai-shek,
1943

and was the first of the great powers to make equitable relations with the government in Beijing. And in the mid-1920s, the anti-imperialist movement was a further great blow to the dominance of the Western powers in China. But despite the efforts of the Nationalist regime to amend them, the Unequal Treaty remained valid for the time being, even if its provisions were more and more difficult to implement in practice.[3] Furthermore, China saw itself confronted with the greatest assault

of imperialism ever with the advance of Japan starting at the end of the 1920s. But finally it was not the direct military conflict with its eastern neighbour that led to the reversal in China's international position, but rather changes in the overall global strategic situation.

The shift of the overall strategic situation and the end of the unequal treaties

The war that is still called the Anti-Japanese War of Resistance today (*Kang Ri zhanzheng*), can be broken down into three phases. The first phase, from 18 September 1931 until mid-1937, was a limited war, during which Japan under a pretext occupied Manchuria and in the following years other parts of Northern China, establishing collaborative regimes, above all the state of Manchukuo (1932). Furthermore, the Japanese Navy attacked Shanghai. Anti-Japanese resistance emanated from local military forces, whereas the National Government negotiated with Japan, which resulted in an armistice at the end of May 1933. China received political and diplomatic support from the League of Nations, whose commission to Manchuria, led by Lord Victor Bulwer-Lytton, recommended the restoration of the status quo, just as non-member USA did. But these demands were ignored in Tokyo, and the Japanese government dispensed with such tedious objections by withdrawing from the League of Nations in the spring of 1933.[4]

The war entered its second phase with the exchange of fire between Chinese and Japanese troops on the Lugou or Marco Polo Bridge near Beijing on 7 July 1937. The occasion was trivial, but it occurred at a time when the situation in China and on the global political stage had fundamentally changed. In view of the increasingly aggressive position of the Third Reich and Italy, Stalin oriented Soviet policy towards entry into the League of Nations starting in 1934 as well as towards the support of anti-fascist people's fronts including bourgeois political parties. In the course of this reorientation, he also demanded that the Chinese Communists, who had just suffered heavy losses in their flight from Nationalist troops to Northwestern China on the "Long March", make peace with Chiang Kai-shek.[5] His imprisonment in Xi'an in December of 1936 by Zhang Xueliang, the former warlord of Manchuria who had fled the Japanese, paved the way for the formation of an anti-Japanese united front. This political and military reversal was reinforced by the pressure of public opinion. The Chinese government thus no longer saw itself in a position to yield to even a small Japanese provocation. Thus an interim armistice could not hold, the more so as the Japanese government was sending reinforcements to China at that very moment.[6]

The Japanese invaders initially advanced in a broad front and occupied the most important cities of Northern and Central China, including the financial centre Shanghai and the capital Nanjing. Guangzhou, the most important metropolitan area in Southern China, fell in October of 1938. As Japanese momentum waned, the country was divided into two parts. The coastal regions were under the control of the Japanese and the western half of the country, which is more difficult to access, became "Free China" with Chongqing as its capital under the rule of Chiang Kai-shek and the National Party. Industries and also educational institutions were relocated to this zone in an astonishing, if unplanned and stepwise exodus, and untold masses of refugees made their way there (the numbers vary from three to 95 million).[7] The Communist base areas in the Northwest and North were not subject to Chiang's direct control, but their troops were formally incorporated into the Nationalist armed forces.

Daily life during the war was characterised by the sorrowful experiences of the Chinese civilian population. Among these were the brutal advance of Japanese troops, the massacres, above all the almost unsurpassably cruel mass murder and rape during the capture of Nanjing from 13 December 1937 until February 1938; the terror bombing including dropping biological weapons (with plague-infected fleas) between 1940 and 1942, and even the use of poison gas at the end of 1941 (which however was quickly prohibited upon the protest of the USA), the human experiments of the infamous Unit 731 in Northern Manchuria, the forced prostitution, ill-treatment of prisoners of war and so on. But the actions of the Nationalist Army also had devastating effects. When Chiang Kai-shek had the dikes of the Yellow River pierced while defending Kaifeng in the summer of 1938, the resulting flood catastrophe claimed the lives of a half-million people and made 3 to 5 million more homeless. A combination of drought and mismanagement by the National Government led to famine in the province of Henan in 1942 and 1943, claiming another 3 million victims. Cities were often set on fire before the advancing Japanese; officials did not always evacuate the population in time.[8]

Map of the East Asian theatre of war, excerpt from ABCA map no. 72

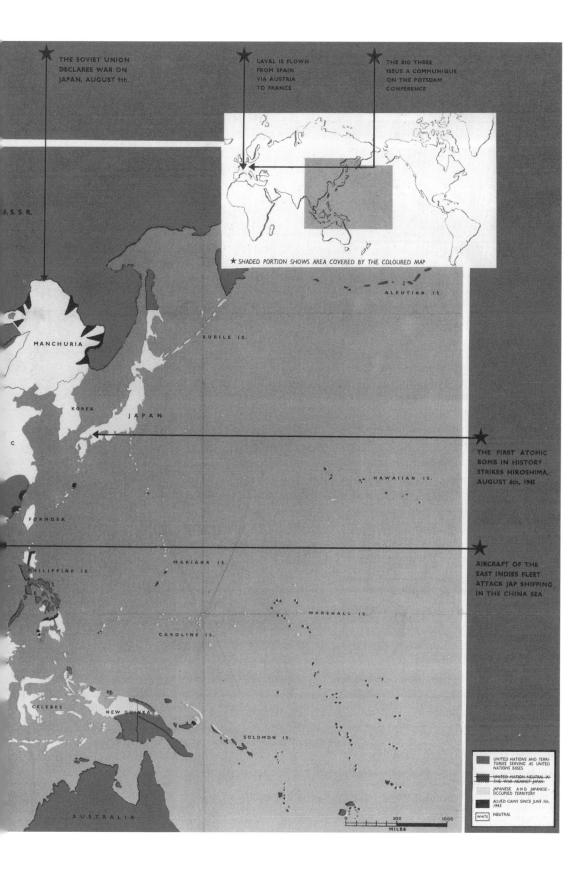

THE SOVIET UNION
DECLARES WAR ON
JAPAN, AUGUST 9th.

LAVAL IS FLOWN
FROM SPAIN
VIA AUSTRIA
TO FRANCE

THE BIG THREE
ISSUE A COMMUNIQUE
ON THE POTSDAM
CONFERENCE

★ SHADED PORTION SHOWS AREA COVERED BY THE COLOURED MAP

U.S.S.R.

ALEUTIAN IS.

MANCHURIA

KURILE IS.

KOREA

JAPAN

C

THE FIRST ATOMIC
BOMB IN HISTORY
STRIKES HIROSHIMA,
AUGUST 6th, 1945

HAWAIIAN IS.

FORMOSA

MARIANA IS.

AIRCRAFT OF THE
EAST INDIES FLEET
ATTACK JAP SHIPPING
IN THE CHINA SEA

PHILIPPINE IS.

MARSHALL IS.

CAROLINE IS.

CELEBES

NEW GUINEA

SOLOMON IS.

UNITED NATIONS AND TERRI-
TORIES SERVING AS UNITED
NATIONS BASES

UNITED NATION NEUTRAL IN
THE WAR AGAINST JAPAN.

JAPANESE AND JAPANESE-
OCCUPIED TERRITORY

ALLIED GAINS SINCE JUNE 5th,
1945

WHITE   NEUTRAL

AUSTRALIA

0   500   1000
MILES

In this second phase of the war, China carried the entire burden of fighting, but was not entirely without support. The governments of the USA, Great Britain and France helped the government in Chong-qing with loans, which were not to be used to buy weapons, however. Starting in 1940, aid became more generous, and at the end of 1941, the USA also began sending armaments as part of the Lend-Lease Act.[9] These were initially transported up the Burma Road and in later years airlifted over the so-called "hump" to the territory of the GMD, which was cut off from the coast. The American flight officer and later General Claire Chennault organised foreign pilots who volunteered for action in China (predominantly Americans) in a formation that would later become famous under the name "Flying Tigers".[10] Until 1941, however, the Soviet Union functioned as the main supplier of aid in the form of oil, medication and armaments, above all tanks and airplanes, and thus gave China more support during this time than all the Western democracies combined. Some of these goods were transported by rail and lorry and some via airlift. Soviet volunteers also reinforced the Chinese Air Force.[11] However, the Chinese National Army never succeeded in decisively driving back the Japanese, and the Communist partisan strategy were only thorns in the side of the invaders, although their resistance did hurt the Japanese.

Even if we regard 7 July 1937 as the beginning of the war in Asia and thus the beginning of the Second World War as a whole, it

Japanese soldiers followed by Chinese civilians, April 1939

was the Japanese attack on Pearl Harbor and Southeast Asia on 7–8 December 1941 that changed the overall situation. The official declarations of war on Japan by the USA, the Allies and China following the attack initiated the third and final phase of the Anti-Japanese War of Resistance, which now formed part of the world war. China became a cornerstone of America's global strategy that had already been drafted at the beginning of 1941. According to the American planning, the European Theatre was to have priority, whereas the fighting in the Asia-Pacific were to be defensive in nature. Since the Soviet Union appeared to have its back to the wall in light of the German advance at the end of 1941 and had also signed a Neutrality Agreement with Japan in the spring of 1941, China as the sole fighting nation in Asia became America's most important partner on the continent. China's role was on the one hand to tie up as many Japanese troops as possible and on the other to make bases available for air and sea attacks on the Japanese main islands when the Land of the Rising Sun was to be wrestled to the ground after the victory over Germany.[12] Moreover, Chiang Kaishek's anti-imperialist credentials were a useful tool in keeping anti-colonial politicians and organisations in the Allied camp, which became especially obvious during his visit to India in February of 1942.[13]

However, if China's alliance with the USA was tense, it was even more so with the British. This was often frustrating for both sides, since the Allies were either unwilling or unable to consider Chinese sensitivities and their desire for true parity. They frustrated the hopes of the Chinese leadership to make China an important theatre of war on an equal footing. Instead, they treated the country as subordinate to the other theatres of war. That China only received a fraction of the aid Washington provided through the Lend-Lease programme made this both symbolically and materially clear—in 1941 and 1942, China's share was a mere one and a half per cent. In the following two years, it even shrank to only 0.4 per cent. Only in 1945 did it increase to a meagre 4 per cent.[14]

These conflicts were personified by the man the USA sent to China upon Chiang Kai-shek's request for an American chief of staff: Lieutenant General Joseph Stilwell. The disputes between caustic "Vinegar Joe" and Chiang, whom he pejoratively named "Peanut" in his journals, were not only caused by personal animosity, but had deeper structural reasons. Washington regarded Stilwell, who held various military and administrative leadership positions and was responsible to both the Americans and the Chinese, as being the same rank as the Chinese Generalissimo; by contrast, the Chinese leadership saw Stilwell as a subordinate to their own commander-in-chief. Already during the fighting in Burma from 1942 to 1944, the only campaign that Chinese troops participated in outside of China's territory and as part of a multinational force, these tensions became obvious. They reached a climax in the spring of 1944, when Stilwell insisted on taking command of all Chinese armed forces, including the

Communists, after the initial success of Japan's Operation Ichi-gō, the largest Japanese offensive in China in the second half of the war. Although President Roosevelt initially supported him and even threatened Chiang with the withdrawal of American aid, the pugnacious general had overbid his hand this time. Offered the choice between him and the virtually indispensable Chiang, Roosevelt had to relent and appoint the more amiable Albert C. Wedemeyer as Stilwell's successor.[15]

Although the Western Allies found it hard to concede full parity to their Chinese partner, they were aware that their special rights in China could hardly be reconciled with the common alliance against the Axis powers. Although the outbreak of the Pacific War played an important role in the suspension of these special rights, the process to end them goes back to the end of the 1920s. Through trade agreements, the 1928 National Government was able, for the most part, to restore the customs sovereignty of the Republic of China. By contrast, negotiations with the British and the Americans regarding the exterritoriality of their nationals in China were cancelled upon the Japanese invasion of Manchuria. The Sino-Japanese War led to drastic changes to Western privileges, since Japan had taken action to end the treaty privileges of the Western powers for the territories it occupied since the middle of the 1930s. In addition, Japanese armed forces in many cases recognised neither the territorial status of foreign concession areas nor the rights of individual foreigners.

By the end of 1938 Great Britain and the USA thus showed their willingness to end their treaty regime. Accordingly, initiatives of both countries gained considerable momentum after the outbreak of the Pacific War. In October of 1942, the British and the Americans told Chiang Kai-shek's government in Chongqing that they were willing to give up all treaty privileges. The corresponding agreement was signed on 11 January 1943. Japan used intermittent disagreements between China and Great Britain over the future status of Hong Kong to hand back all rights from the unequal treaties to the collaborationist Wang Jingwei regime in Nanjing just two days before. Italy and the French Vichy government followed. Due to the temporary existence of two competing Chinese national governments, the revision of the privilege agreements with smaller states, whose economic interests were as a rule in the Japanese-occupied part of China, was delayed until after the war. The entire process was only completed in 1947. China was, from then on, *de jure* a full-fledged member of the international community.[16]

China and the war conferences: from Cairo to Potsdam

The end of the unequal treaties with Great Britain and the USA in January 1943 meant a tremendous formal break for China. Just how the global political role of the country would look like in practice depended not least on the consultations of the Allies regarding a common strategy and the design of the post-war order. In this pro-

Japanese soldier
in front of Chiang
Kai-shek's former
headquarters at Wuhan,
1938

cess, it quickly became clear that Chiang Kai-shek was of secondary importance to the Big Three—US President Roosevelt, British Prime Minister Churchill and the Soviet dictator Stalin.

Chiang as President and Commander-in-Chief of China was only invited to one of the war conferences. From 22 to 27 November 1943, he participated in the Cairo Conference together with his wife Song Meiling, who was promoted as a real media darling in the USA, but to the meeting with Stalin in Tehran that followed on the heels of that in the Egyptian capital, Roosevelt and Churchill went without Chiang. At least, the Cairo Conference bestowed upon the Chinese president a gain in prestige and also promised the liquidation of Japanese imperialism in China. As set forth in the communiqué, all parts of China "stolen" from Japan since 1895, namely Taiwan, the Pescadores Islands and Manchuria, should be returned to China, and this indeed took place in 1945 without a formal peace treaty.[17] The Generalissimo declared himself as agreeing with Roosevelt's suggestion to put Indochina under an international trusteeship instead of returning it to the former colonial power France. By contrast, Great Britain, as Churchill later explained to Roosevelt, wanted to hold on to its colonial possessions in Asia including Hong Kong—a point that caused great concern to Chiang.[18]

At the Tehran Conference, where China was more a side topic, Stalin specifically promised for the first time that the Soviet Union would enter the war against Japan after the victory over Nazi Germany. He thus fulfilled a request that the Americans had been making since August of 1942. But the Soviet leader was sceptical of upgrading China to one of "four policemen", as Roosevelt had envisioned in his version of the global post-war order.[19] However, the Americans were able to push this point through. China sent a delegation to the Dumbarton Oaks Conference (August to October 1944), which prepared the founding of the United Nations, and became a founding member of the UN in April 1945, receiving a permanent seat with veto rights on the UN Security Council, an expanded version of the "Four Policemen" idea.[20]

The entry of the Soviet Union into the Pacific War promised to limit the expected American war losses during the planned capture of the main Japanese islands. It also diminished the value of its alliance with China, which obviously was not able to defeat the Japanese on its own soil. Maybe this is the reason that the Americans hardly resisted Stalin's demands regarding the Far East. The objective of the dictator's policy was to restore the position of Tsarist Russia before its defeat in the war against Japan in 1904–05. This involved the reclamation of former Russian territories such as South Sakhalin and the Kurile Islands as well as areas claimed by China. In Outer Mongolia, Stalin wanted to maintain the status quo, which meant the independence guaranteed by Russia since 1915. In Manchuria, the Liaodong Peninsula and the ports of Dalian and Port Arthur would again be leased to the Soviet Union as well as the East Chinese Railway, originally built by Russia, and the Japanese South Manchuria Railway.

Chiang Kai-shek,
Franklin D. Roosevelt
and Winston Churchill
at the Cairo Conference,
November 1943

Although Roosevelt agreed with the first point, he reduced the second demand. Both ports were again to be in Russian hands, but Dalian should be internationalised. Both railway lines would be administered by a Sino-Soviet company. In any case, Soviet interests were to be respected, and the approval of the Chinese government was regarded by Roosevelt as a mere formality.[21]

Stalin's demands put him in the ongoing tradition of long-term Soviet policy. Although Soviet Russia had relinquished its privileges from the Unequal Treaty with China in 1919 in the Karakhan Manifesto, it attempted to regain its lost positions after the fact. A great victory of this policy was the agreement made with the weak Beijing government in 1924, which reaffirmed the USSR's extensive controlling rights over the East Chinese Railway, refunded real estate and even gave Soviet businessmen a de facto exterritoriality.[22] At the conference of Yalta, held from 4 to 11 February 1945 the Soviet Union received even much more than this for its assurances to enter the war, to recognise Chinese sovereignty in Manchuria and to conclude a friendship and alliance treaty with China, which was signed on 14 August 1945.

1933. SPRINGBOARD TO AGGRESSION

1941. PEARL HARBOUR TO HONG KONG

1942. AN EMPIRE WON

TWILIGHT OVER TOKYO

On Monday, August 6th, the first atomic bomb in history came down to earth, with a shattering effect on the Japanese base of Hiroshima and a sobering effect on the minds of all mankind. Winston Churchill commented :—" This revelation of the secrets of Nature, long mercifully withheld from man, should arouse the most solemn reflections in the mind and conscience of every human being capable of comprehension."

Two days later, as the Imperial Cabinet was discussing what to do about the atomic bomb, Russia declared war on Japan. M. Molotov later revealed that, in the middle of June, the Mikado requested the Soviet Union to mediate with the Western Allies for peace terms.

The ring round the last of the aggressors was now complete.

THE SON OF HEAVEN—" Ever anxious to enhance the cause of world peace."

TOKYO RADIO, AUGUST 10th, 1945.

At second Meanw of Mar

Th Tokyo Declar does ne of His as bein

Th author rule th the Al

Th

44. THE TIDE TURNS

LUDE TO INVASION

. THE POTSDAM TERMS

SOLETE ATOM

th there was dropped on Nagasaki the
hich rendered the first one obsolete.
y was carving its way into the depths
-west and from east.
er the "vapourising" of Hiroshima,
acceptance, on terms, of the Potsdam
understanding that the said declaration
nand which prejudices the prerogatives
gn ruler." The Emperor was described
enhance the cause of world peace."
"From the moment of surrender the
or and the Japanese government to
abject to the Supreme Commander of

yet.

In order to lessen the humiliation of the Chinese National Government, the Friendship Treaty provided for a referendum in Outer Mongolia. It was little surprise, however, that this resulted in a unanimous vote for independence of the Soviet satellite. The provision regarding the internationalisation of Dalian was accepted, although China was to lease shipyards and warehouses to the Soviet Union. Port Arthur was planned as a joint Sino-Soviet naval base, just as the USSR and China were to jointly administrate the East Chinese Railway. However, the agreement assured that the Soviet side would have the majority, both in the number of members and the number of chairman positions in each governing body. Since this again limited the process of restoring Chinese sovereignty begun in 1943, it has rightly been described as the last unequal treaty. It was based on the provisions of Yalta, where Roosevelt and Stalin had made agreements at the expense of China, without its participation and behind the back of its government.

China was thus both defeated—and a victor.[23] The disparity created in Yalta was only corrected five years later in the treaty between Stalin and Mao—against the background of the escalating Cold War. The Chinese Communists were hardly present on the world stage in 1945. Stalin thought they were too weak and was convinced he had to make agreements with the Nationalist Chiang Kai-shek as the leading political power of his southern neighbour.[24]

From the Chinese perspective, the Potsdam Conference added nothing essential to the facts already established. Over the short term, its most important element was the Potsdam Declaration of 26 July, which was drafted by the Americans and the British and also signed by Chiang Kai-shek; Stalin did not participate, since the USSR was not yet in a state of war with Japan. It demanded Japan's unconditional surrender and threatened to bring justice to militarists and war criminals, although it consciously omitted the future status of the Tennō, however. It also announced a temporary occupation regime but promised to guarantee the population human rights and also to leave Japan an industrial base, not for the purpose of re-arming, however, but for the payment of reparations. On the one hand, the signing countries wanted the terms to be harsh to carry domestic public opinion with them, but at the same time offered the Japanese an incentive to surrender.[25]

Excerpt from
ABCA map no. 72

The fact that the anti-imperialistic National Government was among the signatories was quite astonishing, since it was a document that clearly outlined Western interests.[26] But this also shows the ambivalent role China played at the end of the Second World War. The East Asian ally received a certain amount of recognition from the Big Three in the fact that it was given responsibility for the disarmament of the Japanese armed forces in Indochina north of the 16th parallel, whereas the British were responsible south of this line.

At the same time, decisions of long-term importance to China were reaffirmed in Potsdam. After the new US President Truman received the message in the Prussian royal seat that the atomic bomb was available, American interest in a Soviet entry into the war noticeably subsided. However, the agreements had already been made and could not be cancelled, since Stalin, who had been making preparations for a war in the Far East since 1942, had told Truman that Soviet troops would start their invasion of Manchuria in mid-August at the latest; it began on 8 August.[27]

The presence of the Red Army in this region played a key role in 1946, when the civil war reignited between Chinese Nationalists and Communists. They enabled Mao Zedong's forces to take Manchuria and thus created a base for their final victory over the Chinese Nationalists and the assumption of power over the country in 1949. Potsdam confirmed once again the ambivalence of China's position in the post-war years—sovereign and formally on equal footing, but at the same time a second-class victor that had to submit to the decisions made by the USA and the USSR. Even so, this was without a doubt an improvement over the situation at the beginning of the 1930s. One of the ironies of history is the fact that not Chiang Kai-shek and his Nationalists, who had borne the main responsibility of the war years, were the beneficiaries, but the Communists under Mao Zedong. |DC

Notes

1 Ying Mei Su shounao Bocitan huiyi baogao 1946. / **2** Weggel 1989, 69–71. / **3** Fishel 1952, 154, 170–73. / **4** Zöllner 2006, 291–96; see also Mitter 2000. / **5** Mitter 2013, 63–67. / **6** Zöllner 2006, 297–98. / **7** MacKinnon 2008, 44–54. / **8** Mitter 2013, 161. Zöllner 2006, 305, 310–15, cites numbers more than twice as large. / **9** Eastman et al. 1991, 144–45. / **10** Mitter 2013, 234; Ford 2016. / **11** Tschudodejew 1986, 8–13; see Eastman et al. 1991, 145. / **12** Miller 1979, 59. On the Japanese-Soviet agreement, see Kindermann 2001, 243. / **13** Yang Tianshi 2015, 132–35, 139. / **14** Eastman et al. 1991, 145. / **15** Wang 2014 offers a good summary of the entire problem as well as a depiction of the "Stilwell incident" from the perspective of Chiang's journals. See also Mitter 2013, 239–63, 302–05 and 334–49; Tuchman 1971, 313–14. / **16** Fishel 1952, 188–215. Based on this, but with additional source material, Li Yumin 2005, 888–936. / **17** Heiferman 2011, 111–14. / **18** Heiferman 2011, 120–21, 125, 127. / **19** A summary of the Tehran Conference is found ibid. 117–28. / **20** Schlesinger 2004, especially 46–51. / **21** Kindermann 2001, 284–86. / **22** Elleman 1997. / **23** Kindermann 2001, 286–88, 301–03; the analyses ibid., 288, 303. The damage to China from the secret diplomacy at Yalta from the Chinese perspective is emphasised by Zhang Xianwen and Chen Qianping 2017, 247–53. / **24** On the treaty of 1950, see Zhang Shenfa 2010. On Stalin's analysis of the balance of power in China, see Neiberg 2015, 231–32. / **25** According to the plausible interpretation of Neiberg 2015, 244–45; on Indochina ibid., 246. The Text of the Potsdam Declaration is found in the National Diet Library, Text of the Constitution and Other Important Documents, www.ndl.go.jp/constitution/e/etc/c06.html [accessed 23 September 2019]. See also the article by Robert Kramm in this volume. / **26** See also the article by Robert Kramm in this volume. / **27** Neiberg 2015, 232–244. See also Zhang Xianwen und Chen Qianping 2017, 247–49.

Korea –
the Potsdam
Declaration
and Korean
Independence

Jong Hoon Shin[1]

On 26 July 1945, during the Potsdam Conference, US President Truman, the President of the Republic of China Chiang Kai-shek and the British Prime Minister Churchill published the Potsdam Declaration, which gave an ultimatum to Japan to surrender. This declaration indirectly mentions the future of the Japanese colony of Korea. Article 8 (of 13) of the Potsdam Declaration reads: "The terms of the Cairo Declaration shall be carried out and Japanese sovereignty shall be limited to the islands of Honshu, Hokkaido, Kyushu, Shikoku and such minor islands as we determine."[2] In the Cairo Declaration, the three heads of state promised that in consideration of the enslavement of the Korean people, Korea would become free and independent in due course.[3] Japanese Foreign Minister Mamoru Shigemitsu officially recognised the provisions of the Potsdam Declaration when he signed the Instrument of Surrender on board the battleship *USS Missouri* on 2 September 1945.[4] Three years later, on 15 August 1948, the government of the Republic of Korea was formed.

Due to these facts, we can assume that the Potsdam Declaration is an important document to Koreans, since it sheds light on the independence of Korea in the context of international relations. Indeed, Koreans regard the Potsdam Declaration as the last international assurance of Korea's independence. However, contemporary Korean historians have seldom made the Potsdam Declaration an object of study.[5] The lack of research has meant that basic historical facts regarding the Potsdam Conference, not to mention the Potsdam Declaration, have been incorrectly and falsely represented in Korea until now.

If we look at the importance of the Potsdam Declaration to the independence of Korea, it is quite strange that Koreans have no exact knowledge of its origins. The following is an initial attempt to illustrate the false knowledge of Korean society regarding the Potsdam Conference and the Potsdam Declaration using several examples from Korean school textbooks. Afterwards, the preparation and the draft of the Potsdam Declaration before and during the conference in Potsdam will be explained in detail. And finally, the independence of Korea and the formation of the South Korean government in the context of international relations will be briefly discussed.

← US delegates Admiral
C. Kinkaid and Lieutenant
General John R. Hodge
signing Japanese surrender
documents in Seoul,
Korea, 9 September 1945

The treatment of the Potsdam Conference
and the Potsdam Declaration
in Korean school textbooks

The fact that all high school textbooks on Korean history cover the Potsdam Conference and the Potsdam Declaration implies that these topics are regarded as important to Korean history. However, the accounts given in Korean school textbooks are full of mistakes. The following four examples illustrate this.

1) "US President Truman, British Prime Minister Churchill and the Chinese General Chiang Kai-shek met in July of 1945 in Potsdam to discuss the handling of Germany and the war against Japan. After the meeting, the Potsdam Declaration, signed by the heads of state and government of the four countries including the Soviet Generalissimo Stalin, was published."[6]

2) "When the war in Europe ended with the capitulation of Germany, the Allies, who expected Japan to quickly surrender, met in July of 1945 in Potsdam. At this conference, the USA, Great Britain and China demanded that Japan unconditionally surrender. In August, Stalin participated in the Conference and signed the Potsdam Declaration."[7]

3) "In July of 1945, representatives of the USA, Great Britain and China met in Potsdam. The heads of state and government of the Allies decided in Potsdam to demand the unconditional surrender of Japan. ... The Potsdam Declaration confirmed the independence of Korea."[8]

4) "After the surrender of Germany, leading politicians from the USA, Great Britain and China met in July of 1945 in Potsdam to discuss the question of the post-war order. There they demanded the unconditional surrender of Japan. After the Soviet Union declared war on Japan, it participated in the conference."[9]

The quoted examples show that most Koreans have no knowledge of the following basic facts: At the Potsdam Conference, held from 17 July to 2 August 1945, the heads of state and government of the USA, Great Britain and the Soviet Union were present. The Chinese head of state Chiang, in contrast, was not present. And during the Potsdam Conference, Stalin had neither an official position on the Potsdam Declaration nor did he sign it. Only after the conference did Soviet Foreign Minister Molotov say as part of the Soviet declaration of war on Japan on 8 August 1945 that the Soviet government joined the Allies' Declaration of 26 July, meaning the Potsdam Declaration.[10]

The main topics covered by the Potsdam Conference were the preparation for signing peace treaties and the creation of a post-war order in Europe. Therefore, the agenda set forth as the official order of business for the Potsdam Conference was largely limited to the question of the post-war order in Europe. The issue of the end of the Pacific War and the East Asian post-war order were not even put on the agenda of the full meetings of the conference.[11] The Communiqué of Potsdam, which recorded the most important resolutions

Surrender of Japanese
troops in South Korea,
striking the Rising Sun Flag
at Seoul, 9 September 1945

Surrender of Japanese
troops in South Korea,
hoisting of the American flag,
9 September 1945

of the conference, did not mention the question of the end of the Pacific War or the Potsdam Declaration.[12]

The Potsdam Declaration, which was published by the Allies waging war against Japan as an ultimatum for Japan's surrender, was a separate event which had nothing to do with the order of business of the Potsdam Conference. The Soviet Union, which had signed a neutrality agreement with Japan on 13 April 1941 and had a neutral attitude towards Japan at the time the Potsdam Declaration was published, did not participate in the drafting of the Potsdam Declaration. As a result, the document was not signed by the Soviet side.[13] A day after the publication of the Potsdam Declaration, American Secretary of State Byrnes informed Soviet Foreign Minister Molotov that the Soviet Union had not been informed of the Declaration in advance because it was not at war with Japan.[14] Also, before the meeting in Potsdam, it was not planned to publish the Potsdam Declaration during the conference on the initiative of the USA. However, the successful atomic test near Alamogordo in New Mexico on 16 July 1945, one day before the start of the conference, changed the situation completely. Encouraged by this success and with the expectation that the war against Japan, contrary to plan, could end early, it was held that the Potsdam Declaration could and should be published as a kind of final warning to Japan.[15]

But how could Korean society become so catastrophically uninformed regarding the Potsdam Conference and the Potsdam Declaration? First and foremost, the reason is likely attributed to the fact that Koreans do not really understand the difference between the two events, the Potsdam Conference, on the one hand, and the Potsdam Declaration, on the other. In his study *Potsdam and its Legends* of 1970, Robert Cecil expressly describes the Potsdam Declaration as a noteworthy episode which took place during the Potsdam Conference, thus making it clear once again that the Potsdam Conference and the Potsdam Declaration are two different events.[16] Unfortunately, this fact was not known to several Korean historians. Instead, they saw the Potsdam Declaration as an important event at the Potsdam Conference. This misunderstanding on the part of the Koreans has to be corrected and, in this context, a revision of the representations in Korean school textbooks is urgently necessary.

JAPANESE TYRANTS IN KOREA

1 There is, in the Pacific Ocean, a small country called Korea. It is drawn in red on the globe above.

2 Korea is very near to Japan as you can see here. The red part is Korea, the black part Japan.

3 The people of Korea are quite different from the people of Japan and wear a pretty national costume.

4 A long time ago artists from Korea were invited to Japan to teach painting and writing there.

5 The Japanese were always very polite to these wise men because they wished to learn their skill.

6 In 1904 Japan and Russia went to war. Japan won the war in the end.

7 So Japan signed a treaty with Korea promising that the country would still be free.

8 But the Japanese did not keep their promise and they forced the Emperor to give them his country.

9 And in 1910 Korea became a part of Japan in spite of the treaty that had been signed.

10 Soon Koreans were made to work for the Japanese and were turned into slaves.

11 The people of Korea were made to leave their farms by the Japanese and were paid no money for them.

12 Korean officials in government departments had their jobs taken away by Japanese officials.

13 The Koreans were forced by the Japanese to make roads but the Japanese settlers were not.

Pamphlet issued by the British Department of Information, "Axis Criminals", by Ronald Carl Giles, 1942

GAPC0429A-ZE

14 The Japanese had no respect for the Koreans' burial grounds and profaned their graves.

15 There were many examples of Koreans being murdered by the Japanese when they complained.

16 Even women and children were quite often beaten in the streets by Japanese soldiers.

17 In a village called Chaison all religious men were shot and bayonetted in their church.

18 Then the church was set on fire and all the houses except six in the village burned.

19 Ten thousand people were put in prison and the prisons were so crowded they could not sit down.

20 One thousand of these were later killed, 1,500 injured and the rest were beaten.

21 Admiral Saito, a Japanese Governor, was murdered by his own countrymen for being too kind.

22 Japan cannot grow enough rice to feed her own people so she takes rice from Korea.

23 Korean gold is stolen by Japan to pay for the things Japan needs to buy from other countries.

24 There is a shortage of food and clothing in Korea, the Japanese have taken everything.

25 They even force the Koreans to change their own names to a Japanese name.

26 Only Japanese history is taught in Korean schools and the children must learn to speak Japanese.

27 Koreans are not allowed to worship their own gods any more. They must worship Japanese gods.

28 Co-prosperity means only poverty, hunger and unhappiness. Japan has murdered Korea.

In order to understand the background of the Potsdam Declaration, it is necessary to know what the American government had planned regarding the surrender of Japan before the Potsdam Conference. Although the Pacific War had been going in favour of the Allies after the surrender of Germany, the Joint Chiefs of Staff (JCS) of the USA came to the conclusion that landing on the Japanese mainland would be necessary to finally force Japan to surrender. The plan drafted by the military leadership of the USA for landing on the Japanese mainland was divided into two operations. First, 14 divisions of the US Army would land on 1 November 1945 on the island of Kyushu (Operation Olympic) and later, 24 divisions were to attack the island of Honshu, where Tokyo is located, on 1 March 1946 (Operation Coronet). It was accepted that both operations would incur enormous losses to the landing US soldiers, and this number was difficult to calculate in advance.[17]

In a meeting in the White House with the military leadership on 18 June 1945, President Truman approved of carrying out Operation Olympic as planned, but at the same time recommended postponing the decision to carry out Operation Coronet after considering the given circumstances.[18] In this meeting, the question of Russian participation in the Pacific War was discussed. In order to keep the loss of US soldiers to a minimum and to weaken the morale of the Japanese Army, it was important according to the JCS that the Soviet Army fight against Japan in Manchuria and if necessary in Korea. Truman declared accordingly that in the context of the upcoming conference in Potsdam, one of his objectives would be to receive the maximum support possible from the Soviet Union for the war against Japan.[19]

At the beginning of the Potsdam Conference, the US government estimated that the war with Japan would go on at least until the beginning of 1946. For this reason, one of Truman's most important goals at the conference was to involve the Soviet Union in the war against Japan as quickly as possible.[20] This goal was consistent with the basic idea of the Briefing Book papers worked out in advance of Potsdam, according to which the President during negotiations should advocate for essentially continuing the collaboration with the Russians.[21] The actual plan to involve the Soviet Union in the war against Japan lost its importance, however, because the successful atomic test one day before the opening of the conference completely changed the conditions for ending the Pacific War.

The interim brief report about the atomic test, which Truman received from Secretary of War Stimson on the evening of 16 July, reads, "Operated on this morning. Diagnosis not yet complete but results seem satisfactory and already exceed expectations."[22] After they received this report, Truman and Byrnes could hope to have the opportunity to avoid the heavy American casualties predicted in the event of a landing on the Japanese mainland. Beyond that, they recognised that through the use of the atomic bomb, it would be possible to force Japan to surrender before the Soviet Union entered the war.[23] Therefore, during the conference, Truman, in a change of plan, took no specific steps to convince the Soviet Union to get involved in the war as quickly as possible, but in fact attempted to delay Soviet entry into war. And with this in mind, Byrnes also attempted to delay the ongoing Sino-Soviet negotiations regarding Chinese concessions for Soviet entry into the war, in the assumption that Stalin would not enter the war without Chinese approval.[24]

In this light, the American leadership prepared the Potsdam Declaration during the conference in Potsdam. Already in advance, the US government had prepared a draft of a final warning to Japan, demanding that the country surrender. In a meeting called at the initiative of Secretary of War Stimson on 26 June, a sub-committee including staff from the Department of War, the Department of the Navy and the Department of State was charged with drafting a document stating the warning to Japan.[25] Stimson conveyed the sub-committee's draft to Truman[26] on 2 July, and explained to the President that this draft should serve as a basis for discussion at the meeting in Potsdam.[27] In this draft, which several amendments later became the Potsdam Declaration, the countries that demanded Japan's surrender included the USA, Great Britain, (the Soviet Union) and China. The fact that the Soviet Union was put in brackets indicates that Moscow was not to be one of the signatories if it was not involved in the Pacific War at the point in time when the Declaration was published.[28]

From 17 July on, when news of the successful atomic bomb experiment reached Potsdam, US government leaders began to discuss sending Japan an ultimatum to surrender.[29] The discussions regarding the final wording of this ultimatum occurred among those on site in Potsdam as well as in communication with those government officials still in Washington.

In preparing the warning to Japan, there were differences of opinion relating to the conditions of Japanese surrender. Whereas the Allies and the American Secretary of State supported unconditional surrender, Stimson and high-ranking military officials argued against the removal of the virtually "divine" Japanese Emperor in order to end the war more quickly and to more easily facilitate the policies of the occupation.[30] Indeed, a sentence in Article 12 of the draft was deleted upon the recommendation of the JCS because the Japanese could have misinterpreted this to mean that the Emperor would either be removed or executed.[31]

However, Truman and Byrnes feared that moderate terms of surrender guaranteeing the status of the Emperor could lead to unpleasant political consequences, for example, strong opposition from the American public against too lax demands.[32] The final wording of the Potsdam Declaration can thus be seen as a compromise between the military leadership and the Secretary of State. On the one hand, they demanded the unconditional surrender of all Japanese armed forces; on the other, they would allow the Japanese, after the withdrawal of occupation forces, to form a government of their choosing, and the issue of the handling of the Emperor and political institutions was not mentioned at all.[33] According to historian Michael Neiberg, who recently analysed the Potsdam Conference, the declaration is a political document whose objective it was to satisfy a domestic audience who demanded hard terms but also gave the Japanese reason enough to surrender instead of fighting on.[34]

According to Stimson's journal entry, Truman planned to publish the ultimatum calling for the Japanese surrender after he had confirmation of day that the atomic bomb would be technically operational and when he had received the approval of the text of the ultimatum from the Chinese government.[35] On 23 July, Stimson received a report from Washington that the use of the atomic bomb would be possible starting 1 August at the earliest to 10 August at the latest— the time frame can be explained by the preparation process and changing climatic conditions.[36] On 24 July, Truman issued his approval to drop the atomic bomb on any day suitable starting from 3 August, after the end of the conference.[37] And on the same day, the American President sent the first draft of the Potsdam Declaration to his ambassador in China, Patrick J. Hurley, to find out whether Chinese President Chiang Kai-shek would be willing to accept the declaration; Churchill also received a draft on the evening of the same day.[38]

The wording of the declaration was corrected again at the last minute due to Chiang Kai-shek's demand that the order of the listing of heads of state and government be changed.[39] In the declaration draft, the British Prime Minister was listed before the Chinese President. In the Potsdam Declaration of 26 July, the order of the heads of state and government was thus listed as follows: "the President of the United States, the President of the National Government of the Republic of China and the Prime Minister of Great Britain".[40] On 26 July, Byrnes sent Molotov a copy of the final draft of the Potsdam Declaration and informed him that it would be announced to the world the following day.[41]

Japanese Prime Minister Suzuki announced on 28 July that his government rejected the demands of the declaration and that they would fight on to victory.[42] Atomic bombs were then dropped on 6 August on Hiroshima and on 9 August on Nagasaki. On 15 August, the Japanese Emperor finally announced the surrender of Japan. In the meantime, the Soviet Union had declared war on Japan on 8 August and the Soviet Army was able to march into the north of Korea before the Japanese surrender. On 14 August, to prevent the Soviet Union from occupying all of Korea, the USA suggested to the Soviet Union that the 38th Parallel become the interim line to divide Korea into two zones of occupation, one for each country. The Soviet Union accepted the American suggestion a day later.[43] Thus the first unwitting step to divide Korea had been taken.

Final comments

As explained before, the Potsdam Conference and the Potsdam Declaration are to be seen as two separate events, apart from their common time and location. The Potsdam Declaration, not the Potsdam Communiqué, was an important document for Korea's contemporary history because this declaration confirmed the implementation of the Cairo Declaration of Franklin D. Roosevelt, Churchill and Chiang Kai-shek of 27 November and 1 December 1943, which promised Korean independence.

The first draft of the Cairo Declaration, in which the future independence of Korea was affirmed for the first time, recommended that Korean independence should be achieved "as early as possible". But this wording had to be corrected for US President Roosevelt, who doubted the political abilities of the Koreans, to the effect that Korea should be free and independent "in due course".[44] During the Tehran Conference of 1943, Roosevelt even expressed the opinion to Stalin that the Koreans might require about 40 years to finally receive their independence.[45] In May of 1945, Roosevelt's former advisor, Harry L. Hopkins, who was also Truman's envoy to Stalin, suggested to the Generalissimo that the trusteeship of Korea should last a maximum of 25 years.[46] In the end, however, during the Moscow Conference in December of 1945, it was decided that the occupation of Korea would last for a maximum of five years.[47]

At the Moscow Conference, the Secretary of State of the USA and the Foreign Minister of the Soviet Union also agreed that a Korean government should be formed for the entire country.[48] The partition of Korea after the occupation was not originally intended at the beginning of its occupation and division. In the course of the escalation of the Cold War, however, the Soviet Union rejected the implementation of this agreement. And, thus, two separate governments were formed in South and North Korea on 15 August 1948 and 9 September 1948, respectively, finalising the partition of Korea.[49]

This essay is dedicated to the task of correctly rendering the facts of the origin of the Potsdam Declaration and its importance to Korean history. On this basis, it should be a matter of concern to Korean historians to research and present in more detail the role of the international community and the competing interests of the great powers as influencing factors on the independence and partition of Korea. |DC

Notes

1 Professor of History at Gyeongsang National University (South Korea). The content of this article is mostly based on an essay published in 2016 by the author in Korean, which was primarily written with the objective of correcting false portrayals of the Potsdam Conference and the Potsdam Declaration in Korean school textbooks, see Shin 2016. / 2 Proclamation by the Heads of Governments, United States, China and the United Kingdom, FRUS 1945, The Conference of Berlin (The Potsdam Conference), vol. 2, 1474 et seq. / 3 Cairo Communiqué, 1 Dec 1943, National Diet Library of Japan, www.ndl.go.jp/constitution/e/shiryo/01/002_46shoshi.html [accessed 1 August 2019]. / 4 See Official Documents 1945, Surrender of Japan, 264–65. / 5 Only three essays in Korean which refer to the Potsdam Declaration have been published in Korea to date: 정동귀, 「제2차 세계대전중에 있어서의 미국의 대 한국정책 구상」, 「사회과학 논총」 vol. 6 (1988); 박노순, 「2차 대전 중 연합국의 대 반도정책」, 「통일로」 292호 (2012); 와다 하루키, 「카이로 선언과 일본의 영토문제」, 「영토해양연구」 vol. 5 (2013). / 6 History of Korea for Secondary Schools, 금성출판사, 2014, 354. / 7 History of Korea for Secondary Schools, 두산동아, 2013, 254. / 8 History of Korea for Secondary Schools, 지학사, 2014, 337. / 9 History of Korea for Secondary Schools, 비상교육, 2014, 337. / 10 The English version literally states: "Loyal to its Allied duty, the Soviet Government … has joined in the declaration of the Allied powers of July 26." Soviet Declaration of War on Japan, 8 August 1945, Avalon Project at Yale University, https://avalon.law.yale.edu/wwii/s4.asp [accessed 15 August 2019]. / 11 See Fischer 1969. The question of conducting war against Japan was only briefly mentioned during the third full meeting in the context of the discussion regarding the allocation of German naval and merchant vessels. See ibid., 223 et seq. / 12 See Official Documents 1945/Conference of Berlin, 245–57. / 13 Soviet-Japanese Neutrality Pact 13 April 1941, Avalon Project at Yale University, https://avalon.law.yale.edu/wwii/s1.asp [accessed 15 August 2019]. / 14 See "Bohlen Minutes" of the discussion between the USSR Foreign Commissar Molotov and US Secretary of State Byrnes, 27 July 1945,https://history.state.gov/historicaldocuments/frus1945Berlinv02/d710a-126 [accessed 13 February 2020]. / 15 See Neiberg 2015, 239 et seq. / 16 See Cecil 1970, 464. / 17 See Miscamble 2007, 178. / 18 Minutes of meeting, 18 June 1945, FRUS 1945, The Conference of Berlin (The Potsdam Conference), vol. 1, 909. / 19 FRUS 1945, The Conference of Berlin (The Potsdam Conference), vol. 1, 905, 909. / 20 Miscamble 2007, 187. / 21 Drechsler 1997, 36. / 22 Miscamble 2007, 195; The Acting Chairman of the Interim Committee (Harrison) to the Secretary of War (Stimson), 16 July 1945, FRUS 1945, The Conference of Berlin (The Potsdam Conference), vol. 2, 1360. / 23 See Miscamble 2007, 196. / 24 See Bernstein 1975, 44 et seq. / 25 Minutes of a Meeting of the Committee of Three, 26 June 1945, FRUS 1945, The Conference of Berlin (The Potsdam Conference), vol. 1, 888. / 26 Proclamation by the Heads of State. US-UK-[USSR]-China, FRUS 1945, The Conference of Berlin (The Potsdam Conference), vol. 1, 893–894. / 27 The Secretary of War (Stimson) to the President. Memorandum for the President, 2 July 1945, FRUS 1945, The Conference of Berlin (The Potsdam Conference), vol. 1, 888–89. / 28 Proclamation by the Heads of State. US-UK-[USSR]-China, FRUS 1945, The Conference of Berlin (The Potsdam Conference), vol. 1, 893; The Secretary of War (Stimson) to the President. Memorandum for the President, 2. July 1945, ibid., 891–92. / 29 According to his journal, Stimson, at the meeting of the morning of 17 July attended by Truman, Byrnes and Stimson, insisted on the necessity to immediately warn Japan. But Byrnes argued against an immediate warning. Stimson thus no longer mentioned the issue during the meeting. See The Secretary of War (Stimson) to the President, 16 July 1945, FRUS 1945, The Conference of Berlin (The Potsdam Conference), vol. 2, 1266, ann. 6. / 30 See Villa 1976, 70–71.; Neiberg 2015, 236–37. / 31 The deleted sentence reads, "This (sc. the Japanese government after the occupation) may include a constitutional monarchy under the present dynasty if it be shown to the complete satisfaction of the world that such a government will never again aspire to aggression." The Joint Chiefs of Staff to the President, 18 July 1945, FRUS 1945, The Conference of Berlin (The Potsdam Conference), vol. 2, 1268–69. / 32 The results of a 1945 opinion poll in the USA on the issue of what to do with the Japanese emperor: execute him: 33 per cent, let the courts decide: 17 per cent, leave him alone: 4 per cent, use him as a puppet to run Japan: 3 per cent and no opinion: twenty-three per cent. See 강만길 외, 「한국사 17. 분단구조의 정착-1」, 한길사 1994, 138–139; Bernstein 1975, 53 et seq. / 33 Proclamation by the Heads of Governments, United States, China and the United Kingdom, FRUS 1945, The Conference of Berlin (The Potsdam Conference), vol. 2, 1476. / 34 See Neiberg 2015, 245. / 35 See The Secretary of War (Stimson) to the President, 16 July 1945, FRUS 1945, The Conference of Berlin (The Potsdam Conference), vol. 2, 1266 et seq, ann. 6. / 36 The Acting Chairman of the Interim Committee (Harrison) to the Secretary of War (Stimson), 23 July 1945, FRUS 1945, The Conference of Berlin (The Potsdam Conference), vol. 2, 1374. / 37 See Groehler 1997, 203. / 38 The President to the Ambassador in China (Hurley),

24 July 1945, FRUS 1945, The Conference of Berlin (The Potsdam Conference), vol. 2, 1278; President Truman to Prime Minister Churchill, 25 July 1945, ibid., 1279. / **39** Chiang demanded that the President be listed before the Prime Minister. Moreover, he thought that it would help his status in China if the Chinese head of state were listed after that of the USA. The Ambassador in China (Hurley) to the President and the Secretary of State, 26 July 1945, FRUS 1945, The Conference of Berlin (The Potsdam Conference), vol. 2, 1283. / **40** Proclamation by the Heads of Governments, United States, China and the United Kingdom, FRUS 1945, The Conference of Berlin (The Potsdam Conference), vol. 2, 1474–75. Because Churchill and Chiang were not present in Potsdam at the time the Declaration was published, Truman had to sign for both of them on their behalf. See ibid., 1476, ann. 5. / **41** The Secretary of State to the Soviet Foreign Commissar (Molotov), 26 July 1945, FRUS 1945, The Conference of Berlin (The Potsdam Conference), vol. 2, 1284. / **42** See Wagner 1997, 185. / **43** See 강만길 외, 『우리민족 해방운동사』, 역사비평사 2000, 286; Neiberg 2015, 286. / **44** See 와다 하루키, 『카이로 선언과 일본의 영토문제』, 97–98. / **45** See 강만길 외, 『우리민족 해방운동사』, 역사비평사 2000, 286; Neiberg 2015, 283. / **46** See Feis 1960, 115. / **47** See 강만길 외, 『한국사 17. 분단구조의 정착-1』, 147. / **48** See Potter 1950, 709. / **49** See Potter 1950, 709–10.

Iran's Struggle for Sovereignty

Jana Forsmann

In a joint military campaign, British and Soviet troops occupied large portions of Iran at the end of August 1941. Bound in this way to the Allied war cause, the country felt considerable effects from the Second World War, even if no fighting took place there. The ongoing occupation plunged Iran into political and economic turmoil. The country hoped for American commitment whilst the post-war order was created—not least because it had been subject to the far-reaching influence by both the powers of Great Britain and (Soviet) Russia since the nineteenth century. Starting in 1943, the Iranians repeatedly called for the withdrawal of troops. However, this only played a subordinate role at Allied conferences. The conference diplomacy of the Big Three could not prevent the growing confrontation in Iran. The Iran Crisis of 1946 was thus the first case of conflict put before the United Nations Security Council.[1]

The Anglo-Soviet invasion of August 1941

The German attack on the Soviet Union in June of 1941 forced the governments of Great Britain and the Soviet Union into an undesirable coalition. However, the now common enemy, Germany, ensured the powers' quick agreement with regard to Iran. The government in Moscow saw the oil producing regions around Baku, indispensable for the Soviet war effort, threatened by the German advance as well as by pro-German forces in Iran. The treaty of 1921 with the former Persia guaranteed the Soviet Union extensive rights of intervention. The British saw the opportunity and the necessity of a joint military action with the Soviets. At the beginning of the century, they had bought a concession to take over oil exploration in Persia. The rich oil reserves in Southwest Iran, discovered in 1908, fell into the hands of the British government with a majority stake in the Anglo-Persian Oil Company shortly before the First World War. For the defence of the British Empire, it was also essential during the Second World War that the production facilities in Abadan remain intact and under British control.

The invasion was also to secure the Trans-Iranian Railway as a corridor for war material deliveries to the Soviet Union. The prospect of massive deliveries of Western aid would help keep the Soviet Union in the war and defuse the question regarding the establishment of a second front on the European continent.

The diplomatic pretext for the planned invasion referred to the danger posed by the many Germans in Iran. In three joint memoranda to Shah Reza Pahlavi, which increasingly had the character of an ultimatum, the British and the Soviets demanded that Iran end all relations with Germany and deport all Germans from the country. Indeed, trade between the German Reich and Iran had greatly increased since the end of the 1930s. Germany was importing numerous raw materials important to their war effort without delivering a

← British Commonwealth troops in the Middle East. An Indian soldier watching over an Anglo-Iranian Oil Company refinery, 4 September 1941

209

recto and verso of a
postcard back home, 1944

comparable volume of goods to Iran.[2] German experts were involved
in building the Trans-Iranian Railway. After the naval blockade of
shipping in the Persian Gulf starting in September 1939, a German-
Soviet trade agreement in March 1940 enabled the resumption of
German-Iranian trade over land through Soviet territory. The Third
Reich enjoyed the support of the Shah and many Iranians, based on
the hope of weakening the overbearing influence of Great Britain
in Iran through closer economic ties to Germany. On the other hand,
more than a few Iranians hoped the Germans would protect them
from the Soviets and Communism.[3]

Shah Mohammad Reza
Pahlavi, around 1942

The Shah seemed not to believe the Anglo-Soviet threat of joint action—he deeply mistrusted both governments. He reacted to the memoranda from London and Moscow by referring to his country's neutrality since the outbreak of the war and to its sovereignty. Deporting all Germans would have violated both. The Soviets and the British disregarded this argument, because the invasion had already been planned beforehand as part of their respective defence strategies. The joint intervention began on the morning of 25 August 1941, concurrently in the north and southwest of the country. There were only isolated pockets of military resistance. The command structures of the Shah's army hardly functioned and desertion was rampant. On 29 and 31 August, Anglo-Indian and Soviet troops met, both in the western part of the country and northwest of Tehran.

On the day of the invasion, the Shah turned to US President Franklin D. Roosevelt and asked for help. Not only did he hope for support from Germany, but also the USA in the defence against British and Soviet influence. However, the USA had been filled in on Great Britain's plans and approved the invasion in the end. The longed-for assistance from Washington thus failed to appear.

Years of crisis – Iran during the Second World War

In the middle of September, the Shah was forced to abdicate on account of the military pressure of British and Soviet troops advancing towards Tehran. The Shah, whose power was essentially based on his support from the army, had overestimated the stability and acceptance of his regime by the people. Since the middle of the 1920s, he had forced through policies of modernisation and Westernisation following Mustafa Kemal Atatürk's model in Turkey. Even if he had laid the foundation of a modern Iranian state, the measures brought few palpable advantages for most of the population. Beyond that, his reforms were met with considerable resistance, particularly from Shiite spiritual leaders. The Shah made even more enemies with his policy of centralisation, the struggle against nomadic tribes and national minorities, and the deprivation of parliamentary power.[4]

Nevertheless, the British saw the continuation of the Pahlavis' rule to be the best way to stabilise Iran's domestic situation. They thus enabled the son of Reza Pahlavi, the 21-year old Mohammed Reza, to ascend to the Peacock Throne.

The presence of foreign troops, the use of Iranian infrastructure for Western aid deliveries and not least the somewhat open interference by the British and the Soviets in domestic political affairs plunged the country into continued political and economic crisis. The governments in Tehran changed often, usually only staying in office for a few months. In the National Parliament, which had again gained importance, there was a strong fragmentation of interests and parties. Although this was evidence of the democratisation process after the fall of the authoritarian regime of Shah Reza Pahlavi, the struggle for direction hardly contributed to overcoming the chaotic inner turmoil. The young Shah Mohammed Reza had little experience with government and hardly had any knowledge of the numerous political and social conflicts. He had no loyal basis of power in the administration or in society. But there was not only an uproar at the situation in the capital. Various forces in society also gained new political power on the outskirts. Several tribes in the south of the country demanded the return of the autonomy rights

WAR SUPPLIES FOR RUSSIA . . . A convoy of British and American lorries streams along the Persian route to Russia.

B.C.S. 40   Printed in England

they had lost under the old Shah regime. National minorities such as the Kurds and the Azerbaijani pushed for greater independence.

The occupation also caused major economic upheaval. The Western aid programme, led by the USA, included comprehensive deliveries of vehicles and airplanes as well as other materiel important to the Soviet Union's war effort. It was soon clear that the British-led expansion of infrastructure was much too slow to enable the delivery of the contractually-agreed amount of aid. Therefore, starting in 1942, the USA strengthened their commitment to Iran and took over the expansion of infrastructure from the southwest of the country to Tehran. By the end of 1943, the USA had around 28,000 troops stationed in Iran. By the end the war, around 4.6 million tonnes of war materials had been transported through the Iranian corridor, including 5,000 planes and 200,000 lorries. This was about a fourth of all Western aid deliveries to the Soviet Union. Around a million tonnes of civilian aid goods were delivered to Iran itself. Provisions for foreign troops and the building measures that were part of the Allied aid programme caused a massive increase in prices due to soaring demand. The cost of living in Iran virtually exploded. At the same time, there were soon food shortages everywhere in the country, which had various causes. The Soviets transported agricultural goods from the areas they occupied to the Soviet Union. Train connections and streets were constantly blocked by Allied deliveries and grain and other foodstuffs became favoured objects of speculation.

People moved from every province to Tehran or along the railway lines and the planned motorway network in order to work for the Allies. This led to a great wave of internal migration and became a real problem when many of these people were suddenly unemployed after the stop of the aid programme in the summer of 1945 when US troops withdrew.

The US commitment:
political goals and economic interests

In the summer of 1941, the USA was still a neutral but friendly observer of the events taking place in Iran. America wanted to prevent Iran from again being divided up into zones of influence, as it had been during the First World War. They thus prodded the British and the Soviets to sign a treaty with Iran after their invasion. This was to establish that their military action was necessary to the war effort, but also to limit its duration and to guarantee the sovereignty and territorial integrity of the country.[5] At the end of January 1942, the British, the Soviets and the Iranians signed a Tripartite Treaty, which also provided for a complete withdrawal of troops by six months after the end of the war at the latest.

Ending its role as an observer, the USA soon played a formative role. The premise for this was Roosevelt's desire to put the liberties stated in the Atlantic Charter of 1941 to the test. Due to its fragile position between two imperial powers, Great Britain and the Soviet Union in the tradition of Tsarist Russia, the President felt that Iran seemed especially suited to profit from such a realignment of international relations. The State Department's Bureau of Near Eastern Affairs even described Iran as a test case for implementing the principles of the Atlantic Charter and the creation of the United Nations.

Starting in 1942, several advisory missions requested by Iran and commissioned by the US government met in Iran to initiate reforms in the areas of finance, the military, the police and food supply. Despite the sometimes extensive expertise provided, the success of these missions remained modest. This was also due to domestic Iranian resistance, especially from landowners. Only the military mission and the police mission remained in Iran after the war upon the request of the Shah, laying the foundation for building a new army.

In the Middle East, numerous other oil reserves were considered to exist in addition to the oil fields already discovered. American oil companies, with the support of the State Department and at the instigation of the Shah, made several attempts at securing extraction rights in Iran at the beginning of the 1940s. In the competition for Middle Eastern oil, the ambivalence of US policy became clear, since it sought to secure its own economic and strategic interests in Iran for the post-war years and did not only serve as a purported altruistic counterweight to British and Soviet influence.

ABCA map no. 88,
The Middle and Near East

214

GEORGIA

U.S.S.R.

Caspian Sea

U.S.S.R.

SYRIA

TEHERAN

PERSIA

AFGHANISTAN

Aleppo

DAMASCUS

IRAQ

BAGHDAD

PALESTINE

BEIRUT

LEBANON

JERUSALEM

AMMAN

TRANS-JORDAN

SAUDI ARABIA

Persian Gulf

AL KUWAIT

Red Sea

McKERROW

FOREIGN OIL CONCESSIONS - MOSTLY BRITISH AND AMERICAN

S.S.R.

SAUDI ARABIA

PERSIA

IRAQ

BASIN

LIBYA

EGYPT
17½ MILLION POPULATION

TURKEY
18 MILLION POPULATION

SYRIA
22 MILLION

IRAQ
4 MILLION POPULATION

PERSIA
12-15 MILLION POPULATION

SAUDI-ARABIA
9 MILLION POPULATION

U.S.S.R.

RUMANIA

BULGARIA

★ SHADING SHOWS AREA OCCUPIED BY MAIN MAP

ACCURATE CENSUS FIGURES NOT AVAILABLE FOR MUCH OF THIS AREA.

WORLD SETTING: WHERE EAST AND WEST MEET

TURKEY

U.S.S.R.

U.S.S.R.

SYRIA

IRAQ

PERSIA

EGYPT

★ SHADING SHOWS MEMBER STATES OF THE ARAB LEAGUE

SAUDI-ARABIA

POLITICAL PATTERN: BACKGROUND TO ARAB ASPIRATIONS

RRENT AFFAIRS

PRINTED FOR H.M. STATIONERY OFFICE BY FOSH & CROSS LTD., LONDON

Stalin, Roosevelt and
Churchill in front of
the Soviet embassy at
the Tehran Conference,
November – December 1943

The Tehran Declaration of the Big Three, Tehran 1943

At the end of 1943, the heads of government of the three main war allies, Roosevelt, Stalin and Churchill, the so-called Big Three, met personally for the first time. The choice of the conference's location had only little to do with the occupation of Iran. Stalin insisted on Tehran as a meeting point due to the presence of Soviet troops and the geographic proximity to the Soviet border. The journey to Tehran was much more arduous for Roosevelt and Churchill. The American president made the trip despite his physical disability. He absolutely wanted to meet Stalin in order to advance the project dear to his heart: the creation of the United Nations.[6]

In preparation of this first conference of the Big Three, the foreign ministers of the three countries met at the end of October in Moscow. A common Iran policy was also on the agenda. Despite Tehran's request to the Soviet Foreign Ministry, Iran's representatives were not invited to the talks. The Iranian government's suggestions for a joint position of the Allied powers were also ignored. Instead, the British prepared a draft for a joint declaration on Iran. This was to recognise Iran's efforts in the fight against their common enemy and guarantee the country support in coming to grips with the effects of the present war. The draft was only approved by the Americans. In contrast, the Soviets refused to discuss the issue and saw no necessity for this kind of declaration on account of the Tripartite Treaty of January 1942.

During the Tehran Conference from 28 November to 1 December, "Iran" was only a side topic. The Iranian leadership was mostly marginalised during the meeting. They were neither officially received nor honoured by the Allied delegations with a joint visit. Roosevelt granted the Shah and representatives of the Iranian government a one-hour meeting on 30 November. The meeting essentially dealt with Iran's economic problems due to the occupation and the desire to attract the USA to a stronger and longer-term commitment to alleviate these problems.[7] The Shah only spoke with Winston Churchill in passing. Stalin was the only leader to visit the Shah in his palace for a two-hour meeting. The Iranian cabinet members present were finally able to convince Stalin to officially acknowledge Iran's contribution in the fight against the Axis powers as well as the provisions of the agreement of January 1942 in a declaration.[8]

Already the previous day, the Iranian government had brought specific ideas to American and British diplomats for a joint declaration of the Big Three. These included the recognition of Iranian war efforts, the guarantee of Iran's independence, consideration of the country's economic needs during future peace negotiations, the surrender of all domestic matters to the Iranian government and its ministries and, finally, material compensation for the war efforts rendered. These demands were sent in identical memoranda to the three foreign ministries on 1 December.[9] During the Tehran Conference, the Americans were the ones who took up Iran's concerns and brought them up during the consultations. They prepared a new declaration draft. It affirmed the good relationship between the Big Three and Iran, commended the efforts of the country in the present war, confirmed the validity of the Tripartite Treaty and promised economic help after the war. The American draft was accepted by the British. The Iranian government, however, had to work towards Soviet approval of the declaration themselves.

On the evening of 1 December 1943, at the conclusion of the Tehran Conference, only the English version of the declaration draft was briefly discussed by the three government heads and then signed. Stalin agreed to a declaration although he had rejected it just a few weeks before. This reversal of opinion was possibly due to the desire to use the first meeting of the Big Three and the joint Iran Declaration for propaganda purposes. Stalin was thus able to present himself in Tehran as an equal power to the US president, even though his country had been considered the pariah of the international community of nations only a few years prior. Stalin also received a firm commitment to open up a second front on the European continent— a great success for the Soviets.

The Tehran Conference was celebrated worldwide as a milestone in the struggle against the Axis powers. Hope burgeoned that an agreement of the Big Three might bring about an early end to the war and help put in place a stable post-war order.

Despite the declaration, the Iranian government demanded the withdrawal of all foreign troops only a few weeks after the conference. With its declaration of war on Germany in September of 1943 and its announced accession to the United Nations, Iran had fulfilled all of the Allies' demands from the summer of 1941. They further advanced their arguments before the conference in Yalta in February 1945, but these were also to no avail. Iran had to subordinate its interests to the Allied war effort and to the security interests of the British and the Soviets.

Allied and Iranian lines of confrontation

By the next meetings of the Big Three in Yalta and Potsdam, the relationship of the Allies in Iran and the operations of the Iranian Parliament had changed profoundly. An important cause was the competition for Iranian oil. The Soviets also aspired to secure oil extraction concessions from Iran parallel to American overtures. Soviet geologists used their occupation of Iran's Northern provinces to explore for suitable oil reserves. The State Defence Committee (GKO) prepared a draft for an Iranian-Soviet extraction agreement in 1944.

The foreign concession demands led to a confrontation which reached its climax in the autumn of 1944 and irreparably damaged relations between the Allies in Iran. Resistance against the approach

American aircraft
for the Soviet Union at
Abadan Airport, Iran

of the Allies became more and more considerable inside Iran as well. Pro-American and pro-Soviet politicians who endorsed a concession for the USA or the Soviets, respectively, were opposed by pro-British and strictly nationalist forces. On 2 December 1944, the Iranian Parliament, at the initiative of Mohammad Mossadegh, passed a law that forbid any Iranian government from granting an oil extraction concession to a foreign power before the end of the war. The competition for Iranian oil, except for the British concession area in the South, was thus temporarily at an end without an Allied power being granted oil rights. The growing Allied tensions in Iran starting in 1944 affected the relations of the Big Three in a way that is not to be underestimated. In direct talks involving differing visions for the global post-war order and fundamentally different political systems, the limits of what the Big Three could achieve soon became clear. Roosevelt's goal of free, sovereign and unified nations was met with resistance by both Churchill and Stalin, who in different manifestations aspired to a continuation of the policy of zones of influence, especially in Iran. The mutual mistrust of all three main allies, which was slightly alleviated in Tehran at the end of 1943, grew again with the imminent end of the war. The competition for Iranian oil concessions exacerbated this, but also the partition of the Northern provinces by the Soviets and the delaying tactics used by the British in expanding the trans-Iranian aid corridor.

Dashed expectations:
the Potsdam Conference

A few days after the end of the war in Europe, the Iranian cabinet again called upon the governments in Washington, Moscow and London to withdraw all troops from the country. The British and Soviets bilaterally agreed that the six-month withdrawal deadline would only begin with the end of hostilities in the Pacific theatre. In contrast, the USA, under its new President Harry S. Truman, made it clear that it wanted to withdraw its troops as quickly as possible. Considering this scenario, the Iranians attempted to again involve the USA in the Anglo-Soviet withdrawal issue. It was the Iranians' foremost concern to liberate their country from all foreign troops and to regain its full sovereignty. At the beginning of July of 1945, the Iranian government requested to the American ambassador in Tehran that the US government should use the upcoming meeting of the Big Three to push through a stop of all foreign influence, especially in light of the upcoming parliamentary elections in Iran at year's end.[10] The Shah also consulted with the US ambassador in Iran. He complained that the Soviets in the north of the country were making massive efforts to influence the current government cabinet and to place Soviet-friendly members in the future parliament.[11] Iran was experiencing a parliamentary crisis and had no functioning government in the summer of 1945. US diplomats assessed this situation to be the result of the ongoing Anglo-Soviet rivalry and a danger to the newly won peace. The American delegation should therefore openly and comprehensively cover the Iran question with both Allies at the Potsdam Conference.

Accordingly, the presence of troops in Iran was discussed on 21 July. The British delegation submitted a draft outlining a three-stage troop withdrawal. It was decided that British and Soviet troops would immediately withdraw their troops from the capital Tehran. The USA agreed to withdraw the rest of its troops from Iran within 60 days. Only 1,500 soldiers were to remain at the airfields near Tehran and in Abadan.[12]

Despite these concessions, the Potsdam Conference was rather disappointing to Iran. The complete withdrawal of troops was further delayed, and it was feared that Iran would again be subjected to dealing with the British and the Soviets alone. Another problem was that no other issues regarding Iran were resolved but postponed to the following meeting. Still, British troops were the first to leave Tehran on 7 August 1945. By the time all foreign troops had left the Iranian capital, in mid-September, the greatest and most devastating war in the history of humanity had ended—on 2 September 1945, Japan surrendered. The USA insisted that this day marked the beginning of the term for the agreed troop withdrawal as stated in the Tripartite Treaty. Accordingly, the withdrawal would have to be completed by 2 March 1946. The Iranian government also referred to this fixed time period in memoranda to London and Moscow.[13]

The Iran crisis becomes an open conflict
between the Allies

The ongoing occupation and the Soviet influence in the northern provinces of Iran considerably worsened relations between the Allies at the foreign ministers' conferences that took place starting in September of 1945. The conferences were supposed to clear up all pending issues regarding the post-war order. Just as many other nations, Iran did not participate in settling issues that were relevant to its own people. The escalating crisis in Iran thus remained a smouldering conflict between the British, the Americans and the Soviets.

During the meeting in London, the Soviets refused to discuss the Iran question. This occurred with the suggestion that sufficient treaty provisions existed and that these would be observed. The Soviets' refusal to negotiate aroused the mistrust of the British and the Americans, but also that of the Iranians, with regard to Moscow's intentions. As a reaction to the failure they perceived at the London meeting, the Iranian Parliament decided in mid-October 1945 to postpone parliamentary elections until after the complete withdrawal of all foreign troops. This step cemented Iran's domestic political crisis. At the same time, this was an affront to the Soviet leadership in Moscow, since the current composition of the parliament was regarded as hostile to the Soviets. Therefore, the Soviets had already begun to groom numerous pro-Soviet parliamentary candidates in the Northern provinces in the summer of 1945 and to push forward the founding of the Azerbaijani Democratic Party. At the beginning of October, the Soviet leadership decided to give military support to the Iranian province of Azerbaijan, which was striving towards autonomy. At the same time, albeit to a lesser degree, the Soviet government also promoted the autonomy efforts of Iranian Kurds and the founding of the Kurdish Republic of Mahabad. The Iranian government was not able to quell either of these autonomy movements, because the Soviets had forbidden the deployment of Iranian troops in the provinces by referring to security risks to the oil producing regions in Baku.

On 23 November, the USA sent a protest memorandum to the Soviet Union.[14] It criticised Soviet interference with the internal affairs of Iran and reminded Moscow of the joint Tehran Declaration of 1943. Moscow denied any wrongdoing or unlawful involvement and emphasised that the will for autonomy was a purely Iranian domestic affair.

The Conference of Foreign Ministers in Moscow in December also failed to solve these issues. On the contrary, like the conference in London, the USA, Great Britain and the Soviet Union were only able to agree on mutual confirmation of what had already happened on the ground in many countries. In Iran, however, no clear balance of power had been determined. US Secretary of State James F. Byrnes informed Stalin during the meeting in Moscow that the Shah and the Tehran government had suggested putting the Iran question on the agenda of the first General Assembly of the United Nations. Neither the Americans nor the British thought this a good idea, although for different reasons. The Soviets had absolutely no interest at all. The British alternative suggestion of an Anglo-American-Soviet commission to resolve the Iran crisis was also rejected by the Soviets. It was also met with massive resistance from the Iranians, who felt reminded of former times of imperial interference.

On 19 January 1946, during the first General Assembly of the United Nations, the Iranian delegation delivered a letter of protest to the Security Council. It accused the Soviet Union of interference in the domestic affairs of Iran. The Security Council referred the issue back to the conflicting parties and requested to be kept informed of the status of the negotiations. However, bilateral talks in Moscow did not yield any results. The term for the withdrawal of troops thus lapsed at the beginning of March. Further Iranian protest at the United Nations in mid-March ensured that the issue remained in focus on an international level. At the same time, the USA openly and increasingly unequivocally showed that they were on Iran's side of the issue and did not shy away from a dispute with the Soviet Union. The prospect of a confrontation finally caused Stalin to relent. On 4 April 1946, Moscow and Tehran signed a treaty which regulated the complete withdrawal of Soviet troops from Northern Iran. By summer, the Soviets, according to the estimates of Western observers, had indeed left Iran.

Thus, Iran had achieved its greatest objective—the withdrawal of all foreign troops. The country was also able to regain its sovereignty, apart from the Anglo-Iranian Oil Company. However, this did not occur through a reconciliation of interests of the Big Three. The events of the beginning of 1946 are more reminiscent of a political showdown won by the USA, liberating Iran from Soviet influence. | DC

Notes

1 This article is based on the author's dissertation, see Forsmann 2009. This text exclusively quotes recent literature and published sources. / 2 Saikal 2019, 29. / 3 Azimi 2008, 111–12. / 4 Ibid., 71–72, 93 et seq.; Katouzian 2013, 67. / 5 FRUS 1941, The British Commonwealth, The Near East and Africa, doc. 418. / 6 Butler 2015, 6–7. / 7 FRUS 1943, The Conferences at Cairo and Tehran, doc. 370. / 8 Bomati and Nahavandi 2013, 116. / 9 FRUS 1943, The Conferences at Cairo and Tehran, docs. 390 and 399. / 10 FRUS 1945, The Conference of Berlin (The Potsdam Conference), vol. 1, doc. 634. / 11 Ibid., vol. 2, doc. 1327. / 12 Ibid., docs. 1335–37. / 13 FRUS 1945, The Near East and Africa, doc. 372. / 14 Ibid., doc. 419.

A Country in Search of its Erstwhile Grandeur: France and the Potsdam Conference

Matthias Simmich

When General de Gaulle, cheered by thousands of Parisians, paraded down the Champs-Elysées on 26 August 1944, the German occupation of France was finally coming to an end. The country was regaining its sovereignty, and no one embodied France's *grandeur* and *gloire* more clearly and confidently than Charles de Gaulle. "The enthusiastic crowd roared with joy at being", the later Foreign Minister Georges Bidault described the mood at the time. "It saw and heard the victorious leaders only; ... everyone called out 'Long Live de Gaulle.'"[1] The general, in fact, did his utmost to retrieve the lost position of France in the world.

German resistance quickly collapsed after the Allied landing in Normandy on 6 June 1944 and the American-French landing in southern France on 15 August. Around the turn of 1944–45, all French territory, with a few exceptions, was finally liberated from the Wehrmacht. On 23 October 1944, the Provisional Government of the French Republic under de Gaulle was officially recognised by the Soviet Union, Great Britain and the USA. In November, France received a place in the European Advisory Commission in London, which dealt with the conditions for German surrender and the post-war occupation regime.[2] At the Yalta Conference in February 1945, France was finally granted, albeit in absentia, its own zone of occupation in Germany. When the Wehrmacht capitulated unconditionally at Reims on 7 May 1945, a French representative was present as well. With the Berlin Declaration of 5 June 1945, the four major victorious powers of the Second World War jointly assumed supreme authority over German territory. France seemed to have arrived among them.

However, when the Potsdam Conference at Cecilienhof Palace ended on 2 August 1945, there was no French representative to sign the final communiqué. Point II.B called upon the country to accept the resolutions, "to adopt this text and to join in establishing the Council".[3] The Allies obviously treated France as a "second-class victorious power".

← Liberation celebrations
on the Champs-Élysées,
26 August 1944

The situation in France

France was among the victorious powers of the Second World War on paper, but not on the same footing as the Big Three. This became obvious when the country was not invited to the Yalta Conference in February 1945. Only at Churchill's insistence did *La Grande Nation* receive its own zone of occupation in Germany. France was granted voting right in the Allied Control Council, but only because Churchill and Roosevelt managed to overcome Stalin's fierce resistance.[4] On the international stage, France was a lightweight that depended on the Allies' benevolence. De Gaulle tried to disguise this subordinate status from the French public by repeated displays of ostentatious self-confidence and by acting in his own interest.

He was an uncomfortable conversation partner for the Allies, and his relationship with British Prime Minister Churchill was always tense. As for American President Roosevelt, who found de Gaulle high-handed and impertinent, one could almost speak of enmity. Stalin only met de Gaulle in December 1944. For the Soviet dictator, it was not the personality of de Gaulle that mattered, but France's real power. France, according to Stalin, "had contributed little to this war" and de Gaulle acted "as though he were the head of a great state, whereas, in fact, he actually commands little power"—no wonder Paris and Moscow failed to develop a close relationship.[5]

If the Allies wanted France at their side, however, there was no way around accepting and involving de Gaulle. His outstanding achievement was to keep France at war—even after its rout in 1940. Until 1944, this admittedly involved perseverance with limited resources. But after the Normandy landings, French troops actively participated in their country's liberation and even played an increasingly important role in the advance towards Germany. At the end of the war, France had 18 divisions with approximately 1,300,000 men under arms. De Gaulle earned even greater merit by preserving French sovereignty and allowing his country to assume a potential powerful role as a major European great power.

In his capacity as President of the Provisional Government of the French Republic, exercised since 3 June 1944, de Gaulle also managed to reconcile the country with itself and to restore the nation's self-confidence.[6] His government of national unity, in which all political currents and Resistance groups were represented, was supported by the great majority of the population. The agenda now was to rebuild political life after the disgraceful end of the Third Republic in 1940 and the subsequent reign of the Vichy regime. To this end, the government in Paris had to assert its power across the country, and it managed to do so by sending commissioners with extensive powers. The power vacuum created during the war was removed, and the authority of the state, restored.[7]

In the run-up to the general elections on 21 October 1945, in which a vote was also taken on whether France should receive a new

Charles de Gaulles as
President of the Provisional
Government, speaking
to the citizens of Cherbourg,
20 August 1944

Henri Giraud, Franklin
D. Roosevelt, Charles
de Gaulle and Winston
Churchill at the
Casablanca Conference

A TOUS LES FRANÇAIS

La France a perdu une bataille !
Mais la France n'a pas perdu la guerre !

Des gouvernants de rencontre ont pu capituler, cédant à la panique, oubliant l'honneur, livrant le pays à la servitude. Cependant, rien n'est perdu !

Rien n'est perdu, parce que cette guerre est une guerre mondiale. Dans l'univers libre, des forces immenses n'ont pas encore donné. Un jour, ces forces écraseront l'ennemi. Il faut que la France, ce jour-là, soit présente à la victoire. Alors, elle retrouvera sa liberté et sa grandeur. Tel est mon but, mon seul but !

Voilà pourquoi je convie tous les Français, où qu'ils se trouvent, à s'unir à moi dans l'action, dans le sacrifice et dans l'espérance.

Notre patrie est en péril de mort.
Luttons tous pour la sauver !

VIVE LA FRANCE !

C. de Gaulle.

GÉNÉRAL DE GAULLE

QUARTIER GÉNÉRAL
4, CARLTON GARDENS,
LONDON S.W.1

AXOME Développements / PIXOLAVE Signalétiques

constitution (Fourth Republic), the political landscape was rearranged. The *Mouvement Républicain Populaire* (MRP), the Popular Republican Movement, was founded as a Christian Democratic Party, with de Gaulle as its figurehead. The Socialists (SFIO) were close to the MRP. Their political counterpart, the Communist Party (PC), had been banned in September 1939 on grounds of its support for the German-Soviet non-aggression pact; it now became the strongest force in the country.

De Gaulle had not forgotten the French Communists' championing of the Soviet Union in 1939 and 1940. Because of its strong ties with Moscow, he feared that, even after the war, the Communist Party might take on the role of Stalin's fifth column and, where necessary and in cases of doubt, attach greater weight to the International's than to France's interests.[8]

Due to their leading role in the Resistance, the Communists enjoyed great support among the population.[9] Not least because of the declining French economy and general social misery, a large majority of the French shared the PC's goals of nationalising banks and key industries as well as the desire for social reforms. From the first post-war elections, the Communists emerged as the strongest party, winning 26 per cent of the vote.[10] The Franco-Soviet Assistance Pact, which de Gaulle signed in December 1944, should be understood in this context as a signal of the intention to integrate the French Communist Party. Good relations with Moscow were in the interests of most French—and in de Gaulle's, too, if France were to play a self-determined role among the "Great Powers".

France's foreign policy objectives ahead of the Potsdam Conference

The basic objectives of French policy after liberation had already been formulated in the National Resistance Council's action programme of 15 March 1944: "The defence of the nation's political and economic independence, to restore to France her power, her greatness and her universal mission."[11] In terms of foreign policy, this translated into an active policy intended to demonstrate the French claim to great power status.

France faced two fundamental foreign policy problems in 1945, both equally pressing: 1. How should the defeated Germany be dealt with and how can this former opponent be prevented from resurging? 2. What status was to be given to the French colonies and what would their future look like?

France's occupation zone gave it direct formative opportunities in defeated post-war Germany.[12] The main goal was to ensure French security, and it was to be achieved by weakening the former opponent and punishing those responsible for the war. To this end, Paris sought to decentralise Germany. The idea was to forestall a unified central

De Gaulle's appeal of 18 June 1940, poster distributed in the UK on 3 August 1940

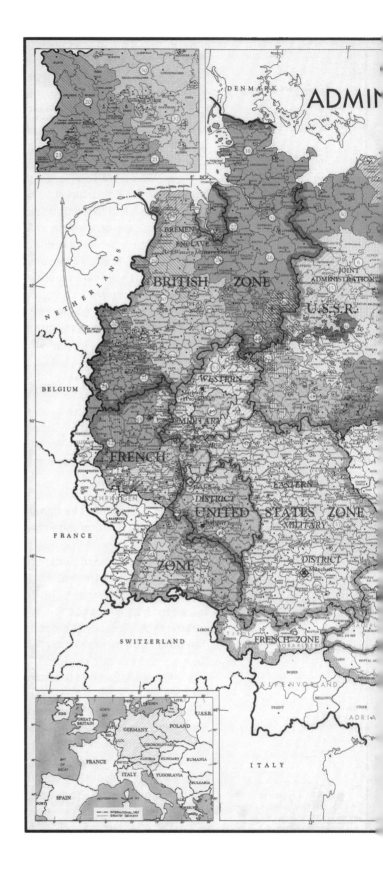

Map of German administrative
districts (July 1944) with
occupation zones in Germany
and Austria, 1945

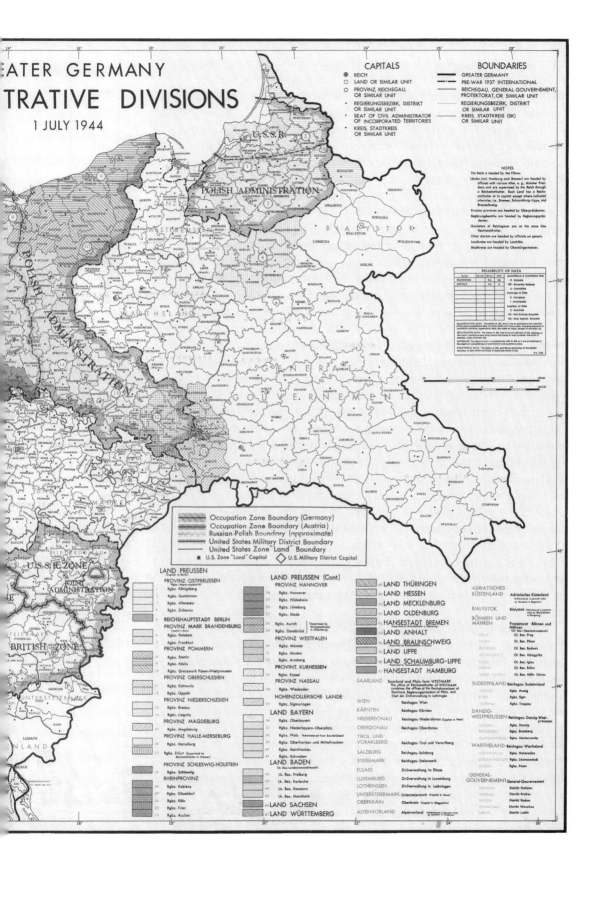

state and to instead create several German sub-states based on historical models.[13] At the time of the Potsdam Conference, however, France was alone in demanding the systematic weakening of Germany. The other Allies had already jettisoned this goal at the Yalta Conference.

Also, former territorial demands for pushing France's "natural borders" up to the Rhine were reasserted and made public in the so-called Massigli plan. Here, French Ambassador to London, René Massigli, had outlined the basic principles of military security and economic recovery relevant to France's policy towards Germany. The plan was to occupy the Rhineland, the Palatinate and the Saar region and to place the Ruhr region under international control. It further provided for French control of some regions on the right bank of the Rhine around Mannheim and Frankfurt am Main, which were to remain part of Germany under constitutional law.[14] De Gaulle even claimed that this was "the political structure which was natural to [Germany]"; in it, "[e]ach region would have recovered its former autonomous statehood".[15] Germany was to be controlled and held down by awarding special status to the Rhineland (military occupation, creation of a separate Rhine state), by internationalising the Ruhr area (control over Germany's "war smithy") and by politically separating the Saar region and economically affiliating it to France.[16]

The French government's radical anti-German attitude under de Gaulle, fed by the experience of three wars within seventy years, led to a deep scepticism towards the neighbouring country: "France also notes that, in the space of one man's lifetime, its soil has been invaded three times, each time more ruinously and horribly than the last, and always by the same enemy. With Germany, which chronically produces Bismarcks, Wilhelm IIs and Hitlers, there can be no peace without material guarantees, not just words."[17] The demand for extensive reparations, intended to contribute to France's economic recovery and strengthen it vis-à-vis Germany, was to be seen in this context. Also, German prisoners of war were to remain in France for a longer period to support the country's reconstruction.[18]

However, the tough stance against Germany ("concept of dominance"), which was supported by the Communists, changed at the end of 1945, when de Gaulle had to realise that in this regard he could count on little support from the Allies. Even if the Franco-German rapprochement ("integration concept") was still to take place, a rethinking was already becoming evident during a visit that de Gaulle paid to the French zone of occupation in October 1945. He there spoke of "healing wounds" and the future need for French and Germans "to cooperate". In a conciliatory note, he looked towards the future: "the River Rhine, our river, was a barrier, a frontier, a line of battle. Today ... the Rhine can again play the role that history and nature gave to it. It can again become a link for the West."[19]

France not only made a claim to absolute dominance over its defeated neighbour but also to global leadership. The idea of the *Union française*, which de Gaulle had already presented at the Brazzaville Conference in January 1944, promoted the colonies' equality with the mother country.[20] During the war, the French colonies had been important allies and, at times, the only place from which the struggle against Germany could continue. De Gaulle held out the prospect of reorganising relations between the French motherland and its colonies. He did so in order to acknowledge their soldiers' contribution to the war and to further rely on their support, but also to develop a sustainable concept for the post-war period. Although independence was not yet in the offing, the colonies were to be accorded a certain degree of autonomy.[21]

In 1945, however, the idea of gradually emancipating the colonies came too late. In Syria and Lebanon, which had been French mandates since the end of the First World War, outbreaks of violence occurred among the population. Some of these outbreaks were very strong and caused great tensions between London and Paris—the British General Staff even drew up plans for military intervention. Naturally, this boded ill for negotiations in Potsdam, where de Gaulle was dependent on British support.

But de Gaulle also failed in his endeavour to put Franco-American relations on a new footing. Efforts to meet with US President Truman ahead of the Potsdam Conference were thwarted. The French government could thus not send a delegation of its own, nor even observers, to the conference, and remained dependent on Britain's goodwill. Despite difficulties with de Gaulle, Churchill was France's only real advocate in Potsdam—maybe because of the similar geopolitical situation of the two countries, which both had irretrievably lost their former *grandeur* and world power status.[22]

France and the Potsdam resolutions

In a total of 7 out of 13 sessions, France was an issue or was mentioned at Potsdam. In some of the negotiations, it was clear to all the participants that without French representatives, there could be no thorough discussion of the problems. During the seventh plenary session, for instance, which dealt with occupied Vienna, Stalin inquired about the situation in the French sector, but there was no one who could give an answer.[23]

In the first and seventh session, the issue of Syria and Lebanon was brought up at Stalin's urging. In the run-up to the conference, the above tensions there had occasioned an exchange of notes between London, Washington and Paris. Despite the Anglo-French conflict on issues affecting the two countries, Churchill acted as an advocate for France. Aware of the great importance de Gaulle attached to the Levant as the "platform for the liberation of Europe", the British Prime Minister refused to make decisions about Syria and Lebanon in the absence of France.[24] There is thus no mention of the two countries in the final communiqué.

However, Churchill's clear commitment to the French ally was by no means altruistic. France and Great Britain fought as colonial powers for their non-European territories. Like de Gaulle, Churchill was aware that if the peoples' right to self-determination, as enshrined in the UN Charter, were to apply to the colonies, both countries would foreseeably lose their colonial empires. Churchill, therefore, can hardly be considered to have acted as an "honest broker" on this question in discussions with the Big Three.

During the negotiations, he repeatedly raised the issue before Stalin of having to ask questions to the French government. But the Soviet dictator never acquiesced, arguing that other countries would then also have to be consulted on issues affecting them.

France's desire for territorial growth, which was known to all delegations, was never discussed. In spite of de Gaulle's support for Polish territorial demands against Germany (expressed during his visit to Moscow in December 1944), his own hope that Stalin would acknowledge French border revisions in the West was not fulfilled. Eventually, de Gaulle had to accept that what was at stake were spheres of influence: Stalin claimed Poland for the Soviet sphere of influence and, despite the French Communists' strong position, would stay out of matters concerning France.[25]

Neither was the French demand for an internationalisation of the Ruhr area included in the protocol. This is all the more astonishing because US President Truman made similar demands regarding German rivers and waterways. Only Tangier in Morocco was mentioned: it was to be placed under international administration and discussed at the next summit, this time with the participation of France.[26]

On France's credit side, there was the decision to form a Council of Foreign Ministers involving a French representative (Section II.1) and intended to draw up peace treaties with the former Axis powers (Section X). On the other hand, resolutions concerning the removal of reparations from Germany (Section IV) and the general political and economic principles for its treatment (Section III A and B) were determined without France being able to comment on them. France was neither involved in the division of the German Navy and merchant fleet, nor was it asked to put forward arguments when it came to dealing with Franco's Spain, its direct neighbour (Section X).

Just how self-evident the Big Three in Potsdam claimed the right to decide on matters regarding France and other countries becomes clear in an episode from the meeting on 20 July. London was jointly designated as the future seat of the Council of Foreign Ministers. Truman, who was aware that this decision should have been taken together with the other members of this body, succinctly noted: "I think that in due time our three Foreign Ministers will be joined by the Foreign Ministers of China and France."[27]

At their session on 31 July 1945, the foreign ministers decided to inform France by telegram about the "political principles to govern the treatment of Germany in the initial control period" and to invite the country to take part in the Council of Foreign Ministers.[28] In keeping with this, American Ambassador to France, Jefferson Caffery, only informed the French government of the Potsdam resolutions on 31 July and 1 August, shortly before the end of the conference. In several spoon-fed notes, he briefed Foreign Minister Bidault about individual decisions already taken by the Big Three, mostly adding the wish that France should accept them ("the Government of France will be able to associate itself with these principles.").[29]

The French answers were given by submitting several memoranda on 7 August 1945. De Gaulle asked Bidault to comment on individual issues in six letters. With the exception of one letter regarding the persecution of war criminals (Section III.A.4), which the French government fully agreed to, these letters expressed undiluted criticism. In some cases, there were serious concerns that sounded less negative only because they were diplomatically camouflaged.[30] In particular, the establishment of a central German government was rejected as "inadmissible".[31] Bidault angrily remonstrated with the three Allies for deciding on a part of the German border—the border with Poland—in the absence of a victorious power, arguing that "the problem of the borders of Germany should be dealt with in its entirety and considered jointly."[32]

Given these clearly negative answers, it is all the more surprising that American Ambassador Caffery came to a rather positive assessment. In a telegram, he briefed the US Secretary of State that Bidault's replies were to be understood as substantial consent and had a negative ring only because of expressions such as "reservations" and "regret".[33]

Unlike their government, which was indignant about the Potsdam resolutions, the French people received these rather well. Daily newspapers reported on the summit in a benevolent and neutral tone, and journalists were amazed at the discrepancy between public opinion and statements of government officials: "All nations are happy about the results achieved, which are remarkable. All governments except ours, it seems, are complimenting themselves on the agreement that has been negotiated on key issues."[34] The author of these lines had accurately perceived the situation. Indeed, already in the run-up to the conference, de Gaulle had made it clear how he intended to deal with decisions taken by the Big Three alone: "We have informed our Allies and we have said publicly that France would, of course, be bound by nothing that she had not had the opportunity to discuss and approve on the same grounds as the other nations."[35]

Conclusion

During the conference, French daily newspapers regularly reported on the progress of the negotiations. Partly accompanied by photos, these articles were no less detailed than, for example, the reports published in the British or American press. However, reports on France's domestic political problems soon prevailed again, all the more since little material from the conference was leaked to the outside world at large—even journalists on site faced the same problem. In particular, the lawsuits against Marshal Philippe Pétain and Pierre Laval as the Vichy regime's major representatives and collaborators with Nazi Germany soon became the focus of news coverage and very quickly pushed Potsdam out of the headlines.[36] Only when General de Gaulle, from 22 to 25 August 1945, paid a visit to President Truman in Washington did Potsdam become a news topic again—as it did whenever the Council of Foreign Ministers would meet.

After the end of the Conference, France had no time to be angry or grieved. Decolonisation continued unabated, and the French army left Syria and Lebanon, the first countries to be granted independence, by the summer of 1946.[37] The attempt to keep Indochina as a colony in the "Union française", on the other hand, failed in 1954. After a long, bloody war, Algeria finally gained independence in 1962.

Likewise, France had to give up its resistance against the establishment of a central German government. In the face of the escalating conflict between East and West, the tough and unyielding stance France had initially taken on Germany (for instance, by refusing to accept displaced persons from the former Eastern territories of Germany in its zone of occupation) was superseded by a constructive approach. While population, in the other three occupation zones, grew between 12 and 20 per cent, it only increased by about 4 per cent in the French zone, which meant that fewer people than before the outbreak of the war lived here—with all the economic consequences.[38] In March of 1948, Paris approved the merger of the French with
the British and American zones of occupation into the Trizone—a year later, it would back the foundation of the Federal Republic of Germany. The attempt to annex the Saar region was abandoned after a referendum in 1956.

At the time of the Potsdam Conference, General de Gaulle was his country's outstanding personality. Despite all the setbacks, he managed to bring France back to the "Concert of the Great Powers". Similar to Churchill during the war, de Gaulle used elaborate public speeches or proclamations to gather support for his policies. Given France's economic and military weakness, he would often have no choice but to rely on the power of his word. Historical references always played a major role here, even in the run-up to the Potsdam Conference, when he congratulated America on its Independence Day in 1945, emphasising what both nations had in common: "We are

old friends. Our two countries have never fought against each other. We have been on your side from the beginning. We saw the birth of your strength, and we saw it grow when first you came to the aid of old Europe. We have just seen that strength spread over the battlefields forever glorious of this war."[39]

With the neat allusion to France's support in the American War of Independence, de Gaulle seemed to imply that it was now up to the United States to support France. His reasoning was based on the triad of past (German threat, France fighting against Hitler from the very beginning), present (victim, destruction and military strengthening of the country, zone of occupation in Germany, member of the United Nations Security Council) and future (Communist danger, Germany's depression, peacekeeping, balance of power in Europe).

There is a touch of tragedy in the fact that de Gaulle, despite attempts to influence the outcome of the Big Three's negotiations according to his own wishes, did not manage to assert himself due to the relative economic and military weakness of his country as compared with his allies. It was not possible for him to create a fait accompli, as the USSR had done by ceding German territory to Poland. Instead, he invoked arguments such as the common struggle against Germany and the sacrifice and plight of France. De Gaulle appealed to his allies, asking them to support his demands for economic, financial and territorial reparation.

What filled him with hope was the fact that Britain and the United States would not be able to do without France, all their differences notwithstanding. Only a reinvigorated France would guarantee a minimum of balance in Europe and prevent the continent from being further drawn into the Soviet sphere of dominance. Eventually, Washington and London accepted de Gaulle's demeanour, even if they considered it pompous and presumptuous.

It is doubtful whether France's participation would have significantly changed the outcome of the Potsdam Conference. In the end, France had no choice but to content itself with the "fiction of a Great Power".[40] Admittedly, this may seem sobering, but given the country's humiliating 1940 defeat, it is still a remarkable foreign policy success. For the *Grande Nation* was now represented on the major international bodies: the Council of Foreign Ministers, the Allied Control Council and the United Nations Security Council. Both to France and de Gaulle, this restored a sense of former grandeur. Only in the years that followed did it become apparent that France was willing to maintain and develop its position through its veto right in the United Nations Security Council, the Council of Foreign Ministers and the Allied Control Council. |CN

Notes

1 Bidault 1967, 54–55. / **2** See Deuerlein 1963, 182–87. / **3** Communiqué (Report on the Tripartite Conference of Berlin), https://history.state.gov/historicaldocuments/frus-1945Berlinv02/d1384 [accessed 29 January 2020]. What is meant here is the "Council of Foreign Ministers", which was supposed to prepare peace treaties with the former Axis powers. / **4** See Fischer 1968, 113–15. / **5** Ibid., 19 and 114. / **6** Defrance and Pfeil 2011, 41. / **7** Rémond 1994, 394–96 and 411–15. / **8** Lowe 2015, 343–44. / **9** Rioux 1987, 54; the number of party members increased from 380,000 to 800,000 between 1945 and the end of 1946. / **10** Kershaw 2016, 668–71; Results of the National Assembly elections on 21 October 1945: Communists (PCF) 26.2 per cent, Christian-Democratic Republicans (MRP) 24.9 per cent, Socialists (SFIO) 23.8 per cent, Moderate Parties (Conservative) 13.2 per cent, "Radicals" (Liberal) 11.1 per cent. As a result, a tripartite alliance of Communists, Socialists and MRP was established under de Gaulle's leadership. / **11** Quoted from: Grosser 1986, 22; Art. II.1, adopted by the *Conseil National de la Résistance*. The main Resistance groups, political parties, unions and the press were represented in this central body. / **12** Deuerlein 1963, 79–82. / **13** De Gaulle 1959, 46 and 377. / **14** Tyrell 1987, 522–23. / **15** De Gaulle 1971, 227. / **16** Woyke 1987, 19. / **17** Bidault 1967, 84. / **18** Koop 2005, 144–77. Between 1945 and 1948, a total of around 1,000,000 German prisoners of war were imprisoned in France. / **19** Poidevin 1983, 21–22; the two competing concepts are explained in Loth 1983, 28–33. / **20** The "France of 100 million inhabitants" was to grant the same rights and obligations to all its citizens, regardless of race and religion. / **21** Kreis 2015, 252–55. In his opening speech on 30 January 1944, de Gaulle justified his rejection of autonomy by invoking the "progress of civilisation", which would only be possible with the help of France. / **22** Grosser 1986, 22. / **23** FRUS 1945, The Conference of Berlin (The Potsdam Conference), vol. 2, 310. / **24** Ausubel 1946, 208. Speech before the National Assembly on 15 May 1945. / **25** Beevor 2012, 98. / **26** See Protocol of the Proceedings of the Berlin Conference, Section XVI, https://history.state.gov/historicaldocuments/frus1945Berlinv02/d1383 [accessed 31 January 2020]. / **27** Fischer 1968, 242. / **28** FRUS 1945, The Conference of Berlin (The Potsdam Conference), vol. 2, 500. / **29** All memorandums in: FRUS 1945, The Conference of Berlin (The Potsdam Conference), vol. 2, Nos. 1395–1400, 1543–47. / **30** The exact French wording can be found in: Documents français 1947, 7–11. / **31** De Gaulle 1984, 52. / **32** Documents français 1947, 11, which reads: "le problème des frontières de l'Allemagne forme un tout et qu'il ne saurait recevoir de solution qu'après avoir été examiné en commun." / **33** FRUS 1945, The Conference of Berlin (The Potsdam Conference), vol. 2, no. 1405, 1550–51. / **34** *Ce Soir* (Paris), 5–6 August 1945, 1: "Tous les peuples se réjouissent des résultats obtenus, qui sont considérables. Tous les gouvernements, hormis le nôtre, semble-t-il se félicitent de l'accord réalisé sur les problèmes essentiels." / **35** Broadcast address 2 February 1945, in Ausubel 1946, 55. / **36** The lawsuit against Pétain began during the Potsdam Conference on 23 July 1945 (and ended on 15 August). Laval's trial lasted from 4 to 9 October 1945. / **37** Chaigne-Oudin 2000, 108–205. / **38** Abelshauser 1983, 130. / **39** De Gaulle 1984, 40–41, "Nous sommes de vieux amis. Jamais nos deux pays ne se sont combattus. Nous étions avec vous dès les commencements. Nous avons vu naître votre force. Nous l'avons vue grandir quand vous êtes venus une première fois au secours de la vieille Europe. Nous venons de la voir se déployer sur les champs de bataille à tout jamais mémorables de cette guerre." / **40** Wolfrum 1991, 62.

Bibliography

Abelshauser 1983
Werner Abelshauser, "Wirtschaft und Besatzungspolitik in der Französischen Zone 1945–1949", in Claus Scharf and Hans-Jürgen Schröder (eds), *Die Deutschland-politik Frankreichs und die Französische Zone 1945–1949*, Wiesbaden 1983

Adams 1995
Henry Adams, *The Education of Henry Adams*, edited with an introduction by Jean Gooder, London 1995

Addison 2004
Paul Addison, "Churchill's Three Careers", in David Cannadine and Roland Quinault (eds), *Winston Churchill in the Twenty-First Century*, Cambridge 2004, 9–25

Addison 2010
Paul Addison, *No Turning Back. The Peacetime Revolutions of Post-War Britain*, Oxford and New York 2010

Adenauer 1951
Konrad Adenauer, "Speech before the Bundestag on 27 September 1951", www.konrad-adenauer.de/quellen/erklaerungen/1951-09-27-regierungserklaerung [accessed 4 March 2020]

Alperowitz 1965
Gar Alperowitz, *Atomic Diplomacy. Hiroshima and Potsdam. The Use of the Atomic Bomb and the American Confrontation with Soviet Power*, New York 1965

Aly and Schlögel 2002
Götz Aly and Karl Schlögel, "Verschiebebahnhof Europa. Völker, die Geschichte leiden. Umsiedlung, Deportation und Vertreibung prägten das 20. Jahrhundert", *Süddeutsche Zeitung*, no. 70 (23–24 March 2002)

Amtsblatt 1946
Mitteilung über die Dreimächtekonferenz von Berlin, 2 August 1945, "Politische Grundsätze", *Amtsblatt des Kontrollrats in Deutschland. Ergänzungsblatt*, no. 1, 1946

Anders 1999
Friedhild-Andrea Anders, *Schlösser in der Stunde Null. Die Berliner und Potsdamer Schlösser während der Kriegs- und Nachkriegszeit*, Potsdam 1999

Angermann and Brüggemann 2018
Norbert Angermann and Karsten Brüggemann, *Geschichte der Baltischen Länder*, Stuttgart 2018

Antipenko 1973
Nikolaj A. Antipenko, In der Hauptrichtung, Berlin (East) 1973

Antoni 1985
Michael Antoni, *Das Potsdamer Abkommen – Trauma oder Chance? Geltung, Inhalt und staatsrechtliche Bedeutung für Deutschland*, Berlin 1985

Arlt and Stang 1995
Kurt Arlt and Werner Stang, "Kampf um Potsdam Ende April 1945", in Werner Stang (ed), *Brandenburg im Jahr 1945. Studien*, Potsdam 1995, 167–94

Asato 2003
Eiko Asato, "Okinawan Identity and Resistance to Militarization and Maldevelopment", in Laura Hein and Mark Selden (eds), *Islands of Discontent. Okinawan Responses to Japanese and American Power*, Lanham 2003

Attlee 1954
Clement R. Attlee, *As It Happened*, London 1954

Ausubel 1946
Nathan Ausubel (ed), *Voices of History 1945–1946*, New York 1946

Awaya 1980
Kentarō Awaya (ed), *Shiryō nihon gendaishi*, vol. 2, Tokyo 1980

Awaya and Kawashima 1994
Kentarō Awaya and Takane Kawashima (eds), *Haisenji zenkoku chian jōhō*, vol. 2, Tokyo 1994

Azimi 2008
Fakhreddin Azimi, *The Quest for Democracy in Iran*, Cambridge 2008

Badstübner 1985
Rolf Badstübner, *Code "Terminal". Die Potsdamer Konferenz*, Berlin (East) 1985

Bailey 1980
Thomas A. Bailey, *A Diplomatic History of the American People*, Englewood Cliffs 1980

Bajohr and Wildt 2009
Frank Bajohr and Michael Wildt (eds), *Volksgemeinschaft. Neue Forschungen zur Gesellschaft des Nationalsozialismus*, Frankfurt am Main 2009

Balabkins 1971
Nicholas Balabkins, *West German Reparations to Israel*, New Brunswick/New Jersey 1971.

Ball 1946
Joseph H. Ball, "How We Planned for the Postwar World", in Jack Goodman (ed), *While You Were Gone. A Report on Wartime Life in the United States*, New York 1946

Barber and Harrison 2015
John Barber and Mark Harrison, "Patriotic War, 1941–1945", in Ronald Grigor Suny (ed), *The Cambridge History of Russia,* vol. III. *The Twentieth Century*, Cambridge et al. 2015

Beer 2011
Mathias Beer, *Flucht und Vertreibung der Deutschen. Voraussetzungen, Verlauf, Folgen*, Munich 2011

Beevor 2012
Antony Beevor, *Berlin 1945. Das Ende*, Munich 2012

Beevor 2014
Antony Beevor, *Der Zweite Weltkrieg*, 3rd ed., Munich 2014

Berg 2005
Manfred Berg, *"The Ticket to Freedom". The NAACP and the Struggle for Black Political Integration*, Gainesville 2005

Berg 2017
Manfred Berg, *Woodrow Wilson und die Neuordnung der Welt. Eine Biografie*, Munich 2017

Bernstein 1975
Barton J. Bernstein, "Roosevelt, Truman, and the Atomic Bomb, 1941–1945. A Reinterpretation", *Political Science Quarterly* 90 (1975), no. 1, 23–69

Bernstein 2007
Barton J. Bernstein, "Introducing the Interpretive Problems of Japan's 1945 Surrender. A Historiographical Essay on Recent Literature in the West", in Tsuyoshi Hasegawa (ed), *The End of the Pacific War. Reappraisals*, Stanford 2007

Bessel 2007
Richard Bessel, "Gewalterfahrung und Opferperspektive. Ein Rückblick auf die beiden Weltkriege des 20. Jahrhunderts in Europa", in Jörg Echternkamp and Stefan Martens (eds), *Der Zweite Weltkrieg in Europa. Erfahrung und Erinnerung*, Paderborn et al. 2007, 253–67

Betzell 1970
Robert Betzell, *Teheran, Yalta, Potsdam. The Secret Protocols*, Hattiesburg 1970

Biddiscombe 2007
Alexander Perry Biddiscombe, *The Denazification of Germany. A History 1945–1950*, Stroud 2007

Bidault 1967
Georges Bidault, *Resistance. The Political Autobiography of Georges Bidault*, London 1967

Biella 1946
Letter from Friedrich Biella to Lotte Dorka, Dankelshausen, 21 December 1946 (private collection Andreas Kossert)

Biewer 1992
Gisela Biewer (ed), *Die Konferenz von Potsdam*, Neuwied and Frankfurt am Main 1992

Binden 1998
Dieter Binden, *Die Polenpolitik der Bonner Republik von Adenauer bis Kohl 1949–1991*, Baden-Baden 1998

Bix 1996
Herbert Bix, "Japan's Delayed Surrender. A Reinterpretation", in Michael J. Hogan (ed), *Hiroshima in History and Memory*, Cambridge 1996

Blake 2009
Kristen Blake, *The US-Soviet Confrontation in Iran, 1945–1962. A Case in the Annals of the Cold War*, Lanham et al. 2009

Bolewski 2004
Andrzej Bolewski, *Z drogi do Poczdamu*, 3rd ed., Warsaw 2004

Bomati and Nahavandi 2013
Yves Bomati and Houchang Nahavandi, *Mohammad Reza Pahlavi. Le dernier Shah 1919–1980*, Paris 2013

Borodziej 2010
Włodzimierz Borodziej, *Geschichte Polens im 20. Jahrhundert*, Munich 2010

Borodziej 2012
Włodzimierz Borodziej, "Versailles und Jalta und Potsdam. Wie Deutsch-Polnisches zu Weltgeschichte wurde", in Hans Henning Hahn and Robert Traba (eds), *Deutsch-polnische Erinnerungsorte*, vol. 3, Paderborn et al. 2012

Borodziej 2015
Włodzimierz Borodziej, "Die enthauptete Nation", *Damals* 2015 (4)

Borodziej 2019
Włodzimierz Borodziej, "Der Verrat von Jalta", in Étienne Francois and Thomas Serrier (eds), *Europa. Geschichte unserer Gegenwart*, vol. 1: *Lebendige Vergangenheit*, Darmstadt 2019, 104–13

Borowski 1990
Tadeusz Borowski, Selected Poems, translated by Tadeusz Pióro with Larry Rafferty and Meryl Natchez, Walnut Creek 1990

Bright Astley 2007
Joan Bright Astley, *The Inner Circle. A View of War at the Top*, Durham 2007

Bullen and Pelly 1986
John M. Keynes, "Our Overseas Financial Prospects" (memorandum of 13 August 1945), in Roger Bullen and Margaret E. Pelly (eds), *Documents on British Policy Overseas*, series I, vol. III: *Britain and America. Negotiation of the United States Loan, 3 August–7 December 1945*, London 1986, annex to no. 6, 28–37

Burridge 1985
Trevor Burridge, *Clement Attlee. A Political Biography*, London 1985

Butler 2015
Susan Butler, *Roosevelt and Stalin. Portrait of a Partnership*, New York 2015

Butow 1954
Robert J. C. Butow, *Japan's Decision to Surrender*, Stanford 1954

Byrnes 1947
James F. Byrnes, *Speaking Frankly*, New York 1947

Calic 2016
Marie-Janine Calic, *Südosteuropa. Weltgeschichte einer Region*, Munich 2016

Cecil 1970
Robert Cecil, "Potsdam and Its Legends", *International Affairs* 46 (1970), no. 3, 455–65

Chafe 1991
William H. Chafe, *The Paradox of Change. American Women in the 20th Century*, Oxford 1991

Chafe 2003
William H. Chafe, *The Unfinished Journey. America Since World War II*, Oxford 2003

Chaigne-Oudin 2009
Anne-Lucie Chaigne-Oudin, *La France dans les jeux d'influences en Syrie et au Liban 1940–1946*, Paris 2009

Chakrabarty 2000
Dipesh Chakrabarty, *Provincializing Europe. Postcolonial Thought and Historical Difference*, Princeton 2000

Charmley 2004
John Charmley, "Churchill and the American Alliance", in David Cannadine and Roland Quinault (eds), *Winston Churchill in the Twenty-First Century*, Cambridge 2004

Ching 2000
Leo Ching, "'Give me Japan and Nothing Else!' Postcoloniality, Identity, and the Traces of Colonialism", *The South Atlantic Quarterly* 99 (2000), no. 4, 763–88

Churchill 1953
Winston S. Churchill, *Triumph and Tragedy*, Cambridge, Mass. 1953

Colville 1986
John Colville, *The Fringes of Power. 10 Downing Street Diaries 1939–1955*, New York et al. 1986

Coulmas 2010
Florian Coulmas, *Hiroshima. Geschichte und Nachgeschichte*, Munich 2010

Craig 1993
Gordon A. Craig, "Churchill and Germany", in Robert Blake and William Roger Louis (eds), *Churchill*, Oxford et al. 1993, 21–40

Craig and Radchenko 2008
Campbell Craig and Sergey Radchenko, *The Atomic Bomb and the Origins of the Cold War*, New Haven et al. 2008

Crossman 1947
Richard H. Crossman, *Palestine Mission. A Personal Record*, London 1947

Cumings 1993
Bruce Cumings, "Japan in the World System", in Andrew Gordon (ed), *Postwar Japan as History*, Berkeley 1993

Dallas 2005
Gregor Dallas, *Poisoned Peace. 1945 – The War that Never Ended*, London 2005

Darwin 2017
John Darwin, *Der Imperiale Traum. Die Globalgeschichte großer Reiche 1400–2000*, 2nd ed., Frankfurt am Main 2017

Davies 2006
Norman Davies, *Europe at War 1939–1945. No Simple Victory*, London 2006

DBPO 1984
Rohan Butler and Margaret E. Pelly (eds), *Documents on British Policy Overseas (DBPO)*, series I, vol. I: *The Conference at Potsdam July–August 1945*, London 1984

DBPO 2010
Patrick Salmon et al. (eds), *Documents on British Policy Overseas (DBPO)*, series III, vol. VII: *German Unification 1989–1990*, London 2010

Dear 1995
Ian Dear (ed), *The Oxford Companion to the Second World War*, Oxford 1995

Defrance and Pfeil 2011
Corinne Defrance and Ulrich Pfeil, *Eine Nachkriegsgeschichte in Europa 1945 bis 1963*, Darmstadt 2011

De Gaulle 1959
Charles de Gaulle, *Mémoires de guerre. Le salut 1944–1946*, Paris 1959

De Gaulle 1971
Charles de Gaulle, *Memoirs of Hope. Renewal and Endeavor*, London 1971

De Gaulle 1984
Charles de Gaulle, *Lettres, notes et carnets, mai 1945–juin 1951*, Paris 1984

Deighton 1990
Anne Deighton, *The Impossible Peace. Britain, the Division of Germany, and the Origins of the Cold War*, Oxford 1990.

Deuerlein 1961
Ernst Deuerlein, *Die Einheit Deutschlands*, vol. 1: *Die Erörterungen und Entscheidungen der Kriegs- und Nachkriegskonferenzen 1941–1949*, 2nd ed., Frankfurt am Main 1961

Deuerlein 1963
Ernst Deuerlein, *Potsdam 1945. Quellen zur Konferenz der "Großen Drei"*, Munich 1963

DeVoto 1944
Bernard DeVoto, "The Easy Chair", *Harper's Magazine*, no. 188, 1 March 1944, 344–47

Dilks 1971
David Dilks (ed), *The Diaries of Sir Alexander Cadogan, 1938–1945*, London 1971

Dilks 1996
David Dilks, "The Conference at Potsdam, 1945", in Gill Bennett (ed) *The End of the War in Europe 1945*, London 1996, 77–100

Dirlik 2001
Arif Dirlik, "'Trapped in History' on the Way to Utopia. East Asia's 'Great War' Fifty Years Later", in Takashi Fujitani et al. (eds), *Perilous Memories. The Asia Pacific War(s)*, Durham et al. 2001, 299–322

Dobbs 2012
Michael Dobbs, *Six Months in 1945. From World War to Cold War*, New York 2012

Documents français 1947
Documents français rélatifs à l'Allemagne (aôut 1945–février 1947), Paris 1947

Documents on Germany 1971
Documents on Germany, 1944–1970, edited by Committee on Foreign Relations, United States Senate, Washington D.C. 1971, 5–8

Dokumente zur Berlinfrage 1987
Dokumente zur Berlinfrage 1944–1966, edited by Forschungsinstitut der Deutschen Gesellschaft für Auswärtige Politik e.V., Bonn in collaboration with the Senate of Berlin, 4th ed., Munich 1987

Douglas 2012
Raymond M. Douglas, *Orderly and Humane. The Expulsion of Germans after the Second World War*, New Haven 2012

Dower 1985
John Dower, *War without Mercy. Race and Power in the Pacific War*, New York 1985

Dower 1993
John W. Dower, *Japan in War and Peace. Selected Essays*, New York 1993

Dower 1999
John W. Dower, *Embracing Defeat. Japan in the Wake of World War II*, New York 1999

Draesner 2014
Ulrike Draesner, *Sieben Sprünge vom Rand der Welt*, Munich 2014

Drechsler 1997
Karl Drechsler, "Die USA des Jahres 1945 und die Potsdamer Konferenz. Herausforderungen – Chancen – vertane Möglichkeiten", in Heiner Timmermann (ed), *Potsdam 1945. Konzept, Taktik, Irrtum?*, Berlin 1997, 29–44

Dülffer 1996
Jost Dülffer, "Wir haben schwere Zeiten hinter uns". Die Kölner Region zwischen Krieg und Nachkriegszeit*, Vierow 1996

Dülffer 1998
Jost Dülffer, *Jalta, 4. Februar 1945. Der Zweite Weltkrieg und die Entstehung der bipolaren Welt*, Munich 1998

Dutton 1997
David Dutton, *Anthony Eden. A Life and Reputation*, London et al. 1997

Duus 1985
Masayo Duus, *Haisha no okurimono. Tokushu ian shisetsu RAA o meguru senryōshi no sokumen*, Tokyo 1985

Eastman et al. 1991
Lloyd Eastman et al., *The Nationalist Era in China, 1927–1949*, Cambridge 1991

Eggert and Plasen 2018
Marian Eggert and Jörg Plasen, *Kleine Geschichte Koreas. Von den Anfängen bis zu Gegenwart*, 2nd ed., Munich 2018

Eiynck 1997
Andreas Eiynck (ed), *Alte Heimat – Neue Heimat. Flüchtlinge und Vertriebene im Raum Lingen nach 1945*, Lingen 1997

Elleman 1997
Bruce A. Elleman, *Diplomacy and Deception. The Secret History of Sino-Soviet Diplomatic Relations 1917–1927*, Armonk et al. 1997

Elliger 2006
Katharina Elliger, *Und tief in der Seele das Ferne. Die Geschichte einer Vertreibung aus Schlesien*, 3rd ed., Reinbek 2006

Emmerich and Gassert 2014
Alexander Emmerich and Philipp Gassert, *Amerikas Kriege*, Darmstadt 2014

Erpenbeck 2010
Jenny Erpenbeck, *Visitation*, translated by Susan Bernofsky, New York 2010

Faust 1960
Fritz Faust, *Das Potsdamer Abkommen und seine völkerrechtliche Bedeutung*, 2nd ed., Frankfurt am Main 1960

Feis 1960
Herbert Feis, *Between War and Peace. The Potsdam Conference*, Princeton 1960

Feis 1962
Herbert Feis, *Zwischen Krieg und Frieden. Das Potsdamer Abkommen*, Frankfurt am Main et al. 1962

Ferrell 1980
Robert H. Ferrell (ed), *Off the Record. The Private Papers of Harry S. Truman*, New York 1980

Fisch 2004
Jörg Fisch, "From Weakening an Enemy to Strengthening an Ally. The United States and German Reparations", in Detlef Junker et al. (eds) *The United States and Germany in the Era of the Cold War 1945–1990. A Handbook*, vol. 1: *1945–68*, Cambridge 2004, 271–77

Fischer 1968
Alexander Fischer (ed), *Teheran, Jalta, Potsdam. Die sowjetischen Protokolle von den Kriegskonferenzen der "Großen Drei"*, Cologne 1968

Fishel 1952
Wesley R. Fishel, *The End of Extraterritoriality in China*, Berkeley et al. 1952.

Foerster 1982
Roland G. Foerster, "Innenpolitische Aspekte der Sicherheit Westdeutschlands (1947–1950)", in Roland G. Foerster (ed), *Anfänge westdeutscher Sicherheitspolitik 1945–1956*, vol. 1: *Von der Kapitulation bis zum Pleven-Plan*, Munich et al. 1982, 403–575

Ford 2016
Daniel Ford, *Flying Tigers. Claire Chennault and his American Volunteers, 1941–1942*, Durham et al. 2016

Forsmann 2009
Jana Forsmann, *Testfall für die "Großen Drei". Die Besetzung Irans durch Briten, Sowjets und Amerikaner 1941–1946*, Cologne et al. 2009

Frei 1996
Norbert Frei, *Vergangenheitspolitik. Die Anfänge der Bundesrepublik und die NS-Vergangenheit*, Munich 1996

Frei 2001
Norbert Frei (ed), *Karrieren im Zwielicht. Hitlers Eliten nach 1945*, Frankfurt am Main 2001

Friedrich 2006
Jörg Friedrich, *The Fire. The Bombing of Germany, 1940–1945*, New York 2006

FRUS
United States Department of State, Foreign Relations of the United States (FRUS), diplomatic papers, *1941, The British Commonwealth, The Near East and Africa*, Washington 1959
1943, The Conferences at Cairo and Tehran, Washington 1961
1945, The Conferences at Malta and Yalta, Washington 1955
1945, The Conference of Berlin (The Potsdam Conference), 2 vols., Washington 1960
1945, The Near East and Africa, Washington 1969
[All FRUS documents can be accessed online at https://history.state.gov]

Furukawa 2012
Takahisa Furukawa, *Potsudame sengen to gunkoku nihon*, Tokyo 2012

Gaddis 1997
John Lewis Gaddis, *We Now Know. Rethinking Cold War History*, Oxford et al. 1997

Gassert 2012
Philipp Gassert, "Popularität der Apokalypse. Überlegungen zu einer Kulturgeschichte der Nuklearangst seit 1945", in Johannes Piepenbrink (ed), *Das Ende des Atomzeitalters*, Bonn 2012

History of Korea for Secondary Schools
고등학교 한국사 (History of Korea for Secondary Schools), 두산동아, 2013
고등학교 한국사 (History of Korea for Secondary Schools), 금성출판사, 2014
고등학교 한국사 (History of Korea for Secondary Schools), 지학사, 2014
고등학교 한국사 (History of Korea for Secondary Schools), 비상교육, 2014

Gilbert 1988
Martin Gilbert, *"Never Despair". Winston S. Churchill 1945–1965*, London 1988

Gleß 2006
Karlheinz Gleß, "Peetzig/Piasek – Erinnerungen an ein Dorf an der Oder", in Hans-Jürgen Bömelburg et al. (eds), *Vertreibung aus dem Osten. Deutsche und Polen erinnern sich*, 2nd ed., Olsztyn 2006, 83–93

Görtemaker 1995
Manfred Görtemaker, "Die Potsdamer Konferenz", in Stiftung Preußische Schlösser und Gärten Berlin-Brandenburg (ed), *Schloss Cecilienhof und die Potsdamer Konferenz 1945*, Potsdam 1995

Görtemaker 1999a
Manfred Görtemaker, "Potsdamer Konferenz", in Wolfgang Benz (ed), *Deutschland unter alliierter Besatzung 1945–1949/55. Ein Handbuch*, Berlin 1999

Görtemaker 1999b
Manfred Görtemaker, *Geschichte der Bundesrepublik Deutschland. Von der Gründung bis zur Gegenwart*, Munich 1999.

Gormley 1990
James L. Gormley, *From Potsdam to the Cold War. Big Three Diplomacy*, Wilmington 1990

Grass 2007
Günter Grass, *Peeling the Onion*, translated by Michael Henry Heim, London 2007

Groehler 1997
Olaf Groehler, "Militärfragen auf der Potsdamer Konferenz", in Heiner Timmermann (ed), *Potsdam 1945. Konzept, Taktik, Irrtum?*, Berlin 1997, 195–204

Gronke 2016
Monika Gronke, *Geschichte Irans. Von der Islamisierung bis zur Gegenwart*, 5th ed., Munich 2016

Gross 2012
Jan T. Gross, "Kielce" (article), *Enzyklopädie jüdischer Geschichte und Kultur (EJGK)*, vol. 3, Stuttgart 2012, 345–50

Hansen 2004
Niels Hansen, *Aus dem Schatten der Katastrophe. Die deutsch-israelischen Beziehungen in der* Ära *Konrad Adenauer und David Ben-Gurion*, 2nd ed., Düsseldorf 2004

Grosser 1986
Alfred Grosser, *Frankreich und seine Außenpolitik 1944 bis heute*, Munich et al. 1986.

Harris 1995
Kenneth Harris, *Attlee*, London 1995

Hartmann 2012
Christian Hartmann, *Unternehmen Barbarossa. Der deutsche Krieg im Osten 1941–1945*, 2nd ed., Munich 2012

Hasegawa 2005
Tsuyoshi Hasegawa, *Racing the Enemy. Stalin, Truman, and the Surrender of Japan*, Cambridge, Mass. et al. 2005.

Hayter 1974
William Hayter, *A Double Life*, London 1974

Heifermann 2011
Ronald Heiferman, *The Cairo Conference of 1943. Roosevelt, Churchill, Chiang Kai-shek and Madame Chiang*, Jefferson et al. 2011

Hennessy 2003
Peter Hennessy, *The Secret State. Whitehall and the Cold War*, London 2003

Herbert 1988
Ulrich Herbert, *Fremdarbeiter. Politik und Praxis des "Ausländer-Einsatzes" in der Kriegswirtschaft des Dritten Reiches*, Berlin et al. 1988

Herbst 1982
Ludolf Herbst, *Der Totale Krieg und die Ordnung der Wirtschaft. Die Kriegswirtschaft im Spannungsfeld von Politik, Ideologie und Propaganda 1939–1945*, Stuttgart 1982

Heyde 2008
Jürgen Heyde, *Geschichte Polens*, 2nd ed., Munich 2008

Höhn and Klimke 2010
Maria Höhn and Martin Klimke, *A Breath of Freedom. The Civil Rights Struggle, African American GIs, and Germany*, New York 2010

Hoesch 2009
Edgar Hoesch, *Kleine Geschichte Finnlands*, Munich 2009

Holloway 1994
David Holloway, *Stalin and the Bomb. The Soviet Union and Atomic Energy, 1939–1954*, New Haven 1994

Horne 2004
Gerald Horne, *Race War. White Supremacy and the Japanese Attack on the British Empire*, New York 2004.

Ihlau 2014
Olaf Ihlau, *Der Bollerwagen*, Munich 2014

Ihme-Tuhel 1998
Beate Ihme-Tuhel, *Die Beziehungen zwischen der DDR, der Tschechoslowakei und Polen in den Jahren 1954 bis 1962*, Cologne 1998

Inoue 1995
Setsuko Inoue, *Senryōgun ianjo. Kokka ni yoru baishun shisetsu*, Tokyo 1995

Jahn 2005
Peter Jahn (ed), *Triumph und Trauma. Sowjetische und post-sowjetische Erinnerung an den Krieg 1941–1945*, Berlin 2005

James 1974
Robert Rhodes James (ed), *Winston S. Churchill. His Complete Speeches 1897–1963*, vol. VII: *1943–1949*, New York et al. 1974

James 1987
Robert Rhodes James, *Anthony Eden. A Biography*, London 1987

Janka 1997
Franz Janka, *Die braune Gesellschaft. Ein Volk wird formatiert*. Stuttgart 1997

Jansohn 2013
Uwe F. Jansohn, *President Truman and (the Challenge of) the Potsdam Conference 1945*, Fort Leavenworth 2013

Jirgl 2020
Reinhard Jirgl, *The Unfinished*, translated by Iain Galbraith, London et al. 2020

Kappeler 2017
Andreas Kappeler, *Ungleiche Brüder. Russen und Ukrainer. Vom Mittelalter bis zur Gegenwart*, Munich 2017

Katouzian 2013
Homa Katouzian, *Iran. Politics, History and Literature*, London 2013

Keiderling 1997
Gerhard Keiderling, "Die Potsdamer Konferenz in der Meinung der Berliner Öffentlichkeit 1945", in Heiner Timmermann (ed), *Potsdam 1945. Konzept, Taktik, Irrtum?*, Berlin 1997, 87–102

Keiichi 1986
Eguchi Keiichi, *Jūgonen sensō shōshi*, Tokyo 1986

Kennan 1968
George F. Kennan, *Memoirs 1925–1950*, London 1968

Kennan 1989
George F. Kennan, *Sketches from a Life*, New York 1989

Kennan 1990
George F. Kennan, *Impressionen eines Lebens*, Düsseldorf et al. 1990

Kershaw 2016
Ian Kershaw, *Höllensturz. Europa 1914 bis 1949*, Munich 2016

Kettenacker 1989
Lothar Kettenacker, *Krieg zur Friedenssicherung. Die Deutschlandplanung der britischen Regierung während des Zweitens Weltkrieges*, Göttingen et al. 1989

Kindermann 2001
Gottfried-Karl Kindermann, *Der Aufstieg Ostasiens in der Weltpolitik 1840–2000*, Munich 2001

Kivelson and Suny 2017
Valerie Kivelson and Ronald Suny, *Russia's Empires*, New York u. Oxford 2017

Kleßmann 1984
Christoph Kleßmann, *Die doppelte Staatsgründung. Deutsche Geschichte 1945–1955*, Bonn 1984

Klos 2018
Felix Klos, *Churchill's Last Stand. The Struggle to Unite Europe*, London et al. 2018

Klukowski 1997
Zygmunt Klukowski, *Red Shadow. A Physician's Memoir of the Soviet Occupation of Eastern Poland, 1944–1956*, Jefferson 1997

Knöfel 2015
Dietbert Knöfel, *Das Kriegsende 1945 in Berlin-Wannsee*, Berlin 2015

Kochanowski 2001
Journal entry Alma Heczko, 18 May 1945, quoted after Jerzy Kochanowski, "Völkerwanderung", *Karta. Zeitzeugnisse aus Ostmitteleuropa* 2 (2001), 103–04

Koch 2017
Christoph Koch (ed), *Das Potsdamer Abkommen 1945–2015. Rechtliche Bedeutung und historische Auswirkungen*, Frankfurt am Main 2017

Koch-Thalmann 2000
Dorothea Koch-Thalmann, *Mein Dorf oder die Reise rückwärts*, Dortmund 2000

Koikari 2008
Mire Koikari, *Pedagogy of Democracy. Feminism and the Cold War in the U.S. Occupation of Japan*, Philadelphia 2008

Koop 2005
Volker Koop, *Besetzt. Französische Besatzungspolitik in Deutschland*, Berlin 2005

Kotkin 2017
Stephen Kotkin, *Stalin*, vol. II: *Waiting for Hitler, 1929–1941*, New York 2017

Kreis 2015
Georg Kreis (ed), *Geschichte Frankreichs in Quellen und Darstellung*, vol. 2: *Von Napoleon bis zur Gegenwart*, Stuttgart 2015

Kreiser 2012
Klaus Kreiser, *Geschichte der Türkei. Von Atatürk bis zur Gegenwart*, Munich 2012

Kröger 1957
Herbert Kröger, *Die staatsrechtliche Bedeutung des Potsdamer Abkommens für das deutsche Volk*, Berlin 1957

Krzoska 2015
Markus Krzoska, *Ein Land unterwegs. Kulturgeschichte Polens seit 1945*, Paderborn 2015

Kühne 2000
Thomas Kühne, "Die Viktimisierungsfalle. Wehrmachtverbrechen, Geschichtswissenschaft und symbolische Ordnung des Militärs", in Michael Th. Greven and Oliver von Wrochem (eds), *Der Krieg in der Nachkriegszeit. Der Zweite Weltkrieg in Politik und Gesellschaft der Bundesrepublik*, Opladen 2000

Küsters 2000
Hanns Jürgen Küsters, *Der Integrationsfriede. Viermächte-Verhandlungen über die Friedensregelung mit Deutschland 1945–1990*, Munich 2000

Kurowski 2018
Józef K. Kurowski (ed), *Byli siewcami dobra i miłości…. Kurowscy z Wileńszczyzny we wspomnieniach*, Łódź 2018

Kushner 2006
Barak Kushner, *The Thought War. Japanese Imperial Propaganda*, Honolulu 2006

Lamberton Harper 1996
John Lamberton Harper, *American Visions Europe. Franklin. D. Roosevelt, George F. Kennan, and Dean G. Acheson*, New York 1996

Landwehr 2016
Achim Landwehr, *Die anwesende Abwesenheit der Vergangenheit. Essay zur Geschichtstheorie*, Frankfurt am Main 2016

Laufer et al. 2004
Jochen P. Laufer et al. (eds), *Die UdSSR und die deutsche Frage 1941–1948. Dokumente aus dem Archiv für Außenpolitik der Russischen Föderation*, vol. 2: *9 May 1945–3 October 1946*, Berlin 2004

Laufer 2009
Jochen Laufer, *Pax Sovietica. Stalin, die Westmächte und die deutsche Frage 1941–1945*, Cologne et al. 2009

Lehmann 1979
Hans Georg Lehmann, *Der Oder-Neiße Konflikt*, Munich 1979

Leonhard 2018
Jörn Leonhard, *Der überforderte Frieden. Versailles und die Welt 1918–1923*, Munich 2018

Levering 1978
Ralph B. Levering, *The Public and American Foreign Policy 1918–1978*, New York 1978

Lillteicher 2011
Jürgen Lillteicher, "Claims Conference" (article), *Enzyklopädie jüdischer Geschichte und Kultur (EJGK)*,
vol. 1, Stuttgart 2011, 511–14

Li Yumin 2005
Li Yumin, *Zhongguo fei yue shi*
[Geschichte der Abschaffung der
ungleichen Verträge in China],
Beijing 2005

Loeffler 2018
James Loeffler, *Rooted Cosmopoli-
tans. Jews and Human Rights in the
Twentieth Century*, New Haven et al.
2018

Longerich 2006
Peter Longerich, *Davon haben wir
nichts gewusst! Die Deutschen und
die Judenverfolgung 1933–1945*,
Munich 2006

Loth 1983
Wilfried Loth, "Die Franzosen und
die Deutsche Frage 1945–1949",
in Claus Scharf and Hans-Jürgen
Schröder (eds), *Die Deutschlandpolitik Frankreichs und die Französische Zone 1945–1949*, Wiesbaden
1983

Lowe 2015
Keith Lowe, *Der wilde Kontinent.
Europa in den Jahren der Anarchie
1943–1950*, Bonn 2015

Lutz 2009
Catherine Lutz, *The Empire of
Bases. The Global Struggle against
U.S. Military Posts*, New York 2009

Mackay 2002
Robert S. Mackay, *This Mr. Presi-
dent is the Story of the Little White
House*, Babelsberg 2002

MacKinnon 2008
Stephen R. MacKinnon, *Wuhan
1938. War, Refugees, and the
Making of Modern China*, Berkeley
et al. 2008

Macmillan 1972
Harold Macmillan, *Pointing the Way
1959–1961*, London et al. 1972

Mai 1999
Gunther Mai, "Alliierter Kontroll-
rat", in Wolfgang Benz (ed),
*Deutschland unter alliierter
Besatzung 1945–1949/55. Ein
Handbuch*, Berlin 1999, 229–34

Marcowitz 1999
Reiner Marcowitz, "'One World'
oder Bipolarismus. Der Jalta–
Mythos und seine Folgen",
*Zeitschrift für Religions- und
Geistesgeschichte* 51 (1999), 115–28

Mausbach 1996
Wilfried Mausbach, *Zwischen
Morgenthau und Marshall. Das
wirtschaftspolitische Deutschland-
konzept der USA 1944–1947*, Düsseldorf 1996

McCullough 1992
David McCullough, *Truman*, New
York 1992

McDougall 1997
Walter A. McDougall, *Promised
Land, Crusader State. The American
Encounter with the World since
1776*, Boston 1997

Mee 1975
Charles L. Mee, *Meeting at Potsdam*, New York 1975

Miller 1979
John R. Miller, "The Chiang-Stillwell
Conflict, 1942–1944", *Military
Affairs* 43 (1979), no. 2, 59–62

Miscamble 2007
Wilson D. Miscamble, *From Roosevelt to Truman. Potsdam, Hiroshima,
and the Cold War*, Cambridge 2007

Mitter 2000
Rana Mitter, *The Manchurian Myth.
Nationalism, Resistance and Collaboration in Modern China*, Berkeley et al. 2000

Mitter 2013
Rana Mitter, *China's War with
Japan. The Struggle for Survival*,
London 2013

Moggridge 1979
Donald Moggridge (ed), *The Col-
lected Writings of John Maynard
Keynes*, vol. XXIV: *Activities 1944–
1946. The Transition to Peace*,
London et al. 1979

Moran 2006
Lord Moran, *Churchill. The Struggle
for Survival 1945–60*, London 2006

Morina 2012
Christina Morina, "Der Krieg als
Vergangenheit und Vermächtnis.
Zur Rolle des Zweiten Weltkrieges
in der politischen Kultur Ost-
deutschlands, 1945–1955", in Jörg
Echternkamp (ed), *Kriegsenden,
Nachkriegsordnungen, Folge-
konflikte. Wege aus dem Krieg im 19.
und 20. Jahrhundert*, Freiburg 2012

Müller 1999
Rolf-Dieter Müller, "Albert Speer
und die Rüstungspolitik im Totalen
Krieg", in Rolf-Dieter Müller et al.
(eds), *Organisation und Mobilisie-
rung des deutschen Machtberei-
ches, zweiter Halbband: Kriegsver-
waltung, Wirtschaft und personelle
Ressourcen 1942–1944/45*, Stuttgart 1999, 275–773

Münch 1968
Ingo von Münch, "Berliner Deklara-
tion in Anbetracht der Niederlage
Deutschlands und der Übernahme
der obersten Regierungsgewalt
hinsichtlich Deutschlands vom
5. Juni 1945", in Ingo von Münch
(ed), *Dokumente des geteilten
Deutschland. Quellentexte zur
Rechtslage des Deutschen Reiches,
der Bundesrepublik Deutschland
und der Deutschen Demokratischen
Republik*, Stuttgart 1968

Myrdal 1944
Gunnar Myrdal, *An American
Dilemma. The Negro Problem and
Modern Democracy*, New York 1944

Nałkowska 2000
Zofia Nałkowska, *Dzienniki 1945–
1954*, vol. 1, Warsaw 2000

Neiberg 2015
Michael Neiberg, *Potsdam. The End of World War II and the Remaking of Europe*, New York 2015

Nicolson 1968
Harold Nicolson, *Diaries and Letters 1945–1962*, London 1968

Nobile 1996
Philip Nobile (ed), *Judgment at the Smithsonian*, New York 1996

Nübel 2019
Christoph Nübel (ed), *Dokumente zur deutschen Militärgeschichte 1945–1990. Bundesrepublik und DDR im Ost-West-Konflikt*, Berlin 2019

Official Documents 1945, Conference of Berlin
"United States-Great Britain-Soviet Union: Report of Tripartite Conference of Berlin, July 17–August 2, 1945", *American Journal of International Law* 39 (1945), no. 4, Supplement: Official Documents 1945, 245–57

Official Documents 1945, Surrender of Japan
"United States-China-Great Britain-Soviet Union: Unconditional Surrender of Japan", *American Journal of International Law* 39 (1945), no. 4, Supplement: Official Documents 1945, 264–65

Orwell 1968
George Orwell, *As I Please. The Collected Essays, Journalism and Letters*, vol. 3, Boston 1968

Osterhammel 2009
Jürgen Osterhammel, *Die Verwandlung der Welt. Eine Geschichte des 19. Jahrhunderts*, 4th ed., Munich 2009

Ovendale 1989
Ritchie Ovendale, *Britain, the United States, and the End of the Palestine Mandate, 1942–1948*, Woodbridge 1989

Overy 2013
Richard Overy, *The Bombing War. Europe 1939–1945*, London 2013

Padover 1946
Saul K. Padover, *Experiment in Germany. The Story of an American Intelligence Officer*, New York 1946

Patterson 1996
James T. Patterson, *Grand Expectations. The United States, 1945–1974*, Oxford 1996

Perlzweig 2007
Maurice L. Perlzweig, "Robinson, Nehemiah" (article), *Encyclopedia Judaica*, vol. 17, 2nd ed., Detroit et al. 2007, 356

Pimlott 1986
Ben Pimlott (ed), *The Second World War Diary of Hugh Dalton, 1940–45*, London 1986

Poidevin 1983
Raymond Poidevin, "Die französische Deutschlandpolitik 1943–1949", in Claus Scharf and Hans-Jürgen Schröder (eds), *Die Deutschlandpolitik Frankreichs und die Französische Zone 1945–1949*, Wiesbaden 1983

Polityka 2018
Defilada Zwycięstwa po II wojnie bez Polaków, "Polityka", 30 June 2018, www.polityka.pl/tygodnik-polityka/historia/1758214,1,defilada-zwyciestwa-po-ii-wojnie-bez-polakow.read [accessed 1 December 2019]

Potter 1950
Pitman B. Potter, "Legal Aspects of the Situation in Korea", *American Journal of International Law* 44 (1950), no. 4, 709–12

Quested 1984
Rosemary Quested, *Sino-Russian Relations. A Short History*, Sydney 1984

Reeken and Thießen 2013
Dietmar von Reeken and Malte Thießen, " 'Volksgemeinschaft' als soziale Praxis? Perspektiven und Potenziale neuer Forschungen vor Ort", in Dietmar von Reeken and Malte Thießen (eds), *"Volksgemeinschaft" als soziale Praxis. Neue Forschungen zur NS-Gesellschaft vor Ort*, Paderborn 2013, 9–33

Recker 2002
Marie-Luise Recker, *Geschichte der Bundesrepublik Deutschland*, Munich 2002

Rémond 1994
René Rémond, *Frankreich im 20. Jahrhundert. Erster Teil 1918–1958*, Stuttgart 1994

Resis 1993
Albert Resis (ed), *Molotov Remembers. Inside Kremlin Politics. Conversations with Felix Chuev*, Chicago 1993

Ressing 1970
Gerd Ressing, *Versagte der Westen in Jalta und Potsdam? Ein dokumentierter Wegweiser durch die alliierten Kriegskonferenzen*, Frankfurt am Main 1970

Reynolds 1991
David Reynolds, *Britannia Overruled. British Policy and World Power in the Twentieth Century*, London 1991

Reynolds 2004
David Reynolds, *In Command of History. Churchill Fighting and Writing the Second World War*, London 2004

Reynolds 2006
David Reynolds, *From World War to Cold War. Churchill, Roosevelt, and the International History of the 1940s*, Oxford 2006

Rioux 1987
Jean-Pierre Rioux, *The Fourth Republic 1944–1958*, Cambridge 1987

Roberts 1996
Frank Roberts, "The Yalta Conference", in Gill Bennett (ed), *The End of the War in Europe 1945*, London 1996

Roberts 2017
Geoffrey Roberts, "Antipodes or Twins? The Myths of Yalta and Potsdam", in Christoph Koch (ed), *Das Potsdamer Abkommen 1945–2015. Rechtliche Bedeutung und historische Auswirkungen*, Frankfurt am Main 2017, 215–33

Robinson 1944
Nehemiah Robinson, *Indemnification and Reparations. Jewish Aspects*, New York 1944

Robinson 1945
Nehemiah Robinson, "The Problem of Indemnification and Reparations (A tentative brief review of facts and measures)", 7 April 1945, *American Jewish Archives, The World Jewish Congress Collection*, series C: *Institute of Jewish Affairs, 1918–1979*, subseries 4: *Indemnification, 1939–1975*, box C276, file 2: Reports, memos re: Potsdam Conference, 1945

Robinson 1953
Nehemiah Robinson, How we negotiated with the Germans and what we achieved, New York 1953

Ro'i 1974
Yaacov Ro'i, *From Encroachment to Involvement. A Documentary Study of Soviet Policy in the Middle East, 1945–1973*, New York 1974

Rosenberg 1999
Jonathan Rosenberg, "Before the Bomb and After. Winston Churchill and the Use of Force", in John Lewis Gaddis et al. (eds), *Cold War Statesmen Confront the Bomb. Nuclear Diplomacy since 1945*, Oxford 1999

Ruchniewicz 2012
Krzysztof Ruchniewicz, "Jalta – ein Mythos von langer Dauer", in Krzysztof Ruchniewicz and Marek Zybura (eds), *Zwischen (Sowjet-) Russland und Deutschland. Geschichte und Politik im Schatten von Józef Mackiewicz (1902–1985)*, Osnabrück 2012

Rüther et al. 1998
Letter by Jupp Kappius on the situation in the Ruhr area on 31 January 1945, quoted in Martin Rüther et al. (eds), *Deutschland im ersten Nachkriegsjahr. Berichte von Mitgliedern des Internationalen Sozialistischen Kampfbundes (ISK) aus dem besetzten Deutschland 1945/46*, Munich 1998

Rysiak 1970
"Postulaty Polski w sprawie granicy zachodniej (Memorandum Tymczasowego Rządu Jedności Narodowej, przedłożone rządom Stanów Zjednoczonych Ameryki, Wielkiej Brytanii i Związku Radzieckiego), 10 lipca 1945 roku, Moskwa", in Gwidon Rysiak (ed), *Zachodnia granica Polski na konferencji poczdamskiej. Zbiór dokumentów*, Opole 1970

Saburō 1985
Ienaga Saburoō, *Sensō sekinin*, Tokyo 1985

Saikal 2019
Amin Saikal, *Iran Rising. The Survival and Future of the Islamic Republic*, Princeton 2019

Scharf and Schröder 1983
Claus Scharf and Hans-Jürgen Schröder (eds), *Die Deutschlandpolitik Frankreichs und die Französische Zone 1945–1949*, Wiesbaden 1983

Schieder 2000
Wolfgang Schieder, "Die Umbrüche von 1918, 1933, 1945 und 1989 als Wendepunkte deutscher Geschichte", in Wolfgang Schieder and Dietrich Papenfuß (eds), *Deutsche Umbrüche im 20. Jahrhundert*, Weimar 2000

Schildt 2007
Axel Schildt, "Die langen Schatten des Krieges über der westdeutschen Nachkriegsgesellschaft", in Jörg Echternkamp and Stefan Martens (eds), *Der Zweite Weltkrieg in Europa. Erfahrung und Erinnerung*, Paderborn et al. 2007, 223–36

Schlesinger 2004
Stephen C. Schlesinger, *Act of Creation. The Founding of the United Nations*, Boulder et al. 2004

Schnabel 1985
Thomas Schnabel, *Stadtverwaltung und Kriegsalltag in Freiburg 1944/45*, in Thomas Schnabel and Gerd R. Ueberschär (eds), *Endlich Frieden! Das Kriegsende in Freiburg 1945*, Freiburg 1985

Schwabe 2006
Klaus Schwabe, *Weltmacht und Weltordnung. Amerikanische Außenpolitik von 1898 bis zur Gegenwart. Eine Jahrhundertgeschichte*, Paderborn 2006

Schwarz 1998
Hans-Peter Schwarz, *Das Gesicht des Jahrhunderts. Monster, Retter und Mediokritäten*, Berlin 1998

Sebag Montefiore 2003
Simon Sebag Montefiore, *The Court of the Red Tsar*, London 2003

Segev 2018
Tom Segev, *David Ben Gurion. Ein Staat um jeden Preis*, Munich 2018

Seiler 2015
Michael Seiler, "Die Rettung der Pfaueninsel und ihrer Bewohner am Ende des zweiten Weltkrieges durch Marie Wolter", *Mitteilungen des Vereins für die Geschichte Berlins* 111 (2015), no. 1, 452–62

Shell 1998
Kurt L. Shell, *Harry S. Truman. Politiker – Populist – Präsident*, Göttingen 1998

Shigematsu and Camacho 2010
Setsu Shigematsu and Keith
L. Camacho (eds), *Militarized Currents. Towards a Decolonized Future in Asia and the Pacific*, Minneapolis 2010

Shin 2016
Jong Hoon Shin, 신종훈, 「1945년 여름, 포츠담: 포츠담 회담과 포츠담 선언」, 「서양 역사와 문화 연구」 vol. 38 (2016).

Simmich 2019
Matthias Simmich, "Sternstunden eines Schlosses – die Welt schaut auf einen Landsitz der Hohenzollern in Potsdam, Teil 1: Die Potsdamer Konferenz im Schloss Cecilienhof, Juli und August 1945", Texte des RECS #29, 22/02/2019, https://recs.hypotheses.org/4483

Sipols et al. 1985
Vilnis J. Sipols et al., *Jalta – Potsdam. Basis der europäischen Nachkriegsordnung*, Berlin (East) 1985

Sked and Cook 1993
Alan Sked and Chris Cook, *Post-War Britain. A Political History*, 4th ed., Harmondsworth 1993

Sowjetische Militärische Administration
Sowjetische Militärische Administration Provinz Brandenburg (ed), *Mitteilungen über die Berliner Konferenz der Drei Mächte*, n. p., n. d.

Spevack 2004
Edmund Spevack, "The Allied Council of Foreign Ministers Conferences and the German Question", in Detlef Junker et al. (eds), *The United States and Germany in the Era of the Cold War, 1945–1990. A Handbook*, vol. 1, Cambridge 2004, 44–49

Steinert 1970
Marlies G. Steinert, *Hitlers Krieg und die Deutschen. Stimmung und Haltung der deutschen Bevölkerung im Zweiten Weltkrieg*, Düsseldorf 1970

Steber and Gotto 2014
Martina Steber and Bernhard Gotto (eds), *Visions of Community in Nazi Germany – Social Engineering and Private Lives*, Oxford 2014

Stöver 2007
Bernd Stöver, *Der Kalte Krieg 1947–1991. Geschichte eines radikalen Zeitalters*, Munich 2007

Suny 2015
Ronald Grigor Suny (ed), *The Cambridge History of Russia*, vol. III: *The Twentieth Century*, Cambridge et al. 2015

Suzuki 2011
Tamon Suzuki, *"Shūsen" no seijishi, 1943–1945*, Tokyo 2011

Tanaka 1996
Yuki Tanaka, *Hidden Horrors. Japanese War Crimes in World War II*, New York 1996

Tankielun 2006
Mieczysław Tankielun, "Aus dem Wilnaer Gebiet nach Pommern und Großpolen", in Hans-Jürgen Bömelburg et al (eds), *Vertreibung aus dem Osten. Deutsche und Polen erinnern sich*, 2nd ed., Olsztyn 2006, 370–83

Thießen 2012
Malte Thießen, "Erinnerungen an die 'Volksgemeinschaft'. Integration und Exklusion im kommunalen und kommunikativen Gedächtnis", in Detlef Schmiechen-Ackermann (ed), *"Volksgemeinschaft": Mythos, wirkungsmächtige soziale Verheißung oder soziale Realität im "Dritten Reich"?*, Paderborn 2012

Timm 2017
Angelika Timm (ed), *Friedensinitiativen für Israel und Palästina 1917–2017. 100 Dokumente aus 100 Jahren*, Berlin 2017

Tokarczuk 2004
Olga Tokarczuk, "Eine Freske menschlicher Schicksale" (Foreword), in Helga Hirsch, *Schweres Gepäck. Flucht und Vertreibung als Lebensthema*, Hamburg 2004, 7–10

Tomala 2000
Mieczyslaw Tomala, *Deutschland – von Polen gesehen. Zu den deutsch-polnischen Beziehungen 1945–1990*, Marburg 2000

Trachtenberg 1999
Marc Trachtenberg, *A Constructed Peace. The Making of the European Settlement 1945–1963*, Princeton 1999

Truman 1955
Harry S. Truman, *Memoirs. 1945: Year of Decisions*, New York 1955

Truman 1956
Harry S. Truman, *Memoirs. 1946–52: Years of Trial and Hope*, New York 1956

Tschudodejew 1986
Jurij W. Tschudodejew, "Vorweggesagt", in *Am Himmel über China 1937–1940. Erinnerungen sowjetischer freiwilliger Flieger*, Berlin (East) 1986, 5–16

Tuchman 1971
Barbara Tuchman, *Sand Against the Wind. Stillwell and the American Experience in China, 1911–1945*, London 1971

Tyrell 1987
Albrecht Tyrell, *Großbritannien und die Deutschlandplanung der Alliierten 1941–1945*, Frankfurt am Main 1987

Uchiyama 2018
Benjamin Uchiyama, *Japan's Carnival War. Mass Culture on the Home Front, 1937–1945*, Cambridge 2018

Umemori 2013
Naoyuki Umemori, "The Historical Contexts of the High Treason Incident. Governmentality and Colonialism", in Masako Gavin and Ben Middleton (eds), *Japan and the High Treason Incident*, New York 2013

Villa 1976
Brian L. Villa, "The U.S. Army, Unconditional Surrender, and the Potsdam Proclamation", *Journal of American History* 63 (1976), no. 1, 66–92

Vogelsang 2013
Kai Vogelsang, *Geschichte Chinas*, 5th ed., Stuttgart 2013

Volkogonov 1991
Dmitri Volkogonov, *Stalin. Triumph and Tragedy*, New York 1991

Wagner 1997
Wieland Wagner, "Tokio und die Stunde Null. Der innerjapanische Streit um die Potsdamer Erklärung", in Heiner Timmermann (ed), *Potsdam 1945. Konzept, Taktik, Irrtum?*, Berlin 1997, 181–94

Wang 2014
Peter Chen-main Wang, "Chiang Kai-shek's Faith in Christianity. The Trial of the Stilwell Incident", *Journal of Modern Chinese History* 8 (2014), 194–209

Weber 2019
Claudia Weber, *Der Pakt. Stalin, Hitler und die Geschichte einer mörderischen Allianz*, Munich 2019

Weggel 1989
Oskar Weggel, *Geschichte Chinas im 20. Jahrhundert*, Stuttgart 1989

Weizmann 1950
Chaim Weizmann, *Trial and Error. The Autobiography*, 4th ed., London 1950

Wetzel 2013
Juliane Wetzel, "Displaced Persons (DPs)", *Historisches Lexikon Bayerns*, https://www.historisches-lexikon-bayerns.de/Lexikon/Displaced_Persons_(DPs), [accessed 2 October 2019]

Wierling 2007
Dorothee Wierling, "Krieg im Nachkrieg. Zur öffentlichen und privaten Präsenz des Krieges in der SBZ und frühen DDR", in Jörg Echternkamp and Stefan Martens (eds), *Der Zweite Weltkrieg in Europa. Erfahrung und Erinnerung*, Paderborn et al. 2007, 237–51

Williams 1961
Francis Williams, *A Prime Minister Remembers. The War and Post-War Memoirs of the Rt. Hon. Earl Attlee*, London et al. 1961

Winkler 2014
Heinrich August Winkler, *Der lange Weg nach Westen*, vol. 2, Munich 2014

Wise 1949
Stephen Wise, *Challenging Years. The Autobiography*, New York 1949

Wittner 1984
Lawrence S. Wittner, *Rebels Against War. The American Peace Movement, 1933–1983*, Philadelphia 1984

Wolf 1984
Christa Wolf. *Patterns of Childhood*, translated by Ursule Molinaro and Hedwig, New York 1984

Wolffsohn and Grill 2016
Michael Wolffsohn and Tobias Grill, *Israel. Geschichte, Politik, Gesellschaft, Wirtschaft*, 8th ed., Opladen et al. 2016

Wolfrum 1991
Edgar Wolfrum, *Französische Besatzungspolitik und deutsche Sozialdemokratie. Politische Neuansätze in der "vergessenen Zone" bis zur Bildung des Südweststaates 1945–1952*, Düsseldorf 1991

Wolfrum 2007
Edgar Wolfrum, *Die geglückte Demokratie. Geschichte der Bundesrepublik Deutschland von ihren Anfängen bis zur Gegenwart*, Bonn 2007

Woyke 1987
Wichard Woyke, *Frankreichs Außenpolitik von de Gaulle bis Mitterrand*, Wiesbaden 1987

Yang Tianshi 2015
Yang Tianshi, "Chiang Kai-shek and Jawaharlal Nehru", in Hans van de Ven et al. (eds), *Negotiating China's Destiny in World War II*, Stanford/CA 2015, 127–40

Yekelchyk 2015
Serhy Yekelchyk, "The Western Republics: Ukraine, Belarus, Moldova and the Baltics", in Ronald Grigor Suny (ed), *The Cambridge History of Russia*, vol. III: *The Twentieth Century*, Cambridge et al. 2015

Yellen 2013
Jeremy A. Yellen, "The Specter of Revolution. Reconsidering Japan's Decision to Surrender", *International History Review* 35 (2013), no. 1, 205–26

Ying Mei Su shounao Bocitan huiyi baogao 1946
Ying Mei Su shounao Bocitan huiyi baogao (fu Yingwen yuanben) [Report of the Potsdam Conference Between the Heads of the Governments of U.S.A., United Kingdom and U.S.S.R.], Shanghai 1946

Yoneyama 1999
Lisa Yoneyama, *Hiroshima Traces. Time, Space, and the Dialectics of Memory*, Berkeley 1999

Young 1998
Louise Young, *Japan's Total Empire. Manchuria and the Culture of Wartime Imperialism*, Berkeley 1998

Yoshiaki 1987
Yoshimi Yoshiaki, *Kusa no ne no fashizumu*, Tokyo 1987

Yoshiaki 2000
Yoshimi Yoshiaki, *Comfort Women. Sexual Slavery in the Japanese Military during World War II*, New York 2000

Zaremba 2016
Marcin Zaremba, *Die große Angst. Polen 1944–1947. Leben im Ausnahmezustand*, Paderborn 2016

Zhang Shenfa 2010
Zhang Shenfa, "The Main Causes for the Return of the Changchun Railway to China and Its Impact on Sino-Soviet Relations", in Thomas P. Bernstein and Hua-yu Li (eds), *China Learns From the Soviet Union, 1949 – Present*, Lanham et al. 2010, 61–78

Zhang Xianwen and Chen Qianping 2017
Zhang Xianwen and Chen Qianping, *Zhongguo kang Ri zhanzheng shi 1931–1945* [History of the Chinese war of Resistance against Japan 1931–1945], vol. 4, Beijing 2017

Zhukov 1971
Georgy Konstantinovich Zhukov, *The Memoirs of Marshal Zhukov*, London 1971

Zionist Congress 1946
Twenty-second Zionist Congress, Basle et al. 1946 (reprint Frankfurt am Main 2001)

Zöllner 2006
Reinhard Zöllner, "Ein ostasiatischer Holocaust? Japans Aggression in China (1931–1945)", in Thoralf Klein and Frank Schumacher (eds), *Kolonialkriege. Militärische Gewalt im Zeichen des Imperialismus*, Hamburg 2006, 291–328

Zweig 2009
Ronald W. Zweig, "'Reparations Made Me'. Nahum Goldmann, German Reparations, and the Jewish World", in Mark A. Raider (ed), *Nahum Goldmann. Statesman Without a State*, New York 2009, 233–54

강만길 외, 「한국사 17. 분단구조의 정착-1」, 한길사, 1994.
강만길 외, 「우리민족 해방운동사」, 역사비평사, 2000.
정동귀, 「제2차 세계대전중에 있어서의 미국의 대한국정책 구상」, 「사회과학 논총」 vol. 6 (1988).
박노순, 「2차 대전 중 연합국의 대 반도정책」, 「통일로」 292호, (2012).
와다 하루키, 「카이로 선언과 일본의 영토문제」, 「영토해양연구」 vol. 5 (2013).

Index of Persons

Lenders and Acknowledgements

We wish to thank the following lenders:

Berlin, Stiftung Jüdisches
    Museum Berlin
Dresden, Militärhistorisches
    Museum der Bundeswehr
Hiroshima, The Hiroshima Peace
    Memorial Museum
Swindon, The National Trust for
    Places of Historic Interest
    or Natural Beauty

Walter Frankenstein
Joy Hunter
Thoralf Klein
Kornelia Kurowska
Nicolas Perruchot
Stefan Riemer
as well as our private lenders
who prefer to remain anonymous.

Acknowledgements

Harald Berndt
Jeanette Birk
Vadim Danilin
Anne Fritsche
Joy Hunter
Eldar Ianibekov
Sven Kerschek
Anne-Kathrin Kretschmann
Svetlana Liubenkova
Jens-Christian Lüdeke
Matthias Marr
Verena Mühlegger
Bernd Nogli
Mario Prien
Thomas Rabe
Olaf Saphörster
Ute Weickardt
Franziska Windt

Our special thanks go to all
employees of the Prussian Palaces
and Gardens Foundation Berlin-
Brandenburg and of the Fridericus
Servicegesellschaft der Preußischen Schlösser und Gärten as well
as our many external colleagues.

With the support of

Media Partners

tipBerlin

ZITTY

Picture Credits

pp. 10–11: Bundesarchiv, Bild-Nr. 170-373, Photo: Max Baur

pp. 14–15: U.S. National Archives and Records Administration, NAID: 198799, Photo: Harry S. Truman Library & Museum, public domain

pp. 18–19: U.S. National Archives and Records Administration, NAID: 198943, Photo: Harry S. Truman Library & Museum, public domain via Wikimedia Commons

p. 22: U.S. Central Intelligence Agency, Photo: public domain via Wikimedia Commons

p. 23: U.S. National Archives and Records Administration, NAID: 198840, Photo: Harry S. Truman Library & Museum, public domain via Wikimedia Commons

p. 25: United Kingdom Government, public domain via Wikimedia Commons

pp. 26–27: U.S. National Archives and Records Administration, NAID: 198936, Photo: Harry S. Truman Library & Museum, public domain via Wikimedia Commons

p. 30: Naval History and Heritage Command, Photo No. 80-G-K-14539, Photo: public domain

pp. 34–35: Naval History and Heritage Command, Photo No. 26-G-2340, Photo: public domain

pp. 38–39: U.S. National Archives and Records Administration, NAID: 7865578, Photo: Harry S. Truman Library & Museum, public domain

p. 40: U.S. National Archives and Records Administration, NAID: 198768, Photo: public domain via Wikimedia Commons

p. 43: U.S. National Archives and Records Administration, NAID: 516217, Photo: public domain via Wikimedia Commons

pp. 44–45: U.S. National Archives and Records Administration, NAID: 535840, Photo: public domain via Wikimedia Commons

pp. 50–51: U.S. National Archives and Records Administration, NAID: 66395398, Photo: public domain

pp. 54–55: Naval History and Heritage Command, Photo No. NH 65820, Photo: public domain

pp. 56–57: Naval History and Heritage Command, Photo No. USA-C-2719, Photo: public domain

pp. 62–63: RIA Novosti archive, image #602161 / Zelma / CC-BY-SA 3.0 via Wikimedia Commons

p. 66: U.S. National Archives and Records Administration, NAID: 44268285, Photo: public domain

p. 70: Great Patriotic War Museum Moscow

p. 72: U.S. National Archives and Records Administration, NAID: 7788604, Photo: public domain

p. 73: U.S. National Archives and Records Administration, NAID: 7788604, Photo: public domain

p. 74: U.S. National Archives and Records Administration, NAID: 44266070, Photo: public domain

pp. 76–77: U.S. National Archives and Records Administration, NAID: 7387483, Photo: public domain

p. 78: Great Patriotic War Museum Moscow, Photo No. NVF 1694–7

pp. 82–83: National Archives and Records Administration, NAID: 198863, Photo: Harry S. Truman Library & Museum, public domain via Wikimedia Commons

p. 86 (top): akg-images, Photo No. AKG1574827

p. 86 (btm.): U.S. National Archives and Records Administration, NAID: 198704, Photo: Harry S. Truman Library & Museum, public domain via Wikimedia Commons

p. 89: U.S. National Archives and Records Administratin, NAID: 198919, Photo: Harry S. Truman Library & Museum, public domain

Imprint

Exhibition

**Potsdam Conference 1945
Shaping the World**
at Cecilienhof Palace, Potsdam
1 May – 1 November 2020

An exhibition hosted by the
Prussian Palaces and Gardens
Foundation Berlin-Brandenburg
(SPSG)
General Director: Professor Dr
Christoph Martin Vogtherr

Concept
Dr Jürgen Luh,
Matthias Simmich

Academic Supervisor
Dr Jürgen Luh

Academic Curator
Matthias Simmich

**Project and Commercial
Management**
Heike Borggreve

Registry and Loan Processes
Sylvia Möwes

Research Assistants
Jessica Korschanowski,
Sylvia Möwes, Jacob Riemer,
Truc Vu Minh

Research Advisors
Dr Thoralf Klein,
Dr Andreas Kossert

Research Volunteer
Carolin Alff

**Project Group
Potsdam Conference**
Harald Berndt
Heike Borggreve
Esther Bulgis
Julius Burchard
Matthias Gärtner
Stefan Gehlen
Dr Ulrich Henze
Silke Hollender
Bärbel Jackisch
Jessica Korschanowski
Kerstin Lauterbach
Dr Jürgen Luh
Sylvia Möwes
Wilma Otte
Matthias Simmich
Tina Schümann
Truc Vu Minh

**Marketing and
Event Management**
Heike Borggreve in collaboration
with the SPSG Marketing Depart-
ment under the direction of
Dr Heinz Buri

Fundraising
Sarah Kimmerle, Tina Schümann

Press and Public Relations
Anne Biernath, Dr Ulrich Henze,
Frank Kallensee, Elvira Kühn

Poster Design
Julius Burchard

**Arrangement of Exhibition Rooms
and Technical Implementation**
Kerstin Lauterbach and SPSG's
Harness Yard workshops under
the direction of Heiko Neubecker

Restoration Supervision
Wulf Eckermann, Bärbel Jackisch,
Undine Köhler in collaboration with
the SPSG Restoration Department
under the direction of Kathrin
Lange

Design and Planning of Exhibition
beier+wellach projekte, Berlin
Florian Mittelbach, Josefine-Emilia
Müller, Margaret Schlenkrich,
Birte Schramm, Peter Wellach

Media Installation Hiroshima
Michele Pedrazzi

Media Design
id3d-berlin gmbh, Berlin

Exhibition Construction
Tischlerei Schuster, Bautzen

Graphics Production
Pigmentpol Sachsen GmbH,
Dresden

Catalogue

Arrangement of Exhibits
Zehnpfennig und Weber GbR,
Berlin

Audio Guide
Orpheo Deutschland GmbH,
Weimar

Multi-Media Guide
KULDIG, DroidSolutions GmbH,
Leipzig

Translations
Ekatarina Logashina,
Elizabeth Volk

**Supervisory Staff, Service,
Cleaning**
Fridericus Servicegesellschaft
der Preußischen Schlösser und
Gärten mbH

With the assistance of the
group service and all SPSG
employees.

Edited
on behalf of the General Direction
of the Prussian Palaces and
Gardens Foundation Berlin-
Brandenburg
by Jürgen Luh
in collaboration with Truc Vu Minh
and Jessica Korschanowski

Editorial Staff
Truc Vu Minh, Jürgen Luh,
Jessica Korschanowski

Image Processing
Truc Vu Minh

Translations from the German
Daniel Costello (DC)
Christoph Nöthlings (CN)
Jonathan Pattishall (JP)
(Translators' initials are indicated
at the end of each contribution)

Copy Editing
Christoph Nöthlings

Design
Joachim Steuerer,
Sandstein Verlag

Type and Reprography
Gudrun Diesel, Jana Neumann,
Sandstein Verlag

Printing and Finishing
FINIDR s.r.o., Český Těšín

Typeface
Akkurat, Diamante

Paper
Acroprint Milk, 100 g/m²

Until the end of production, every
effort has been made to locate all
owners of reproduction rights.
Persons and institutions who may
not have been reached and who
claim rights to illustrations used
in this volume are requested to
contact the editors.

The Deutsche Nationalbibliothek
holds a record of this publication in
the Deutsche Nationalbibliografie;
detailed bibliographical data can
be found under: http://dnb.ddb.de

ISBN 978-3-95498-547-0

Illustrations
Cover design: Joachim Steuerer
based on motifs by Julius Burchard,
photo: U.S. Army Signal Corps,
Courtesy of Harry S. Truman
Library, public domain via U.S.
National Archives and Records
Administration, NAID: 198958

Frontispiece: Cecilienhof Palace,
Conference Hall, Photo: SPSG,
Photo No. F0017533

pp. 242–243: Signature of the
United Nations Charter in San
Francisco on 26 June 1945,
Copyright: bpk, Picture
No. 30018640

p. 264: Armoured reconnaissance
tank of UN on patrol in area of
Sarajevo Bosnia, French Foreign
Legion, winter 1993, Photo: Alamy
Stock Photo, Picture No. B91JR8